ALAN WINNINGTON, who
Great Depression as an amate
coin-counterfeiter until he found a steady job with a Fleet Street
photo agency. During the Second World War he was chief sub-
editor at the *Daily Worker*, where he worked closely with Claud
Cockburn, the foreign editor, and the legendary newspaper
designer Allen Hutt. In 1947 he travelled clandestinely to China
in order to cover the final stages of the civil war and then, after
entering Beijing with the People's Liberation Army, helped to
establish a foreign-language news agency there.

When the Korean War broke out in 1950, Winnington
reported on the conflict from the northern side and, accused of
treason, was deprived of his British passport. On his return to
Beijing, he and his family lived in the old city rather than in a
special hostel for foreigners and, as the murderous folly of
Maoism became clearer, his fondness and respect for the Chinese
people grew in tandem with his suspicion and dislike of their
leaders.

Horrified by the Great Leap Forward and Chinese policy in
Tibet, Winnington understood earlier than most foreign
observers the disastrous nature of the course on which China had
embarked, and he left the country in 1960. Moving to Berlin, he
continued to work as a journalist while also writing thrillers and
children's books in both English and German, as well as a highly
acclaimed autobiography, *Breakfast with Mao: Memoirs of a
Foreign Correspondent*. He died in 1983.

THE SLAVES OF THE
COOL MOUNTAINS

*Travels Among Head-Hunters and Slave-Owners
in South-West China*

ALAN WINNINGTON

Serif
London

This edition first published 2008 by
Serif
47 Strahan Road
London E3 5DA

www.serifbooks.co.uk

1 3 5 7 9 8 6 4 2

Originally published in slightly different form in 1959 by
Lawrence and Wishart

British Library Cataloguing in Publication Data.
A catalogue record for this book
is available from the British Library.

Library of Congress Cataloging-in-Publication Data.
A catalog record for this book is available from the Library of Congress.

ISBN 978 1 897959 58 9

Printed and bound in Malaysia by Forum

AUTHOR'S NOTE

FOR a long time I had nursed the idea of finding out what went on among the primitive peoples of modern China, but with only the haziest notion of what I might find. Many times during the actual journey over more mountains than I ever climbed before, looking for something that might not be there, I suspected that intuition had led me astray and I had better go back. I visited the "Black Bone" Norsu slave-owners, the Wa headhunters and lived in a Jingpaw jungle village. These are peoples who inhabit the remotest corners of China, on the borders of Yunnan Province. Nobody will ever again be able to see them as I saw them.

This book is about the impact of the Chinese Peoples Republic on some of the most backward peoples in that vast country—even in the world. In writing it I have tried to do justice to unique events by allowing them to tell their story for themselves. I have tried to set the record straight about their background and customs.

My deepest thanks are offered to all those who helped to make these arduous and exciting journeys possible—especially to my fellow-journalists in the Kunming branch of the New China News Agency and to Big Li, Li Two and Little Li.

ALAN WINNINGTON.

PEKING, 1959

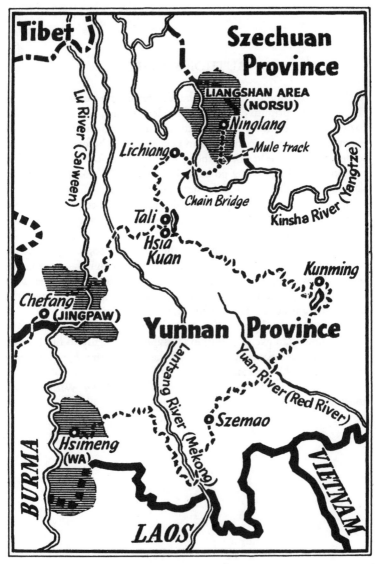

CONTENTS

Part I: THE NORSU

Part III: THE JINGPAW

Part I

THE NORSU

CHAPTER ONE

TWENTIETH-CENTURY SLAVERS

A pocket of the past—On the edge of the world's roof—Mystery of Norsu origins—Tale of a two-tongued sheep—There are no "Lolos"—Attempts to map the Cool Mountains—Death of Lieutenant Brooke—Recent increase in slave raids

BLACK-CLOAKED and black-turbanned, the former slave-owner looked at me from hooded eyes—an aristocrat appraising a bit of common human merchandise. He pondered, took a good swig of rough corn whisky and said: "Your age is against you, but as a curiosity you would have fetched a decent price here until recently. I'd say five silver ingots. Ordinarily a slave of your age would fetch one ingot at best."

The man who reckoned my curiosity value as a slave at £7 10s. was a nobleman named Buyu Heipo—one of the traditional absolute rulers of a little-known group of people called the Norsu who live among the highest mountains in south-west China. Much has been written about these people, known to the western world as the "Lolos", but it was written from hearsay—vague reports that contradicted each other. Nobody dared to penetrate the lofty mountain area where these proud and warlike people lived, with slaves and serfs to do their bidding—a by-passed pocket of human history. From outside, it was only known that from time to time the Norsu swept down from the heights through passes "narrow as a bird's flight" and ravaged the nearby lowlands, returning with struggling men, screaming women and bewildered children to replenish their stock of slaves.

My own determination to visit these people was spurred by a small item in the Chinese press. This scrap of news announced that a number of slaves had been released in the Cool Mountains,[1] where the Norsu live. It said that more would be released in increasing numbers until all slavery was abolished there. Intriguingly, the paper reported that the slaves had been set free as a result of negotiation and agreement with their masters and now had new homes and the means to produce and live in freedom.

[1] Hsiao Liang Shan—Lesser Cool Mountains—are on the Yunnan-Szechuan border. See map.

This press item buzzed in my head, confirming what I had long idly speculated at the back of my mind: that slavery still existed in south-west China. It might still be possible to go there and see the actual process of freeing the slaves, sift out the facts from a sea of legend and dissolve the literary "mystery" that has been built around these people. Such a trip offered most fascinating possibilities because if only a cupful from that ocean of contradictory rumours about the Norsu people were true, their manner of life must be an extremely curious one to be still existing in the twentieth century.

At that time, the end of 1956, although I had read a great deal about them, I scarcely knew where the Norsu actually lived, and since the reader is no doubt in the same situation, a few words about that might not come amiss.

Yunnan Province is the south-west corner of China and borders on Vietnam, Laos, Burma and India. Its northern border marches with Tibet and Szechuan and is one of the most isolated areas in the world. Yunnan has always attracted the inquisitive traveller because it contains some twenty quite different national groups of people, all with widely differing social systems and customs, preserved throughout the centuries. This is partly because of the nature of the place and partly because of the way in which imperial China penetrated it. The province is a high plateau covered with higher mountains. Its mean altitude is 5,000 feet above the sea and communications are the poorest, mostly ancient pack-animal trails hung on the sides of mountains. In its higher parts it is temperate, a land of "perpetual spring", but it is slashed by mighty rivers running into Vietnam, Laos and Burma. At the river levels the climate passes from temperate to tropical, a sudden change unbearable to the plateau dwellers and this partly accounts for their isolation from each other as well as from the rest of China. A profile of the mean altitude drawn from the China Sea to Tibet would show a series of five gigantic steps, the last being the roof of the world—the Tibetan plateau. Fourth of these steps, just below Tibet, is north-west Yunnan, and this is where the Norsu live, guarded through centuries of isolation by the high terrain and surrounded by the giant loop of the fast-running Upper Yangtze River.

Controversy is plentiful about the origin of the Norsu people. Only one thing is certain: that they are a branch of the great *Yi-chia*—"original people"—which is found in various parts of Yunnan and Szechuan Provinces. One story is that the Cool Mountains Norsu moved there about 170 years ago as a result of a dispute over a two-tongued sheep which could make a remarkable noise audible for several score miles. A bitter feud over the theft of this valuable creature led to this branch fleeing over the border into the Cool Mountains where they enslaved the small local population. This is the least credible version of their antecedents. Some Norsu claim that they came long ago from Tibet. More credence could be placed in this if the languages had anything in common, for the Norsu are tall like Tibetans, darkly acquiline of visage and the younger men have smaller waists than the girls. Still others say that the Tibetans are a degenerated branch of the Norsu. What is most likely is that many centuries ago when the Chinese Emperors unified China, some of the Yi-chia fled northwards across the bend of the unnavigable Yangtze River and settled in this impenetrable mountain fastness where they enslaved what few people lived in those heights and remained isolated until the past few years.

The name "Lolo" by which the Norsu have become known in the western world is simply an example of picking up from the old Chinese régime a term of contempt used to describe a number of differing nationalities in Yunnan, in much the same way as some British people use the contemptuous term "wog" for persons who couple darker skins with a failure to dress for dinner. Nevertheless, innumerable scholarly books have been written, largely by missionaries and based on local hearsay only, about the lives and habits of the "Lolos" whom they have never visited.

Attempts to visit the Cool Mountains were made but they failed. Both the British and the French competed to penetrate the whole of Yunnan Province. While the French did actually succeed in building a narrow-gauge railway from Vietnam to the capital of Yunnan—said to have cost a Chinese life for every rail laid—it was not until the Second World War and with the help of the Chinese that the famous Burma Road was built to link that city, Kunming, with Burma. But many attempts to survey the whole province were made by British agents with the economic, political and military possibilities in mind.

In all these attempts, the Cool Mountains remained unpenetrated, unsurveyed and unknown. Even the famous British War Office map of Yunnan compiled by Major H. R. Davies, corrected to 1908, shows this area blank and across it, overstamped in red, the word "Lolo", itself enough to show complete ignorance of the area. Why Major Davies failed to get much co-operation, at any rate from local people, might be explained in his own words, detailing his travels through Yunnan:[1] "I took up my stick amidst looks of incredulous amusement from the spectators, and gave the head mule-man one or two whacks over the head." The major should have known that when embarrassed, especially by another's folly, the Chinese usually smile. And again: "It is in any case far easier to kick a [Chinese] man downstairs than to clear an inn yard." The major seems to have been an imperialist with an epithet.

Another British War Office agent, Lieutenant Donald Brooke, made an attempt to survey the Cool Mountains in 1909. His body was sent out in two pieces without comment.

To give an impression of the aura surrounding this place, I cannot do better than quote a passage written in 1925 by Harry A. Franck, the American traveller, explorer and writer:[2]

"It goes without saying that I should gladly have given my best hat to have visited the 'Independent Lolos' at home now that I was passing within a hundred *li* (33 miles—A.W.) of them. But quite aside from any hesitancy to leave my hide among them, that would have been impossible. Not only do they control the few ferries across the Golden Sand (name of the upper reaches of the Yangtze River—A.W.); the Chinese authorities on the eastern side are diligent beyond their wont in keeping visitors from crossing. . . . There is a certain inter-course between the Norsu of Kweichow and their independent rela-tives beyond the turbulent, rock-strewn northern sweep of the Upper Yangtze; some go back and forth, and even bring back wives from over there—like our immigrants going back to the 'old country' for their brides; but neither foreigners nor Chinese usually find the way open. Once a British photographer eluded the watchfulness of the Chinese authorities and got across, but he was killed, and only one of his coolies, who had been left for dead, came back to tell the story. Then there is the better known case of Lieutenant Brooke, who also left his bones among them."

Between the majority people of China, the Hans—those people whom most foreigners think of as the Chinese—and the other minority nationalities[3] in Yunnan Province, no love was ever lost.

The Hans spread south and west over the centuries, dominating the

[1] *Yunnan: The Link Between India and the Yangtze*, Major H. R. Davies, Cambridge University Press, 1909.

[2] *Roving Through Southern China*, Harry A. Franck, The Century Co., 1925.

[3] There are more than twenty distinct nationalities in Yunnan, with over 100 branches and speaking some seventy languages and dialects.

lush lowlands and forcing the smaller, local nationalities into the less fertile areas, often on the hills. Little enough was known in Peking of what was going on. These outlying "barbarians" would be made to pay a nominal tribute and occasionally kow-tow to the throne, but how much was actually extorted from them by the representatives of the throne was nobody's business.

The Norsu people never submitted. They remained in their mountain fastness, occasionally invaded by a force of sufficient strength from the lowlands and retaliating always with more than interest when their warriors swept down to capture slaves and loot. These harassments were on a fairly small scale until the Chinese Revolution of 1911 and the chaotic days of the warlords.

Matters got much worse from 1918 onwards when the scale and frequency of raid and counter-raid rapidly increased. A single case which I was able to authenticate fully will be enough to give the atmosphere. In the early 'twenties a Han who was both a big landlord and a militia officer in Yung Sheng plain on the southern edge of the Cool Mountains, took 400 armed people on a raid, looted a whole Norsu area, burned houses, killed a few people and retired with some cattle and horses. The Norsu planned revenge.

One night not long after, 1,000 Norsu warriors struck back, burned houses for a distance of seven miles, captured 300 slaves, 1,000 cattle and vast loot. This Han landlord escaped the raid but lost his property and influence. For the next few years he acted as a slave-trader, selling his own people to the Norsu, a man or woman for a few of the blue-looking, adulterated silver ingots which the Norsu prefer to money, until he too disappeared into the Cool Mountains to finish his life in chains, it is said.

Major slaving raids became common-place throughout the rule of the Kuomintang in China. As late as 1948 and 1949 raids were taking place in which several hundred and even a thousand people were driven up the passes into slavery.

This was the place I now intended to try to visit. Nothing much had been reported about what was going on there since the Chinese People's Republic had been founded in 1949, certainly nothing definite until that small news item about the freeing of the slaves in one part of the Cool Mountains in December 1956, and it was almost a year later that I was able to get away from other work and try to visit the Norsu, not knowing what the prospects were.

I escaped the cold Peking winter by plane and on the same day

B

landed in the perpetual spring of Kunming, capital of Yunnan Province, where the camellias were in bloom.

My heart sank when I learned that even in 1957 there was still no way of getting to the Cool Mountains except by walking or riding a horse for at least a week up and down mountains on an ancient track that was said to be bad going even for a Yunnan horse-trail. Not that I feared a week's trekking, but it meant organising a pack-train for bedding and food and possibly tents, riding animals, interpreter, someone who knew the way—a host of problems outside my power both practically and financially. Local people made well-intentioned efforts to dissuade me on the ground that the journey was hard and not worth it. "Slavery is so backward and there are so many new and interesting things to see in Yunnan. Why pick this?" Why indeed? But my journalist's nose had scented a rare story and I felt I must go if any way could be found.

I never would have been able to go but for the help of the Kunming office of the New China News Agency, an old friend Li Ping-tai from the Peking office of the same agency and another who turned out to be in charge of work among the smaller nationalities for the Communist Party of Yunnan Province. An arrangement to split the costs was soon made, the wires were set buzzing and a few days after reaching Kunming we were able to set off in a borrowed Land Rover on the first stage of what became the most interesting trip I ever made. There was myself, Li Ping-tai, Li Chao-yang, a reporter from the Kunming branch of the agency and Li Chih-ping, a young and enthusiastic Szechuanese escort, with a vast sense of humour, a carbine and a terrific appetite for red pepper: Big Li, Li Two and Little Li.

Half-way down the Burma Road, by some magnificent hot-springs, a road leads north, through the famous old walled city of Tali, near the place where Major Davies boasted of beating the mule-man, and soon climbs on to a plateau about 8,000 feet above the sea. There, under a great peak of perpetual snow, lies the little town of Li Chiang —the last point we could reach on wheels. From here, over those impressive peaks that stretched away like distance itself, it must be by foot and hoof.

In this town we must spend a day or two collecting pack-train, riding horses, food and a guide, and send telegrams ahead announcing our future arrival to local authorities on the way. We bought rice, hardtack, pungent Yunnan ham, pickles, dried shrimps and red pepper, things that would keep and give enough flavour to help down the rice; tea and butter, rich rancid yak butter that is blended with tea and salt into a drink more sustaining than food in rarefied mountain air.

Most of the inhabitants of Li Chiang belong to the Nashi people, a minority people who still retain strong traces of the matriarchal system of marriage which is common in these parts. The women are said to rule their men with a rod of iron, though I saw no public signs of this. They wear stiffened, bonnet headdresses exactly like the Dutch women and long flared skirts. But for the snow peak hanging overhead we might have been in Holland, what with women's bonnets, long skirts, cobbled lanes hardly wider than outstretched arms and the lacing of little brooks beside the streets where ducks paddle furiously upstream and float sideways down. The city is a junction of several ancient trading trails leading far north into the wilds to Szechuan and Tibet.

Our *ma-bong* was finally signed on: the word seems to mean both the muleteer and his pack-train in these parts. Old Chen was a tiny, tough and horsy character who drank like a fish but still managed to harangue his animals over 35 miles of unspeakable track every day. Perhaps I got that wrong, and because of the latter he both needed and was able to do the former. He provided three spavined, angular pack horses known to him as Little Flower, Date-coloured Cow and Shorty, to carry our bedding, baggage and food for animals and men. He had also raked together a collection of slightly less mangy riding animals, ranging from a tall grey mule to a powerful-looking chestnut mare which was provided to carry my extra weight.

Our ill-matched cavalcade set off, led by Little Flower, clattering through Li Chiang's cobbled alleys at dawn, past open-fronted shops where men and women hammered silver, nailed shoes, stitched, wove, ironed, bought, sold, ate and drank—out into the mountains.

CHAPTER TWO

INTO THE SLAVE-OWNERS' FASTNESS

Over the Twelve Barriers—Horse hotels and perpetual stew—In sight of the Cool Mountains—Where birds need safe conduct—Silent escort—The first freed slaves—Own language forgotten—Deadliest Norsu insult—Breaking-in human draught animals

TO steel my legs and other parts, I had spent my spare time walking up and down mountains and riding horses. I might have saved the trouble. Tinkering around was of no value as preparation for such a journey. And it is unfortunate that the first mountain that has to be crossed is the worst on the whole trail—a perpendicular monster known as Twelve Barriers. Local people say: "You can't attempt Twelve Barriers unless you eat oil-fried rice for three days."

Half-way up, my "strong" mare gave up the struggle, stood still and refused to lift another hoof. I walked the rest of the way up to the pass. It is not so bad from that side because the climb starts at 8,000 feet on the plateau. But on the other side the mountain falls almost sheer to the raging Yangtze River, which from far above seems to be a slowly wandering stream. "We'll sleep by the river tonight," Little Li remarked. It was only about one o'clock in the afternoon and I said happily "But it's no distance at all down to there." Little Li said: "It's farther than it seems." It was.

After the first three hours of direct descent from rock to rock, sliding down some steep places from tree to tree, slipping and sliding in dry streams of rubble mixed with fine dust, my legs were moving like those of an automatic toy. The dust of an old horse-trail, which clogs eyes and nose, may look like ordinary dust on the ground, but in the air it smells like dehydrated stables, dessicated cattle-yards—the purest essence of four-footed excrement.

By the time that the Yangtze had grown to a river instead of a brook, and the spider web of a chain suspension-bridge became visible, each leg quivered as I put the weight on it carefully, steadying the thigh with a hand just above the knee before trusting myself to lift the other foot. So it went on from boulder to boulder until later the track became more recognisable as something man-made and after nightfall we clattered on to the stone end of Golden Dragon Bridge.

Out in the windy darkness its planks swayed on creaking iron chains which had pitched forty workmen to their deaths half a century ago as they were building it. We spent the night on the floor of the bridge-house.

That was a sample of the trail which itself helped to explain the isolation of the Norsu, though as yet we were in relatively populous, "lowlands" places. After that, from dawn to dusk and later, we walked and rode up and down this ancient trail, carved out of the mountains and stamped into the sides of almost sheer precipices by dead genera-tions of pack animals and their drivers. For my part I mainly walked. True I had the grey mule now, a tractable and experienced animal, but as an inexperienced rider I did not find it restful to ride on such a rough trail.

Nor is there any casual strolling. On this first stage of the march, before entering the Cool Mountains, "horse hotels" exist, separated by "half a day's journey". Half a day may be 20 miles or it may be 15 and two such stages must be done daily to keep a schedule. In a horse hotel a man gets the right to a piece of earth floor in a room where a wood fire smokes all night, water, use of the fire to boil tea and a roof— for fourpence. For less than a penny, horses can stand all night under cover and their owners can also buy hay and dried beans. Now with the growth of producer co-operatives, local peasants supply food at almost any time, making a profitable sideline for themselves. Usually two great concave iron cauldrons are kept going permanently; one containing stew, a sort of perpetual beef stew through which cattle follow one another nose to tail, discarding nothing but horns, hide and hooves; in the other, rice is cooked, eggs fried, trenchers steamed and soup made.

That stew, sauced with a 20-mile march, served with an inch-thick wheat trencher, an onion omelette, soup made from the beef stock and cabbage, a dressing of red pepper, onion, garlic and parsley, and the whole washed down with a couple of ounces of 120 proof sizzling corn liquor and topped off with a bowl of buttered-tea, stands out as one of the most delectable in a lifetime of varied gastronomic experi-ences. The entire meal cost eightpence a head, including liquor.

Our first such meal on the trail was served by a young woman who chopped, flipped and poured with great charm and efficiency. When we returned she had gone. A passing soldier, proving the adage, had stopped there to eat, lost his heart, proposed on the spot and carried her off to Kunming. I wonder if he finds his wife's cooking as delicious in Kunming as when it was flavoured by a 20-mile march in the rare mountain air, and whether the poor girl is now spending her time vainly trying to produce a replica of the meal that won his hungry heart. On the lintels of this co-operative hung two new year messages—modern versions of the old "May you be wealthy" signs. One said "Today we have the two-wheeled plough" and the other "Tomorrow the tractor will come".

On the evening of the second day, the Cool Mountains came into sight, rising tier upon tier from the fertile plain of Chingkuan. Next day a stiff four-hour climb brought our pack-train to Yung Sheng, the last and highest mountain-locked basin before climbing still further and entering Norsu territory. For this was still the "lowlands" and not a single Norsu had yet been seen.

The way into the Cool Mountains is through Bird Pass, a narrow gully between mountains so precipitous and bare that local people have the saying: "Even birds must get permission to fly through Bird Pass once the surrounding peaks are manned."

It would take a first-class horse to carry a man up to that pass and an even better one to carry him down. We had no first-class horse and no second-class ones, so walked up out of necessity. In any case it suited me better to walk for the only thing worse than riding up a dry mountain stream is riding down, especially if nature has left the tap dripping. They are treacherous 45-degree slopes of dust and rubble, or mud and rubble, through which stick rounded boulders skilfully disguised with mud and dust to look quite treadable on. Such a trail, hung perilously from the side of a cliff, seen from the height of a mule and leaning backward over its rump, is enough to make any novice rider get off and trust his two tired legs rather than the animal's four.

Through that narrow rocky pass generations of Norsu raiders mounted on tiny powerful ponies have descended into the plain of Yung Sheng and returned with human loot, leaving a handful of men on the peaks to hold up the pursuit.

It takes less than three hours climbing from Yung Sheng to the pass. Once through it the people are Norsu and everything is different. On Yung Sheng plain, plump, clean Hans and Dutch-looking Nashi women pick plump, clean vegetables even in January. It is fertile and fat and full of fat infants.

Up beyond the pass the people are taller and darker, mainly unwashed, with full black turbans, short black felt cloaks almost a quarter of an inch thick, black trousers ending at the calf, as wide as a split skirt. Their massive turbans when unrolled to their full length of several yards are handy for leading a horse down a difficult descent.

Three such sinister-looking figures slid out of the scrub as we breasted Bird Pass, rifles on shoulders, serious but obviously friendly. Little Li, our Szechuanese manager, went forward and then came back with the diagnosis, "min bing" (Home Guard). These turned out to be former slaves now enrolled in a popular defence force to prevent any possible attempt by slave-owners to stage a comeback or do harm to their former chattels. These shadowy guards kept us company all the way, one group handing over to the next as we left one district and entered another, slipping along the ridges, appearing and disappearing, always there, never the same faces.

There were still several days of marching to get to Ninglang town where the new county government is seated high up in the Cool Mountains. But there were no more horse hotels—only the dirt floors of adobe buildings which house the local Communist Party "work-teams" or peasants and provide shelter for men if not their animals.

Gradually steel balls of pain in calf and thigh become less excruciating and a routine sets in. Each morning, Old Chen who has slept outside wrapped in a Norsu felt cloak though he is a Han, reluctantly leaves the dead wood fire and staggers round giving the animals their dried beans which they crunch with sleep-shattering effect. In the biting cold of mountain pre-dawn he begins to lash our belongings on the pack-frames with furlongs of rawhide, using his teeth and shiny fingers like jointed rods of blue steel. Tentative clucks from the corner proclaim that the chickens are getting up and news arrives that Little Li has gone in search of our black horse which chewed his bridle and escaped.

When I have lashed my bedding, I fan the ashes of the charcoal fire into a blaze with a washing bowl and start to boil brick-tea in two mugs for myself and Big Li. A huge copper pot arrives full of Da Huo Tsai (Big Pot Dish) which consists of the remains of last night's meal with some additions. In all it contains ham, pork, turnips, pota-toes, beans, noodles, truffles, onions and pickles, all swimming in what Huckleberry Finn would have described as juices that have swapped round, and is downed, at six o'clock on a dark morning, with rice and red pepper. A few bowls of that, with a big mug of brick-tea boiled with Tibetan yak butter and salt, and there is no mountain that cannot be tackled.

Before sunrise the cavalcade begins, led by Little Flower, with Date-coloured Cow in the middle, and Shorty third, followed by

Old Chen. For all their appearance of decrepitude, they carried our baggage over those mountain trails for seven days and are no doubt still doing the same job for a few sheaves of hay and some dried beans every day. Little Flower was the pampered darling of Old Chen, being the youngest and most valuable animal. She had the lightest packs while Shorty got the worst. Old Chen seemed to spend his whole time in a rage at the other two horses. Every few minutes he would tap Shorty with the twig he carried. Shorty responded by hurrying for a few paces before relapsing, thus nudging Date-coloured Cow and occasionally producing a mild response from Little Flower. In difficult places, which were plentiful, Old Chen would hurl himself in a frenzy at Shorty's rear, pushing and cursing as though to drive the entire cavalcade through the obstruction by main strength. Usually he could not get through himself and Little Flower, his darling, would seize this moment for a nibble at the herbage. Old Chen, reaching bursting point, would then hurl a stone at the unreachable Little Flower, usually managing to hit Date-coloured Cow. As the din increased, the horse-boy, supposed to be in front to look after the affairs but normally walking along asleep far ahead, would come scurrying back to pull Little Flower's bridle with none of Old Chen's tenderness. I suppose when she gets older, Little Flower will be demoted to second place and the rocks, and will end up with the twig in the twilight of her days.

It is cold before dawn, for all that the mountain sides are covered with camellias even in December, and better to walk than freeze in the saddle. At fords, bare footprints of yesterday are preserved in morning-frozen mud as we climb out of shadowed valleys into sunshine along tinkling ice-bound streams, crackling under the animals' hooves. By ten o'clock it is hot and by noon sunburn a problem.

At the passes, cairns of stones and the Lamaist "Om Mani Padme Hum" (Hail to the Jewel in the Lotus)[1] testify to the mixture of animist Tibetan Buddhism which has passed this way with Tibetan pack-trains, for no good Lamaist would cross a mountain without con-tributing his stone to the pile at the top.

At noon on such a day I met newly freed slaves for the first time. Theirs was a terrible happiness. Such joy is too mixed when men, women and children are happy only to be sitting in the sun, not to be parted from husbands, wives, children, no more to be spreadeagled

---

[1] Buddhist "Paternoster". The Buddha is often depicted sitting in a lotus flower, symbolising heavenly birth.

and flogged, and yet fearful of the future, fearful of change, even with a trace of regret for the familiar past. To a slave, as to his owner, slavery seems a natural thing and a slave's idea of heaven is to be a slave-owner rather than to be free.

When I arrived at Bolo, still two days from Ninglang, slaves who had been set free not long before were being issued with relief cotton cloth by members of the local Communist Party work-team. In this tiny rural district, several hundred slaves had been released. Newly built houses of rammed-earth adobe in Bolo village housed 140 of them and those who were not collecting cloth were sitting stitching it, or merely sitting. Old slaves, young slaves, male, female, beautiful, ugly, brutalised and coquettish, clever slaves and congenital idiots, deaf, blind and lame, with work thickened hands and feet that had never known a shoe, they sat, lay, talked, slept, waiting for someone to tell them what to do next.

They crowded round the stranger, stroking and feeling. I fear I did the western world little good in their eyes, with a five days' growth of beard and a nose several times skinned by the unfiltered sun in that attenuated atmosphere. But they patted and grinned. Somebody explained that despite my ferocious appearance I was all right, a friend of "Gongzo" (work-team) and an opponent of slavery. For all their embraces and clasping of horny hands, the historic mental gap was palpable. To ask one question was to get an answer to another. I never felt so incapable of making contact with other human beings.

As soon as they had their issue cloth, in white, two shades of blue and black, the more able women settled down to make Norsu dresses for themselves and the others. Norsu gowns are ankle length, white at the top, then light blue, with dark blue at the ankle and deeply flounced. They needed only wide-brimmed straw hats with plenty of flowers to remind me of pictures of my mother at the turn of the century. Unmarried girls wore a black triangular cloth headdress with the front angle ending just above the bridge of the nose and tied down with a piece of red cord. Married women wear a bigger headdress not tied on.

Most characteristic feature of the Norsu dress, for both men and women, is the black cloak. This is felted to fit the shoulders, very thick and stiff, impervious to rain and, when its wearer squats, it becomes a little windproof tent. In its more expensive form the cloak is thin and of two layers, deeply fluted in the making and measuring scores of feet round the bottom edge. The cloaks of the newly freed slaves at Bolo consisted of a patchwork of variegated bits of old felt stitched with string on the ghost of what may have been a whole cloak half a century before.

Abolition had taken place so recently there that work was still going on to finish the high wall of rammed-earth surrounding this new village. Walls like this are needed because, in a few places, occasional slave-owners who had pretended to be reconciled to the reform had lain in the dark hills at night and sniped at their former property by the light of the village fires.

I noticed two girls who were obviously Hans but dressed in Norsu style and wearing on the backs of their hands the tattooed black spots, about as big as sixpence, which all Norsu women have. They were Hans, I was told, who had been abducted as children and later tattooed as usual by their mistress. This was one of the methods of preventing flight by the slaves who were told that anyone on the plains would now know them for Norsu and a Norsu would be killed on sight by other nationalities.

These two girls could speak no word of their former language, had no idea where their homes might be and no desire to leave the Cool Mountains. They had been told by their mistress that they were Hans, not with any desire to impart information but because to a Norsu, a Han was a most loathsome thing. Even slaves insult each other by using the Norsu word *swor* (Han) and no deadlier insult is available than "You are a dead Han".

While our rice was being boiled I watched the cloth being issued —12 feet for a man and 36 feet for a woman, this being the amount needed for the flounced skirts which are their greatest pride. Like visiting royalty I bent down to pick up the cloth a woman was stitching but was quietly restrained by someone who knew that even when she is not wearing it, a stranger commits an offence by touching a Norsu woman's skirt.

Among the 140 slaves here—all technically Norsu—were mostly people of Han origin with a sprinkling of Nashi, Lisu, Hsifan, Chung-chia, Mosu and Tibetans. They come from a wide area, as far afield as Szechuan and Li Chiang. Once caught and taken up into the Cool Mountains, marching on the ridges at night, chances of escape were few. Mass raids, though spectacular, were comparatively rare. Most abductions were by small parties of Norsu who grabbed one or two people and took them long distances to confuse them. A runaway slave stood a 90 per cent. chance of recapture and the best he could then hope for was that his captor would be dishonest and keep him as his own slave. If returned to his own master, especially to a wealthy one, he would most likely be killed as an example to the others. At best he would be flogged within a skin's thickness of death and probably hamstrung at the ankle. Loyalty to the slave system as well as the difficulties of dissembling in such a small population generally led to runaways being returned to their original masters, so slaves took a dreadful risk when they decided to escape.

Captured children offered little difficulty to their new masters but adults who had been free took badly to slavery and had to be broken in. This was done normally by chaining, flogging and starvation. I saw one device at Bolo calculated to reduce a new slave to cringing servility—an iron ring which slipped over the knee and locked the bent leg so that it could not be moved or straightened. Another more simple method was to lock a section of tree-trunk on the leg by putting one foot through a mortice in the trunk and driving a spike through just behind the ankle so that it could not be taken off. When the slave wanted to move he must pick up the trunk by means of ropes fitted for this purpose. Captured girls or women gave less trouble and the method of anchoring them by getting them pregnant was both simple and effective.

Tempting as it was to stay in Bolo and similar new villages on the way to find out more from the newly freed slaves, we pushed on after lunch and, as we left, black-clad men with rifles quietly went up to the ridge on each side of the trail to ensure that nobody interfered with the visitors from Peking.

At noon on the seventh day from Li Chiang, our cavalcade, still led by Little Flower, was clambering down from the surrounding mountains to the high plain where lay Ninglang, capital of the Cool Mountains. We were dusty, bearded and very sure that the journey had been worth the effort.

CHAPTER THREE

BLACK BONES AND BLUE BLOOD

*Nobles, serfs, slaves—Nobles' contempt for "free" serfs—Death for inter-
marriage—Feasts for 5,000 guests—Freemen into slavery and slaves into
freedom—The morality of slave society—Caste system among slaves—
Girls worth more—Jingu Hushe sells half of his sister, buys half of his wife*

BY the standards acquired in reaching it, Ninglang is a town.
In fact, it is a single muddy lane with about 15 feet between
the hovels flanking it; a handful of sleepy stalls the size of packing
cases selling a tiny range of identical goods that nobody seemed to
want. Pigs and chickens scratch among a jostle of Norsu, Tibetans,
Hans and Mosu. Women sit delousing themselves, and chatting, while
urchins come up to suckle after a game of tag. Long pack-trains come
pushing by, their lead animals gaudy with flags and tassels of dyed yak
tails, jangling with round brass bells, and unload salt blocks, grain,
yak-butter, tea bricks, bolts of cloth. In the middle of the old town—
which takes about thirty seconds to walk through—is the little new
state store, centre of attraction for miles around. This is always crowded
and sells hundreds of wares: bales of bright cloths, cottons, silks,
velvets, swords, rifle ammunition, horse trappings, Tibetan high boots
and gold-embroidered hats, copper and enamel-ware, china, silver
trinkets, an endless profusion of things loved by the local minority
people, plus vacuum flasks, petrol lighters, electric torches and fountain
pens from Shanghai.

The rest of the town is new but not much bigger—pinkish adobe
buildings with real glass windows. These are the county government,
trading station, bank, hospital and a multi-purpose producer co-operative. Ninglang is the capital of a new county of that name, covering
the Cool Mountains. Its exact borders have not yet been defined but
approximately it is 100 miles from east to west and 125 miles from
north to south, lying between the great U-curve of the Upper Yangtze
River and the Szechuan border.

This was indeed the heart of the Norsu area and I was said to be
the first non-Chinese to reach it. I spent more than a week in this
hamlet of a town, drinking buttered tea from daybreak to late at

night, and talking with Norsu slave-owners, slaves and commoners, Communist Party leaders, people responsible for trade, education and medicine, before leaving to visit places where I could study the abolition of slavery at first hand. By the time I left the town I had a pretty clear picture of Norsu slave-society.

In the Cool Mountains—now officially Ninglang County—the Norsu live on the highlands and the other nationalities[1] live in the level basins between the mountains. People who actually are Norsu, those who reckon themselves as Norsu and those who have descended from abducted slaves and claim no other nationality, make up a total of 56,294, as far as they have been counted. Possibly a few others exist in remote valleys but they cannot be many.

Of these 56,000, fewer than 3,000 are nobles, the hereditary aristocracy and ruling class, alone having full political, citizenship and property rights. They are tall, healthy and warlike, with a strong belief in the inferiority of all other human beings, coupled with an exaggerated view of the characteristics they think they possess. They call themselves the *Nor* which means "black" and claim to have "strong black bone", in the same way as English aristocrats refer to their "blue blood" and think it better than the vulgar sort. (Since *su* means "people", Norsu means "black people".)

According to Norsu legend, the nobles had a common ancestor named Lapudior about thirty generations ago and this original noble had four sons. One of these named Wadja had a wife of doubtful antecedents and so the clan was split, a bastard clan being formed named Loho. The other three clans, Buyu, Lomhm and Zeku refused until recent times to marry into the Wadja and Loho clans so there must have been a reason for the legend at some point of Norsu history.

These five clans of nobles are subdivided into 500 families—each clan and each family a law to itself so far as it can enforce it. No centralised governing organisation ever existed among the Norsu. Marriage within the clan or outside the tiny caste are absolutely forbidden. These two rules are unbreakable; "black bone" must be kept pure.

All other Norsu, about 53,000 of them, are either common bondsmen or slaves. The bondsmen, who are slightly more than half of that

[1] Eleven other nationalities live on the alluvial plains in this one county. Their way of life was feudal and the reform, which took place at the same time, was very different from the abolition of slavery. The nationalities are: Han, 19,341; Mosu, 8,287; Sifan, 4,104; Lisu, 3,074; Nashi, 1,088; Chungchia, 612; Miao, 252; Tibetan, 264; Hui (Moslem), 32; Minchia (Bai), 30; Tai, 3.

number, are born in serfdom, having to render duties to the nobles all their lives.

These commoners are called *Pu Nor* which means "white black" They are not slaves but there is no way in which they can evade the feudal obligations they owe to their aristocratic masters and failure to fulfil these duties leads straight to total enslavement.

Common bondsmen regard themselves as Norsu and there is little doubt that they sprang from the same stock, but there has been so much interflow between bondsmen and captured slaves that the original Norsu strain has been very much thinned out. Only the nobility can be said with any certainty to be Norsu, and they have the common features of dark skin, height and aquiline feature.

Nevertheless, the commoners regard themselves as Norsu and as having better "bone" than all "cheap bone" people. In fact they feel themselves better than all others except their noble masters.

Whatever the commoners may think about themselves, the nobles refer to them with the same contemptuous word they use to describe slaves, *Nji*, and call them "first class slaves".

From birth to death the commoner is in servitude to the noble family into whose bondage he was born. He may become rich and able to substitute the labour of others in fulfilment of his traditional duties, but he can never evade military duty at the call of his master, never become a noble, never marry into the nobility, never commute the payment to his master of the same deference as is paid by the poorest member of the commonalty. If he dies without a son, all his property at once reverts to the noble to whom he belongs by birth, regardless of whether the widow and her girl children are left destitute. In handing anything to a noble, a commoner must look away from him over his shoulder, kneel on one knee, extend the object with one hand, at the same time putting the fingers of the other hand on the extended elbow.

So long as no question of marriage is involved, a noble may seduce a common girl, but there cannot be any recognition of offspring. The child remains a commoner, a few ingots may pass and the girl's family regards the matter as having conferred an honour on them.

It is quite opposite if a noblewoman has a liaison with a commoner. Then both must die. Flight elsewhere is impossible. Inside the Cool Mountains the woman's dialect would instantly betray her as a noble; outside, no other people tolerate the hated Norsu slavers.

These relationships reflect the economic servitude of the commonalty. I was able to list almost forty privileges which the nobles exact by right from their bondsmen, and there are doubtless more. It would be tedious to mention them all; a few will serve to indicate their character.

Births, marriages and deaths of nobles are naturally taken as important events for celebration, which automatically means soaking the commonalty. When a nobleman marries, each family of his father's commoners must give five bottles of liquor, five pounds of oat flour and a fat pig. Similarly for a funeral, except that for deaths the pig from each family is changed to one cow for each five families. A noble's funeral is a big occasion, with as many as 5,000 guests eating their way through seventy or eighty cattle and 300 pigs. Every one may come and the more guests, the brighter the splendour—at the commoners' expense. There are many other occasional and standard events when gifts have to be made—wine and pork at New Year, entertaining overflow guests from the master, and so on.

Failure through poverty to fulfil any of these obligations creates a debt which is calculated in compound interest up to 300 per cent. in the illiterate head of the master (no nobles can write) and after a few years the bankrupted bondsman or some or all of his family must leave the twilight of "free" bondage and enter the full black night of slavery.

There are plenty of duties other than giving presents. When a noble girl gets married, she spends the first years of her married life travelling between her mother's home and that of her new husband where she settles down only when the first child is born. This travelling involves plenty of corvée duty for commoners. A noble daughter must obviously travel with plenty of male and female escorts, and commoners have to leave their farming to go to the devil while they take the young lady long distances, providing their own subsistence. And when the daughter finally settles down, she will take common girls to her new home, sometimes for a few years, sometimes never to see their families, or even their husbands, again.

On the other hand, when a common girl marries, her family must pay the overlord one silver ingot—a custom regarded by some people in Ninglang as a remnant of the *jus primae noctis*.

Commoners provide both the money and most of the manpower for clan warfare, are subject to mobilisation at a moment's notice and pay the indemnities when a feud is mediated. Both winning and losing nobles make a profit from the great game of war. If an indemnity is fixed in negotiation at 2,000 ingots, it would obviously be foolish to go to all that trouble for nothing; 3,000 or more ingots would be collected, the loser keeping the odd 1,000. Ransoms are also passed on to the commoners in the same way.

Corvée is demanded for opening new land—all the farming being by the primitive slash-burn method—for getting firewood, escorting the master or his family whenever he wants to travel, building houses.

Caste and class divisions do not coincide. A noble may be poor and a commoner rich. Commoners can become richer than the general run of nobles, owning many slaves.

Norsu commoners imitate their masters in having clans and banning marriage inside the clan, but members of a single common clan may belong to masters of different aristocratic clans and therefore find themselves in battle against their own clan members. Moreover, when commoners are forced into slavery, they are "married" by their masters to any partner who may suit his slave breeding plans. Norsu custom is therefore only rigidly applicable to the nobles.

About 47 per cent. of all the Norsu living in the Cool Mountains are slaves. Most of these are descendents of other nationalities captured and enslaved, though a very large number are first generation slaves, captured within the past few decades as children. This reflects the intensified abduction of slaves since the early 'twenties.

Slaves exist in two categories: "house-slaves" who live in the owner's house; "separate-slaves" who live in an uncertain state of matrimony in separate households.

These are the two aspects of the Norsu slave's life-cycle.

Separate-slaves are called in Norsu *Apa-i-su*, which means "people sleeping on the side". Their "marriages" are formed by the master and can be liquidated by him at any time. The slave-owner pairs off male and female slaves, provides a wattle "house" and some land and allows the slaves a small part of their time to cultivate for themselves. This encourages the reproduction of what has now become the main form of wealth in Ninglang—slaves. As one separate-slave said to me: "In the daytime we produce in the fields for our master and at night we produce for him in our beds."

Children of separate-slaves become house-slaves.

House-slaves are called *Gashigalu* which means "those at the lower end of the fireplace". They are also known as *A-i-zen* or "small children".[1] They enter the master's house at the age of five or six, when they can perform simple tasks, and their education stops at that point. A slave-owner with enough slaves and a big household may keep one slave doing nothing but carrying water, another milling grain or getting firewood and able to do no other work.

House-slaves are divided among their master's sons and daughters of the same generation when these marry. Boy slaves go to the sons and girl slaves to the daughters. On marriage the girls take their girl slaves to the home of their new husband, who has his share of male slaves. The male and female slaves are paired off as separate-slaves and the cycle begins again.

Slave parents have no rights over their children, as they have none over their own persons. When separate-slaves are old and their children have already been dispersed into various distant households to breed a new generation of slaves, the aging couple are sold to whomever might be interested in a cheap slave, frequently to different owners. If only an extra bottle of wine can be got for separating a couple who have lived all their adult lives as man and wife, the bottle will win and no more attention paid to the tears of the old couple than to the bellowing of cattle.

That is the morality of slave-society, to which it is very hard to adjust. It is staggering to the modern mind to observe the casual manner in which very charming slave-owners are willing to dispense grief in disposing of human flesh and blood while still adhering to their own strict caste régime. A slave-owner who will casually sell a husband and wife in two different directions—for ever—will also go out to die for a cousin he has never met in a clan dispute whose cause he does not know. By the standards of later social forms, slave-society is cruel but to slaves and their owners it seems quite normal, even eternal, so it is better to leave those standards out when examining slavery.

Old Ashi Chesa and his wife were waiting to be sundered at the age of sixty or seventy, nobody knew within a few years—when the abolition of slavery came to Bolo and saved them in July 1957. Originally there were three sons and three daughters, but the eldest son was killed by his master for escaping. Of the other five, four were dispersed into four different households. This left only one valueless slave, a cripple girl—"made lame by the ghosts".

[1] Because of this the local Hans call them *wa-dzu* from the Chinese *wa-wa* for baby, and not by the proper Chinese for slave which is *nu-li*.

C

"I went to bed and lay there to kill the sadness," said Ashi Kwam, the mother. "There were no children left to bring a little firewood and water now and again, or save us a handful of oats."

Ashi Chesa and his wife had belonged to two different slave-owners who had paired them together. This is relatively common. It occurs when slave-owners have more slaves of one sex than the other. An understanding is reached between the masters as to who will own the children. Sometimes one takes all the boys, or they will agree to take every other child.

Ashi Chesa had no idea what the contract might have been and it was not his business, being only a slave. After a few years his wife had been taken away by her owner and Ashi Chesa spent most of the rest of his life getting her back and retaining her. Her master had agreed to sell her to her husband, demanding the absurd price of 300 ounces of silver for a woman whose market price was at best no more than 80 ounces. In this case, as in so many where human relations are involved, it was a seller's market and Ashi Chesa must either agree or allow her to be sold at her real price, but to some different place where he would never see her again.

By various "fiddles"—tending horses on the side, growing opium —he had managed to pay 50 ounces in the bluish alloy that passes for silver in Cool Mountains. He was still in debt after all those years and the return of Ashi Kwam was being more and more vehemently demanded when the reform began. If she had gone it would have left crippled Ashi Chesa and his crippled girl of twelve to fend for themselves in not the most benevolent of environments.

Because separate-slaves are under less strict surveillance and must have some small means of production, they can sometimes get money in the same way as Ashi Chesa did, which they use to buy slaves themselves. Slaves possess slaves, and even the slaves of slaves possess slaves.

So it appears that separate-slaves own some means of production and have some right of inheritance. Indeed there is a saying: "The master eats myself and my children, but my possessions he does not eat". Slaves are also able to use the wealth they acquire in side-occupations to buy their freedom, or they may be released for some signal service to their owner, such as saving his life in battle. Perhaps a slave runs away to place himself under the protection of a strong enemy of his master, to be raised to the level of common bondsman to his new owner as a reward.

Some slaves achieve freedom, but at the same time more than half of the bondsmen, even those who own several slaves, live under the constant menace of being enslaved with their whole families for debt. There is also the risk of being abducted by any casual slaver from some other place, of being taken prisoner in a clan dispute and, in rare cases, a man will run out of money in a gambling game and stake himself or his family on the turn of the dice.

Thus between the mass of commoners and the mass of slaves there is a constant flow of unknown dimensions.

Some local students of the Norsu regard these as signs that this is a society in the process of transition from slavery to feudalism. There are arguments in favour of this view but no statistics exist, and probably none ever will exist, to show whether more slaves have been entering the half freedom of common bondage or more commoners leaving it for slavery.

Others in Ninglang argue that if a master owns his slave and his slave's children, how can he fail to own his slave's cow. Certainly slaves can sell or give away what is theirs, but equally their masters can take over their property at any time on any pretext and flog them to death into the bargain. Separate-slaves prefer not to acquire much visible property.

Nevertheless, it seems to me the argument of the latter school is somewhat formal. And against the argument of the transitional school it may be said that the proportion of slaves greatly increased by capture in the past forty years. Maybe enough evidence will be accumulated eventually to settle these fascinating questions. From what is known, Norsu society seems to be a moribund mixture of social forms.

House-slaves are the most abject of all humans in the Cool Mountains and maybe anywhere in the world. They possess nothing at all, not even the tatters they wear. Unable to "cheat" to any greater extent than growing a little opium secretly, they live at bedrock subsistence level, eating only what they are given by the master and that is very little indeed. Their normal diet is the coarse siftings of the grains they have ground for the master's family, mixed with swill from his table and wild vegetables collected by themselves, served in a wooden trough on the floor.

While they remain in their master's home, generally until they are able to produce children, they are treated like animals—actually rather worse than animals—work all available hours, tend the fire at night and are beaten for the least hint of fault or at the whim of their ill-tempered and opium-sodden master or mistress. They are unimaginably ignorant.

After a while I automatically asked every house-slave, "Were you beaten?" and never heard one reply "No". Abi Vugan, a Han girl who was stolen from her parents at the age of three or four—according to her mistress—was minding the slave-owner's children at the age of seven and his herds at the age of ten. By twelve she was "main" labour, getting firewood from the hills in the morning, farming by day, grinding meal in the evening and keeping the fire alight at night. Beatings were daily, "very hard, but I'd sooner be beaten than be punished by not getting food. That often happened."

Ashu Vuga, another girl of about twenty-two, thought that her parents had been first-generation slaves. She looked like a Han. Her working history was similar to Abi Vugan's. Two of her fellow slaves died of malnutrition and maltreatment. A third committed suicide after a beating of exceptional severity. She stole opium and ate it to commit suicide but failed. "Most often I was beaten with a broom handle," she said.

Lulrl Duve, fourth-generation slave, was originally owned by a rich commoner. He died without sons and she passed into the possession of his overlord. She was taken from her mother at the age of thirteen. "I got so homesick that I ran back to see her. They soon caught me up and dragged me back running behind a horse. Near our house they held me down in the river, sometimes under the water. It was winter. Then I had to kneel in my wet clothes while my master flogged me. I was screaming. He kicked me in the face with his nailed shoe and laid my forehead open here." She has a deep scar running up from her left eyebrow.

"My treatment was the same with both masters. We ate gruel with wild vegetables. Meat? Of course not! Once a year, maybe, at the New Year, we might each get a bit of meat as big as my two fingers.

"My first job was minding a young baby. If it cried I was beaten so I had to nurse it most of the night, trying to doze, and then work all day as well. I was all alone and beaten all the time." Tears began to run down her brown face.

Had she ever heard of a slave who wasn't beaten? There were some. Clever girls who won favour and helped in managing the master's household, doling out food, work and blows to other slaves. "They never marry," she added.

Favourite slaves do not marry but it would not be profitable to allow their child-bearing capacity to go unused. A slave from elsewhere or a likely young commoner is mated with them to produce more slaves. Owing to strong caste prejudices, girl slaves are not much used by their masters for their own sexual gratification, though this happens if the mistress is away and the fact unlikely to become known.

Notwithstanding the considerable interchange between bondsmen and slaves, it is a loss of social prestige for a male commoner to marry a slave and impermissible for a male slave to marry a bondswoman. In this they follow faithfully the *mores* of their joint overlords. If a commoner is too poor to get a wife of his own caste, he will sometimes enter an arrangement with a slave-owner to marry one of his slaves. As a rule, the slave-owner will then claim all the children as slaves, otherwise the arrangement is a loss to him. If other factors enter the contract, the master may have to be content with all the boys, or all the girls. Girls are more valuable than boys and young slaves than older ones. Norsu slave-owners agree with Cato, that perfect slave-owner of whom Plutarch records that he bought slaves young "that is, of an age when they could be easily subjected to education and training like puppies and foals".

It is rare for nobles to have sex relations with slaves, but it happens. There are indigent nobles, swashbuckling wastrels who eat from door to door and scrape what living they can from feuding to slave-grabbing so long as no work is involved. Labour above all is not possible for an aristocrat. These "dry Nor", as they are called, usually have no slaves and so cannot work any land and are usually in no position to exercise their privileges over their commoners. In this case, the noble will generally sell his rights to exact privilege to some other noble for a trifling sum. He cannot sell his bondsmen physically unless they have been enslaved according to normal custom, but he can surreptitiously arrange for somebody to kidnap them as slaves on the understanding that, for a slightly larger amount, he will not raise any hue-and-cry over the theft.

In 1949 there was a case of three "dry Nor" brothers, too poor to get a wife, who clubbed together and bought one female slave with whom all had relations. This set every noble tongue wagging and they were social outcasts from then on.

To a noble, commoners and slaves are all *nji*, but among them there are many social distinctions. At the top, next to the nobles, are commoners who can trace their Norsu ancestry back for several generations of "freedom" and who themselves own many slaves. In itself possession of slaves confers prestige. Nevertheless, a poor commoner without slaves regards himself as superior to a slave who possesses slaves. A slave belonging to a noble considers himself above the slave of a commoner and that slave looks down on the slave of a slave. A "Norsu" slave looks down on a "foreign slave" and an old slave on one recently enslaved, especially on those who have not yet acquired Norsu custom. Those who know their parents scorn those who do not. Crushed, downtrodden and in mental darkness, they accept the ideas of their masters as eternal laws. Norsu society is an object lesson in the absurdity of national chauvinism, it being quite amazing how strongly an enslaved Han can feel about being a "Norsu" and this applies to all castes including the lowest I could discover—the slave of a slave of a slave.

One obvious question that needed to be clarified was why a slave who owned other slaves did not sell them to buy his own freedom. I put this question to a typical representative of this group, Arlul Zeda, a "real Norsu" slave who owned two slaves. He first look puzzled at the question and then eyed me as though I were an ignorant newly-captured Han who might be expected not to know any better.

"I and my wife are very expensive slaves, worth far more than my two slaves. Suppose I sold my two; I wouldn't even get enough to buy myself out, let alone my wife and children. We come from several generations of Norsu slaves."

He went on, making everything as simple as possible for the ignorant foreigner: "A slave of several generations is not likely to run off. I know how to manage things as a slave, how to get along. Since I became a separate-slave, I've been better off than a good many free bondsmen. It's fairly safe that slaves like us won't try to run away. And another thing, if I did run away, where could I go? I am a Norsu. Suppose I went to a Han district. Short shrift I'd get. Nobody likes a Norsu.

"I could only afford to buy cheap, newly-caught slaves; cheap-bone people. But still, it is a good thing to own slaves. Brings a man respect. They could do my work for the master and I could work for myself. A man with slaves is somebody.

"Buying yourself out isn't so easy. The price is always put high and when you are out you start with nothing. Next thing you know you're back again with a new master and maybe no wife. At my age (he said he was over fifty) it's too risky."

In the Cool Mountains every gradation of ownership and part-ownership of slaves can be found. Jingu Hushe told me how, as a separate-slave, he acquired ownership of half of his own wife.

A woman who is provided as the wife of a slave to establish a separate household is of course still the master's property and must spend most of her time working for the slave-owner. Jingu Hushe's wife was a very expensive slave, having cost the top price of fourteen ingots (about £20). She was tall, strong, handsome and a magnificent breeder, having had seven children in about sixteen years, and still looking both younger and more intelligent than her husband.

Two major motives existed for Jingu Hushe to buy a half-share in his wife. First, this would make it difficult for the master to separate the pair by sale later and, second, half of his wife's time could be spent on their own land and household affairs instead of about one-fifth to one-eighth as is normal.

Jingu Hushe inherited a half-share of his own sister, the other half being owned by his master. This was due to his father having been lucky while looking after some horses for another person. A mare had foaled and by custom new-born animals belong to whomever is looking after them at the time. In order to get more help at home, Jingu Hushe's father had sold the young stallion for seven ingots and bought half of his own daughter. When his father died, Hushe had inherited this half of his sister and so he was able to sell her out entirely to the master and buy half of his wife.

His half-share of his wife did not entitle him to any of his own children who all belonged to the master and had already been allocated to various sections of the master's family. They would have been split in all directions by marriage of the master's children but for the abolition.

A nobleman can even be enslaved by a commoner. This has occurred in the past, or so people say, by debt, gambling or abduction to a distant place. In this rare event, the noble is expected to preserve honour by committing suicide.

Some things are fairly clear in this apparently confusing picture: most nobles possess both bondsmen and slaves, the biggest slave-holding known in the Cool Mountains being 158 owned by a Buyu family; some commoners are rich and own many slaves; about half the commoners own some slaves; slaves are divided approximately into two-thirds separate-slaves and one-third house-slaves; slaves themselves own about one-twentieth of all the slaves.

But the majority of commoners do not own enough slaves to free them from the need of work—the most important ideological yardstick in the Cool Mountains.

CHAPTER FOUR

SEX, MARRIAGE AND KINSHIP

Remnants of mother-right—Three unbreakable rules—Women's high position—Daughters richer than sons—Women can stop war—High cost of marriage—Marital rights must be won—Widows always become wives— Marriage by abduction—Elopement is dangerous

SOME of the peculiarities of the Norsu slave system seem to be traceable to the system of marriage, sex relations and consanguinity among the nobility carried over from an earlier, non-slave society. These *mores*, imitated by the commoners and slaves, cannot be fully exercised by them owing to the limitations of their bondage. Only among the Black Bones are they fully—and rigidly—observed.

Norsu society preserves what appear to be strong traces of an earlier matriarchal form. Such traces are common in Yunnan, and indeed the Mosu nationality in the northern Cool Mountains have branches where full matriarchy exists to this day with descent through the mother line.

Among Norsu nobles there are three basic rules of marriage: inside the nationality, inside one's own caste, outside one's own clan. Norsu nobles who cannot afford a wife of noble family prefer to remain single.

Father-line descendants cannot marry because they are members of the same clan. But the children of brothers and sisters, married as they must be into different clans, have priority of marriage. Brother and sister will pledge that if their children are of opposite sexes they will marry. Breach of such a pledge would lead to a feud unless it is by agreement at a later date with compensations paid.

Children of two sisters, however, are forbidden to marry regardless of their clan names and breach of this rule carries the death penalty. This seems to be a direct remnant of matriarchy.

Daughters of sisters are called "sisters" and they refer to their own mother as "Big Mother" (*ahmu*) and to their sisters in order of seniority as "Mother One", "Mother Two", "Mother Three" (*muni ahj, muni ahei, muni gahdz*).

Infringements of marriage rules are an affair of the whole clan and

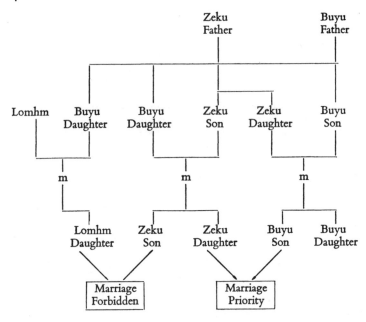

other clans would not condone them. Offenders, facing total social ostracism in this small community, are generally forced to commit suicide and their bodies are burned. Sometimes they are put to death by burning.

Women occupy a high position in aristocratic Nòrsu society, some people even place it higher than that of men. I met one fiery little wine-bibbing warrior with a reputation for fierceness who admitted that if his wife told him: "No drink today", he would not take a drink. Moreover he would go home to his wife and specifically report: "I have heeded your words and taken no drink." I was told that if he failed to obey, it was quite on the cards that she would commit suicide and that this would then become a clan matter, probably leading to war. Threat of suicide by Norsu wives is very common and it is not an idle threat. Norsu women are extremely sensitive to what is regarded as a social affront or loss of face. I was told that it is by no means rare for Norsu girls to commit suicide because of accidentally breaking wind in the company of males. A case is cited which occurred in 1949, showing how heinous an insult it is for a stranger to touch the skirt of a Norsu woman. During the mediation of a feud, a wealthy commoner, trusting in his own nobles to protect him, ostentatiously pretended to lift the skirt of a noble woman in order to annoy the other side. His own people rounded on him and he had to pay an indemnity of 4,000 ounces of silver to the enemy clan to save his own life.

Norsu noblewomen's powerful position seems to derive from two prime sources. Clan protection is one; the other is their economic position. Women inherit their share of the main wealth of the Norsu society—the slaves—in their own right. Daughters of the separate-slaves must become the property of the master's daughters of the same generation, even if there are only girl slaves. Unless this is done, fatally bad luck to the family's slave enterprises would ensue.

Daughters inherit horses, cattle, sheep and silver equally with the sons and they also have other private property. While the males go around fighting and squandering their wealth, mothers save up for their girls from birth onwards. Slaves, horses, cattle, accumulated silver and heirlooms are taken by the betrothed to her husband's house and part of the enormous wedding gifts of the groom to the bride's family is given to the bride to carry back as her own to her husband's house. Since marriages mostly take place between families of approximately equal status a wife's property is generally greater than her husband's.

Women have the determining voice in the household and a wife's agreement must be sought in any important matter. In feuds, if the fighting becomes too fierce and general, the noblewomen on either side may come out and wave their skirts or cloaks. Fighting must then stop at once. It is a heavily sanctioned and grave social crime to kill a woman. Indeed it is generally held that women must not be attacked at all.

One reason for this may be that in any noble household there are usually women from several clans but males of only one clan.

Even if previously-pledged first cousins get married by long term arrangement between a brother and sister, there has to be a middleman, and still more so where the marriage is being arranged between un-related people. He stays weeks—even months—in the house of the girl, using all his eloquence to extol the unheard-of qualities of the would-be groom. Finally the promise is given with a great show of reluctance, fortune telling is carried out by sacrifice, the betrothal gifts are sent and celebrations are held at great expense. The wedding can take place. All very costly—to the commoners.

Every time the middleman goes to the house of the girl, the boy's family must give at least ten bottles of liquor and some meat. But he stays in the girl's house at the expense of her family. If the boy's side is very persistent, the expense of keeping the middleman so long weighs favourably in the balance for the boy. At betrothal the boy's family must give to the girl's family three very good racehorses, ten silver ingots, ten ordinary horses or cattle and 100 sheep. Then there are gifts to the middleman, to the managers of the wedding, wedding gifts, three silver ingots each to the families of the commoners who accompany the bride to her husband's home. The more of these the better for prestige. I estimated the total minimum presents at 2,670 yuan (£400). This is a terrific sum in a place where the average annual spending is loosely reckoned at about £1 10s. per head.

On the surface, the bride is purchased, but actual relations deny this appearance. A noble girl going to her husband's house does not go as a chattel and she cannot be repudiated or divorced. If there is maltreatment or even a fancied cause leading to suicide, the very least that would occur is payment of compensation of 3,000 ounces of silver to her clan and there would most likely be a clan war ending in payment of perhaps more ingots, each worth 10 ounces.

After the marriage feast, the girl may not remain long with her husband but goes back to her own family accompanied by her common girls and her clansmen. Then her husband sends again for her and she again returns to her old home, accompanied each time by presents. This goes on until the birth of a child.

During this period, and up to the birth of the child, the newly-weds can half-openly or "secretly" have affairs with others—especially cousins on the father's side. But if the newly-wed girl has had no sex relations with her husband and gives birth, there is a serious feud between the household of the husband and the wife's lover and, more rarely, a feud between the households of the husband and wife. In this case the presents have to be returned. But still this does not mean divorce. In most cases the feud is settled by blood, or silver wrung from the commoners, and the marriage later resumes its course.

The possibility of such a situation arises from the traditional duty of the wife to resist her husband's advances as long as possible and of any woman to offer a realistic pretence of resistance to the advances of any man. Sometimes two or three years will pass before a husband is able to have relations with his own wife. It is her customary right and duty to resist her husband with especial realism, biting, scratching and generally making intercourse impossible and an acquiescent wife would be regarded by her husband as being of questionable nobility or morals, just as a husband who finally failed to force his wife to acquiesce would become a laughing stock to her and everyone else.

The elder son of a Norsu noble whose name I had better withhold was refused by his wife for three years. In the end he bound her to a plank and whipped her till she submitted and this was regarded by one and all as the hallmark of a marriage destined for success. Cases have occurred of wives resisting their husbands for as long as seven years before being subdued by beatings.

This resistance continues even after the birth of children and is only relaxed when several children have been born.

To other lovers a newly-wed wife would make only a formal resistance, a few scratches on face or arms to enable her to "prove" her resistance satisfactorily to herself and her lover. Sexual promiscuity, however, is only permissible while the wife is still commuting between the two homes and ceases when she lives at the home of her husband. Otherwise there is strict monogamy for the women and almost equally so for the men because of clan protection of the women. A man whose first wife is sterile can take a second wife and if both rich and fecund may also be able to do so after a number of children are born, if he can pay the first wife's family enough.

Inside the husband's household a wife is not required to be entirely faithful. Nothing is said if a wife sleeps with the younger brother of her husband during his absence from home, and her husband is not jealous of this. It would be improper for her to do this while her husband is in the locality and if he found them *in flagrante delicto* the husband would certainly administer a beating to the brother, though no big quarrel would be caused.

An elder brother, far from having this privilege, is not permitted to meet the eyes of his younger brother's wife. This prohibition is not enforced if the younger brother's wife is a first cousin, but in other cases the girl would not eat at the same table with her elder brother-in-law or her father-in-law. She and the brother must avoid meeting face to face and if they should accidentally do so, compensation must be made. The girl presents a bottle of wine to her brother-in-law who gives her a silver ingot and there is a drinking party. After this the two take the greatest care never to confront each other. This rule is also relaxed somewhat after the wife has produced several children. Then they may talk together but never sit at the same table.

A widow becomes the wife of her dead husband's younger brother by "transfer of household", or if there is no younger brother, to an elder brother of the deceased (even if they formerly made compensation for confronting each other). Where there are no brothers, the dead husband's father can take over the widow but only if there were no children of the marriage. Or cousins, near and distant, can be the recipients of the widow. Whatever happens she must be "transferred" or the wife's maternal family will accuse the husband's family of despising her clan and a feud might begin that would last generations.

In such "transfer of household" the man gives a cow or sheep, the neighbours have a feast, the couple sit around trying to look shy and a good bout of drinking ends the ceremony.

In these cases, the man has full marital rights and obligations and though he may have a wife and several transferred wives, this does not give rise to jealousy. During my talks with a nobleman named Zeku Alu, he casually remarked: "I don't have any problem about living. My income is enough to keep me, my wife, four children and the transferred wife of my elder brother."

Marriage by abduction still exists but is not genuine marriage by abduction, which is normal in other parts of Yunnan, for example among the Jingpaw. Norsu boys and girls of equal caste and different clans may fall in love but meet parental disagreement with their marriage. In this case, sometimes the girl tells the boy where she will be collecting firewood and he gets his friends together to take her by "force". Once the issue is raised in such a public manner and the girl undeniably seduced, the parents are usually willing to come to terms. They send out a party to seek the girl and the boy's side sends a party to intercept and negotiate. Usually the wedding presents in these cases are less than in a negotiated marriage.

Marriage by elopement also occurs rarely, usually because the boy's parents cannot afford to pay the presents demanded by the girl's side. After elopement—which damages the reputation of the girl's family— the husband will never be able to visit there. Elopement is dangerous since it involves matters of hard cash. If caught, both parties have sometimes been put to death, regardless of whether they were eligible to marry by custom and equality of wealth and position.

These customs are maintained as far as circumstances permit and at a lower level, by all other castes. The average cost of wedding gifts among commoners I found to be 93 yuan (£13).

Traditional Norsu feelings that the sex-act lowers a woman's status extend down to the separate-slaves among whom a man will show his scratched arms to prove the morality and "superior bone" of the slave-wife his master has married to him.

CHAPTER FIVE

HU TAN'S DELICATE MISSION

Rumours of revolution—The hated Han—"Pastor An" makes a proposi-
tion—Into the Cool Mountains by night—Beginning of the big push—Slave-
owners help to fight the Kuomintang—"Good Hans and bad Hans"—
Shortage of slaves—Sorcerers get busy—Structure of a slave society

UP from mountain-locked Yung Sheng basin, through Bird Pass into the Cool Mountains, rumour trickled along with captured slaves and smuggled rifles that big changes were on the way all over China. It was 1948, and the Communist-led People's Liberation Army had already taken Mukden, surrounded Peking and carved to pieces the bulk of Chiang Kai-shek's armies. People said that the end of the Kuomintang was only a matter of weeks or months. As these tales spread through the Cool Mountains, people recalled that a dozen years earlier, a tattered starving Communist army had marched through this corner of Yunnan and had told them that it would return to set them free from the Kuomintang and its foreign backers, bringing a better life with self-government to the minority peoples.

Slave-owners had very mixed feelings about what they heard of these ragged but evidently capable fighters. The military deeds of Communist Generals Ho Lung and Hsiao Ke became legends. News filtered back from over the Szechuan border of a daring hand-over-hand crossing of the chains of the burned-out bridge at Luting in the teeth of Kuomintang machine-gun fire—a battle which had taken the locking-pin out of Chiang Kai-shek's entire local military plan and permitted the Red Army to pass on its way to Yenan. Feats like this struck a sympathetic chord in the hearts of the Norsu clan leaders, used as they were to podgy sycophancy, corruption and military ineptitude from the Kuomintang.

It seemed that the Red Army fighters had the heroic qualities which the Norsu leaders attributed to themselves and in addition, the winds up Bird Pass told of an army that never took so much as a thread of cotton to mend a coat from the peoples as it passed, paid for anything it wanted, treated people courteously, did not tolerate rape—an army of avenging angels.

Not only were the Kuomintang local leaders guilty of that most spine-chilling crime in the Norsu vocabulary—cowardice—they also committed every other offence in the list and especially that of stealing racehorses. The Cool Mountains have long been famous for their breed of small, rounded, muscle-packed racehorses. A good animal is worth half a dozen slaves and a top-class one worth twenty human cattle in prestige to its owner. Although small, these horses will carry a six-foot man straight up a steep mountain and even have to be held in check.

When the Red Army reached this area, Chiang Kai-shek sent General Kuo to Yung Sheng with an army that devoured the countryside and made raids into Norsu country. By a confidence trick, Kuomintang officers managed to get hold of about twenty of the best racehorses, which they exchanged for twenty of their sore-backed hacks.

Since no fate could be too bad for racehorse thieves, it seemed a very good thing that the Communists were trouncing the Kuomintang. Against this, the Kuomintang had never bothered about whether or not the Norsu had slaves, while the Communists were said to stand for the poor against the rich. It was all extremely confusing.

One thing was clear and unarguable: the Communists were Hans, hereditary enemies of the Norsu. Let them do what they pleased to each other on the plains, the Norsu could always keep them out of the highlands as they had done during dynasty after dynasty.

At this time the chief figure among the Norsu was Buyu Wani, almost undisputed leader of the Buyu clan which is bigger than the total membership of the other four clans. Centre of Buyu Wani's domain was only a day's march through Bird Pass to Yung Sheng where the Kuomintang was garrisoned and it often fell to Buyu Wani, as to his father before, to negotiate settlements with them on the plain below.

When the big drive south against the Kuomintang was being prepared and even the Americans were beginning to feel that maybe the dollars they had lavished on Chiang Kai-shek had been poured down a rathole, two people contacted Buyu Wani.

One was a British missionary, "Pastor An", who chose this nodal point of history to suggest that it was time the church entered the Cool Mountains—no mention being made of radio equipment; the other was Hu Tan, a very young Han Communist who had been given the responsibility for developing underground resistance to the Kuomintang in the same area.

D

In point of time, Hu Tan got there first. In disguise and armed only with a pistol, he avoided Bird Pass, went over the peaks in the dark and into an almost trackless plateau where the pleasantest fate if caught would be a reasonably quick death. He had no knowledge of the Norsu language and only a few topographical facts to guide him in seeking Buyu Wani's home. But this was work of the greatest moment because the Cool Mountains was just such a border area that would attract masses of Kuomintang remnants—an ideal stronghold for a drawn-out resistance which would cost many lives and tie up many troops. Hu Tan's job was to win the Norsu to co-operate with the People's Liberation Army in wiping out the Kuomintang.

This proposition had certain attractive aspects which were quickly apparent to Buyu Wani when Hu Tan contacted him after several days of spying out the ground. Buyu Wani could speak the Han language and night after night he discussed Hu Tan's propositions, hiding the Communist underground worker in his house all day and later riding with him further into the Cool Mountains to hide him in the house of one of his sons.

For people who had the insight to look beyond the hated name of Han, co-operation with the PLA had its points. Anyone could see what would happen if large groups of Kuomintang fugitive troops tried to use the Cool Mountains to make what must be a hopeless but protracted stand.

Preventing that was one thing, but having invited the policeman in, how to get him out again?

Night after night Hu Tan, Buyu Wani and his sons, raised their points and discussed what could be done. "He was most frank," Buyu Wani told me, speaking excellent Han. "He said things were never going to be the same again. His party—the Communist Party—must win and the minority people would be their own masters. China would become great and rich and there would be a reform here, but this would be done only in agreement with the nobility. Everyone would advance and become well-to-do." Buyu Wani, thin, yellowish and frail looking, talked to me many times in Ninglang, where he is now the head of Ninglang County as well as a member of the National People's Congress, China's parliament. From these talks I gradually culled the story which Hu Tan was too modest to tell.

"Hu Tan came and went," Buyu Wani said. "Once when he was hiding in my house, he fell sick and of course we couldn't get a sorcerer. I wanted to kill a sheep and pass it round his head to cure him but he said that was superstitious. We became friendly. I believed what he said. He stayed in Yung Sheng, living secretly, working underground. That place was getting full of Kuomintang bigshots quarrelling among themselves."

Buyu Wani was appointed by the PLA to be commander of the Norsu people's affairs in the Cool Mountains and, using his powerful position as leader of the biggest clan, he began preparing forces to take military action against the Kuomintang in co-ordination with the Han underground forces on the plains.

At this time he was contacted by "Pastor An" who, Buyu Wani said, "seemed a good fellow". He met him in Yung Sheng before the People's Liberation Army began what was to be its last great push that ended in clearing Chiang Kai-shek right off the Chinese mainland. "Pastor An" contacted Buyu Wani in Yung Sheng and said he wanted his people to be allowed to enter the Cool Mountains and spread Christianity. British aircraft at that time were using a strip of the Li Chiang plateau, three days march away, as a landing ground. Buyu Wani told the "Pastor" that things were rather complicated and it would be better to wait. He added that in his view Christianity would not be welcomed by the Norsu. Missionaries had taught a written language to some Lisu and taught them Christianity, and now there were disputes between converts and the rest, he said. "Pastor An" argued that really the British and the Norsu were one "people". He said: "You see, Norsu women wear skirts and so do British women. We are not like the Hans." Buyu Wani commented: "They did not look at all like Norsu women in photographs. Very short skirts, more like slaves. Anyway, I told him we did not want Christianity also because you can't eat certain things."

By early 1949 Yung Sheng was a cockpit where runaway landlords and their bullies, local petty warlords and Kuomintang soldiery were feuding and squabbling beyond the verge of dissolution. Hu Tan told Buyu Wani that it was time to strike. With Hu Tan leading the guerillas from the plains and Buyu Wani the Norsu fighters from the mountains, they sandwiched big Kuomintang forces and cut them up.

"But my forces did not understand the situation well," Buyu Wani said. "Instead of regrouping to polish them off, they looted and took slaves. I was worried and fell sick."

A few months later, 1,000 Kuomintang troops counter-attacked at Yung Sheng, were beaten and fled north to Yenpien over the border in Szechuan.

At this point another big slave-owner with quite a different sort of history entered the scene—Zeku Alu, famous racehorse breeder whose father owned the most renowned of all Norsu racehorses, Aniwanduhi. Zeku Alu was dying to get his own back on the Kuomintang who had stolen his racehorses and silver, burned 300 houses of his clan, looted and raped. But when the PLA came to Ninglang, Zeku Alu fled to the hills and refused to have anything to do with them because they were Hans.

"Then a PLA officer named Ma came along, with a few Norsu nobles to persuade me to come back. That was a brave thing to do and it made a big impression on me. There were meetings, doctrines, and they gave things to the Norsu people instead of taking them away. Captain Ma said there were good Hans and bad Hans.

"After a time I offered to go north to deal with the Kuomintang army there, either to talk them into surrender or help fight them." This was a tough assignment; the local Chiang Kai-shek officers being no less than Generals Hu Tsung-nan and Ho Kuo-kuan. The PLA approved and Zeku Alu was given a company of PLA soldiers to accompany his thirty fighting men.

Zeku Alu's whole life had been fighting, though in appearance he is slender, graceful, with a thin aristocratic face, long gentle fingers, like an intellectual from an Oscar Wilde play. Negotiations with the Kuomintang led to nothing, so he led his company against their 3,000 men and annihilated them in the hills. "I got a banner for that," he said.

"I stayed in Yenpien a month learning politics. They said blood revenge was unreasonable and feuds were bad. My mind started to change. I was a rich man but I wore no shoes and could not write my own name. They told me that all Norsu people could be well-to-do. I had never realised before how poor we were, not always much to eat, only one poor suit and cloak, no proper houses, no factories, nothing.

"They explained that if we went on keeping slaves we would all remain backward because slaves had no reason to work well."

"I had reckoned that as soon as the Communists had helped us to get rid of Chiang Kai-shek's men, they must get out or we would fight them too," said Buyu Wani, making the same point as Zeku Alu. "Bit by bit I saw that we had been deceiving ourselves. I went to Peking with Zeku Alu and some others. That was an eyeopener: trains, cars, factories; we met Chairman Mao and when people saw our black Norsu cloaks they wanted to shake our hands.

"What did we have? Slaves, animals, opium crops, land, feasts for 3,000 people, feed our animals with new grain and potatoes, better than we fed ourselves and then we all went hungry half the year. No security, no peace. Always wars, raids, battles."

How typical were these men? I would say not at all. Very few, a tiny handful of Norsu nobles felt like that in 1952. To the rest, nobles, commoners and slaves, a Han was a Han. Communist Hans might seem better than the Kuomintang Hans, but they were merely doing a confidence trick of a rather more complicated nature. Good behaviour was the sugar round the pill.

Rumours filtered into the Cool Mountains about land reform, how landlords had been stood up at mass meetings, reviled, their land taken away and some of them executed for blood crimes. Slave-owners, too, were "rich", and had flogged, chained and killed their slaves. What could they expect from Communists?

The nobles looked at the "cheap-bone" Hans with contempt for their non-Norsu origin, with respect for their military ability and with disquiet for their known antagonism to slavery and their open sympathy for the slaves.

Abduction inside the Cool Mountains went on but slave-raids into surrounding districts were no longer possible. The main pipe-line of slave supply had already dried up. Things were beginning to look bad and all because of the Hans, as usual.

This was the lowering atmosphere into which one Communist Party work-team arrived at Bolo rural district in the Racecourse area. There were two people in the team: one Mosu[1] and one Minchia girl.[2] A Han *ganbu*[3] arrived a few months later in 1953.

They had only what they brought on their horses and their first job was to build their own house.

"You've seen for yourself the poverty of this place," said Chinluan

---

[1] The Mosu are a small branch of the Nashi people. They preserve the matriarchal system in what seems from hearsay to be almost its pure form. Children only recognise their mothers and their mothers' brothers, and do not know their fathers. To ask a Mosu about his or her father is insulting. It is said that the women live together, taking menfolk in as convenient and ejecting their lovers when they tire of them. Some Mosu live in the most northerly corner of the Ninglang County on the Szechuan border, too far away for me to reach on this trip.

[2] She later married Mu Tan. Minchia are also known as Bai, a common nationality in the Tali region.

[3] *Ganbu* is commonly translated as "cadre" in China. They are working personnel of the government or Communist Party. The term is untranslatable. The two Chinese characters individually mean "to get it done" and "office" or "department", which gives a flavour of the overall meaning. The word is better left italicised.

Denze the Mosu, and still leader of the team. "That is after we have done a lot of relief work. Try to imagine what it was like then. Girls and boys of fourteen and fifteen, long past puberty, did not even have trousers. They covered themselves as best they could in tattered cloaks.

"How they hated us! To them we were Hans—in any case, not Norsu. We could not speak a word of their language. We got on with building our house and in between tried to make contact with the children, giving them little things in exchange for a word of their language. At the end of the day we sat round the camp-fire (wondering if a bullet would come out of the hills), and exchanged the words we had learned. It was a big day when we spoke to an adult, an inquisitive commoner, for slaves were under orders not to talk with us. It was an occasion for real celebration when someone spoke to us first. But gradually they began to believe we were not the same as the Kuomintang people."

Relief goods began to flow down the horse trail from Li Chiang and were distributed by the team. "We had only one slogan: 'Do good and make friends.' It wasn't easy. Rumours were spread that the relief goods we gave away were loans. They said that after a while we would demand payment with interest and take away as slaves those who had accepted them," said Ahjin, the Minchia girl.

She did simple medical work, which did not please the local sorcerers, who spread it round that pills and injections were to sterilise the Norsu people and cause them to die out. None the less it was medicine that broke the ice, as it so often does among the backward peoples.

A slave's child fell in the fire and got badly burned. It was obviously a fatal case in local terms and the sorcerer said, "If you have a sheep, kill it and at least send the child to a proper place." Ahjin offered to cure it. It was a test case. For days the whole place was agog with excitement as Ahjin went to work with penicillin, sulpha, boric and mercurochrome. The infant's health waxed and waned, sorcerers sneered and predicted that the child's spirit would end up badly. Then the crisis was over and the word went round: "*Gongzo's* (the work-team's) medicine is more powerful than the sorcerer's."

After this the work-team's stock was high. A doctor arrived and surgical cases were tackled with success. But then the local Lomhm clan leaders got defeated in a battle with the Buyu clan and stated that this was because the work-team sorcerers were working magic against the Lomhm. Nobody came near them for a long time after that.

By late 1955 they had learned the language and were well enough acquainted with things to begin a survey of their district—one of four rural districts in Racecourse Area.

This was the first time that the actual social composition of Norsu slavery was analysed. It gave the following break-down by caste for Racecourse area:

	Households	Individuals
Nobles . . .	30	123
Bondsmen . .	825	3,737
Separate-slaves . .	358	1,426
House-slaves . .	0	955

A further break-down by slave-ownership is needed to bring the picture into relief:

	Households	Individuals	Percentage
Owning 10 or more slaves	41	168	2·69
Owning 5–9 slaves .	82	381	6·10
Owning 1–4 slaves .	335	1,551	24·86
Bondsmen owning no slaves . . .	397	1,760	28·20
Separate-slaves . .	358	1,426 }	38·15
House-slaves . . .	0	955 }	

The first group (consisting of nobles and rich commoners) which owned more than 10 slaves per household, owned 35·9 per cent. of the slaves and the nobles of that group were overlords of 67 per cent. of the commoners. Each family in this group owned an average 19·93 slaves.

The second group owning 5–9 slaves per family owned 25 per cent. of the slaves and the nobles included in that group were overlords to 23 per cent. of the commoners. Each family averaged 7·05 slaves.

The third group owning 1–4 slaves per family owned 33·9 per cent. of the slaves and included the overlords of most of the rest of the commoners.[1] Each family averaged 2·23 slaves.

---

[1] Some nobles might be "dry" and own no slaves, and some commoners might be bondsmen of nobles living in another area.

Separate-slave families owned 4·8 per cent. of the slaves.

Landholding figures produced by the survey show an enormous preponderance of land in the hands of the biggest slave-owners, that is, mainly the nobles.

(The table below is given in *chia* of land which is a variable measurement roughly equivalent to what an ox can plough in one day. It is approximately one-third of an acre.)

	Chia per Group	Chia per Person	Percentage
Owners of 10 or more slaves	. 46,463	277·00	87·9
Owners of 5–9 slaves . .	. 4,122	10·80	7·8
Owners of 1–4 slaves . .	. 1,656	1·07	3·1
Bondsmen owning no slaves .	398	0·22	0·75
Separate-slaves	237	0·17	0·45
House-slaves	0	0·00	0·00
	52,876		100·00

Almost all of the land—95·7 per cent.—was owned by 8·79 per cent. of the people and those were the people owning five slaves upwards. Only 4·3 per cent. of the land was in the hands of the remaining 91·21 per cent. of the people.

In actual usage of the land, the figures give a different result. Some land is rented out and some lying fallow.

Land actually in use in Racecourse Area, 1956

	Chia per Group	Chia per Person
Owning 10 or more slaves . .	12,556	74·70
Owning 5–9 slaves . . .	5,317	14·00
Owning 1–4 slaves . . .	5,777	3·70
Bondsmen without slaves . .	5,380	3·06
Separate-slaves	3,551	2·50
House-slaves	0	0·00
	32,581	100·00

Typically for slave society, property in slaves is important and property in land not. There is plenty of land in the Cool Mountains which is not used at all. Land has little enough value and is easy to rent, so possession of labour power decides how much land a person can exploit. When ownership of land becomes decisive, this is already a sign that feudalism has the upper hand.

The first two groups—that is, people owning more than five slaves, were also found to be the biggest usurers. Out of a total 10,515 yuan (£1,500) owed in July 1956 in Racecourse Area, 9,043 yuan was owed to members of these groups.

Although the Cool Mountains appears to be a place where enormous crops could be grown, as in Tibet, the level of production is fantastically low. Land is not fixed. Slash-burn cultivation is universal and the tools are of the most primitive kind.

In these historically by-passed highlands, slave and master alike ate porridge and wild vegetables with insufficient salt. Steamed oaten loaves and parched grain were almost luxuries. There was never enough salt. Only the wealthy could eat plenty of meat, poultry and butter with their grain and potatoes.

Bondsmen might feel themselves superior to slaves but they were not much better off and plenty of separate-slaves were more well-to-do than most poor commoners. And even commoners with several slaves were frequently on the verge of entering slavery through years of inexorable approach to bankruptcy. Slave or commoner, the surplus above their bare subsistence level found its way into the hands of their masters to be squandered.

I estimated the general yield of grain per acre at a little above 600 lb. rising at very best to 1,200 lb. An ear of oats has half a dozen grains in the Cool Mountains and sometimes the seed itself is not replaced. Only very wealthy people could be sure of food for the whole year and some surplus. Of the rest, the majority led a life in which hunger played a great part, hunger and scraping a living by picking wild vegetables, getting firewood for others, carrying water and borrowing. This was the last, inevitable recourse, because debt led straight to enslavement.

Norsu society is more backward than some primitive societies. No division of labour exists between agriculture and stock-raising, farming and handicrafts. Settlements are tiny, scattered and without protection from constant feuding. Cities do not exist and Ninglang, the only place approaching a town, was smaller than most people's idea of a village. There is no Norsu commerce, no Norsu mercantile class but sporadic exchange of goods without organised markets.

Buyu Wani was a rich man, though not the richest of his clan. When his father died in 1927, he inherited eleven male slaves. His wife brought five girl slaves and these were paired off with some of his. He had a fair number of cattle and land that produced $1\frac{1}{2}$ tons of grain. Two decades later when Hu Tan penetrated into the Cool Mountains to win Wani's co-operation with the Communists, he owned fifty slaves, eighty cattle, 200 sheep, twenty horses and ten pack mules. His income from opium growing was about 400 ounces of silver a year—4,000 yuan.

"I was rich but still we never could make ends meet," he told me. "There were so many guests, great entertainments. We wasted grain feeding it to animals. I had only one suit of clothes. We Norsu did not wash. Only now we are learning to do that. Even with many slaves it was hard to get anything done and the crops often went wrong."

What he complained of is normal for slave society. Slaves never have had any incentive to work, as so many Greek and Roman writers observed, without seeming to notice at the same time that slaves might be human.

In Greece and Rome the misery of the slaves at least raised the level of human conditions to that point where a leisured class could think, philosophise and invent, leave their indelible mark on history and provide the basis for a still higher stage of human development beyond the slave system. It cannot be said that Norsu society made any contribution to mankind at large to offset the anguish of its slaves. I met not one noble who could read. Sorcerers alone are "literate", that is to say they know by rote how to recognise the mumbo-jumbo of their animistic creed in the ideographs of their dead script, itself a less worthy derivative of the complex Chinese language which they affect to despise. All the piled-up sufferings of their slaves and commoners ended in drunken feasts, opium orgies or buried silver ingots. This was a rotting backwater of human life, strictly in need of cleansing.

CHAPTER SIX

PLANTING SEEDS OF CHANGE

Avoiding head-on clash—"Doing good and making friends"—Limitations of a slave society—"Whose tail is longer?"—Ashi Vugan escapes from her owner—Talk of mass-murder—Life through a slave's eyes—Preparations for the abolition—"Free bondsmen" the key group

NORSU nobles boasted that "a Han cannot go uphill in the Cool Mountains without a company of soldiers, unless he has our safe conduct". Only one cause had ever been known to unite the feud-loving Norsu—to fight against the Hans. Controlling bondsmen directly and the slaves indirectly or directly, the nobles were able to mobilise all able-bodied Norsu males and create swiftly an army of experienced fighters who knew every inch of the mountains. Any attempt to reform slavery in the Cool Mountains by frontal assault would have the inevitable result of uniting the whole people in opposition and defeating its own purpose. Very few nobles, a mere handful, like Buyu Wani and Zeku Alu, were farsighted enough to realise that abolition of slavery was the condition for any improvement in their own way of life.

To avoid a head-on clash, stabilise the nobility and reduce their suspicions were prime necessities for the work-teams and other *ganbu* sent to the Cool Mountains.

The nobles too preferred to avoid a head-on clash with the disciplined and well-behaved People's Army. This was not an army that stole racehorses and food but brought with it more food than it used, distributed relief grain and spent its spare time learning to read.

In meetings with the nobles, the Communist Party Working Committee[1] said that there was no intention of interfering with the internal affairs of the minority peoples either now or in the future. They must settle their fate themselves. The Communists were willing to help. Reform was a matter for the Norsu people to decide. If later they

---

[1] A Working Committee of the Communist Party is a committee of the CCP which is not indigenous to the area. That is, it cannot be a normal organic unit of the Communist Party, which must be composed of its local members and elected by them. Working Committees are temporary bodies until local organisations can be formed.

decided to change their system of living, the Communists were there to help and to see that the living standards of all the Norsu people did not fall. There would always be proper places for the nobility and salaries to ensure no hardship. But the condition was the entry of the army to ensure that the area could not be used as a base for Kuomintang remnants and dissidents to accumulate strength and cause trouble to the new Chinese People's Republic.

For the slave-owners the main thing was their property and their way of life. Deeply suspicious but with no alternative other than challenging this efficient army—which would have led to disunity in their own ranks—they acquiesced.

Work-teams arrived, grain and cloth came in, relief was issued, reform was not mentioned. Concentration was on "unity" and "doing good and making friends".

"Unity" mainly involved the prevention, mitigation and settlement of disputes, a form of activity pleasing to most people. Feudal wars might be small in scale, being mainly based on the family unit taking its own commoners and slaves to fight, but in such a small community everyone got involved sooner or later. Commoners and slaves, gun-fodder of the warring parties on whom the costs of clan war ultimately fell, were especially pleased as fighting was reduced.

Zeku Alu and Buyu Wani, with their great prestige as fighting men, played a big part in mediation and changing the atmosphere. Tension gradually relaxed and after a while a Han could "go uphill" and move freely around without fear of ambush.

Relief goods flowed in. Grain, cloth, medical goods, farm tools were handed out and low interest loans issued. Much of these probably never reached the hands of the slaves at all but were kept by their owners; commoners often had to part with their relief goods to defray their debts. Some work-team members say that most of the relief was ultimately retained by the slave-owners. "But this had two effects", said one work-team member. "It took pressure off the slaves and commoners. Indirectly they were a little better off. They heard about it, too. One slave told me his master had boasted that he got all of the two hundredweights of rice issued to his house-slaves, because they dared not demand it from him. But he gave them more oats instead. The slaves contrasted how *Gongzo* gave things and their masters took them away.

"Another result was that the nobles began to speak well of the Communists, and the commoners and slaves copied what they said.

Nobles took our interest-free loans. The common slave-owners did the same and soon even slaves applied to us for loans.

"When the people here don't understand anything, their masters decide which way they go. This is really the key to understanding how to work here."

At this stage the hope existed that slavery and servitude could be abolished, as in other places in Yunnan, without the direct expropriation of the slave-owners, by developing a higher level of production and gradually changing the social relationships of the people; settling minor problems on the way with subsidies and face-saving political manœuvres.

Work-teams cautiously broached the matter of producing more. By this time work-team members were very well regarded by the slaves and poor commoners. Little gifts of needles, spools of thread, cigarettes, matches, a drink of corn spirit—odds and ends that could not give offence to their masters—had put the work-team members on very good terms with the poorest of the Norsu. Farming tools were quite another matter.

Slaves, and to a less degree, commoners both reacted strongly against new farm tools. In all human history, slaves have never been interested in the results of their labour but only in avoiding work and punishment. Every observant recorder of slave societies in the past has noted that slaves can be given only the crudest instruments of production and even these they break if they can do it without detection. The issue of iron tools, wide hoes, efficient ploughs, harrows, seemed to put the Communist Party on the side of the slave-owners.

This was a period when the slave-owners felt very good and the slaves and bondsmen went back to the view that the new situation was not so new after all. They had felt the Hans to be rather strong and on their side because the slave-owners paid attention to what they said and fighting had more or less stopped. New enslavements also had fallen to an average of only 200 a year since the *ganbu* arrived.

But now the slave-owners were saying, as several slaves told me: "The Communist Party is the government and they want more production. They have given new tools and if you don't produce more you are going against the law." They put pressure on the commoners to produce more and clear off back debts. This call by the Communist Party for more production seemed to be in the interests of the rich and caused some confusion.

What it did not cause was more production.

Neither the slaves nor the poor commoners stood to gain anything by increasing production and they comprised, judging from Racecourse Area, almost exactly two-thirds of the population. Of the rest, a fair proportion of the slave-owning commoners were obviously so deeply in debt as to have no incentive to produce more. The rest were rich enough to do little work or to live entirely from the production of others. It was not a social structure conducive to any advance in productive methods.

While the slave-owners used the "more production" slogan to grind a little more from the faces of the poor, they also used the situation to spread the opinion that they were stronger than the Communists. How strong relatively were the nobles and the Communists was a critical question. Slaves asked: "Is the tail of the Communist Party long or short?"—a Norsu expression meaning is the Communist Party strong or weak. A joking reply by one *ganbu* who held his fingertips close together and said, "So long", taken seriously by his hearers, was spread all over the area and did considerable damage to the Communist reputation.

While abortive efforts were being made to raise production and living standards ("Like pouring water down a well", said one *ganbu*), rumour began to sift into the Cool Mountains about the great nationwide land reform and the struggle of the peasants all over China against the landlords.

Wild tales swept round, both as to what was happening in other parts of China and as to the treatment being prepared for the Norsu slave-owners. "I personally never believed in the relief," an old noble named Buyu Heipo said to me. "We went out capturing Hans as slaves and they come here and give us wheat and cloth. Why? I doubted the motive. It seemed to me that they were only trying to soften us up and get into position to destroy us."

Efforts to calm these fears of the slave-owners were undermined by some of the slaves themselves who began running away and seeking sanctuary with the work-teams. This put the work-teams into a quandary. Try as they might to persuade the slaves not to take matters into their own hands and upset the situation, the slaves kept on fleeing. Once they had fled, it was a hard choice for the working *ganbu* to make: whether to jeopardise the smooth development of the overall situation on account of a few runaway slaves when slavery would soon be abolished anyway, or whether to jeopardise the life of the slave by returning him to a master who might exercise his traditional right to kill the slave. Compromises were sought and the slave-owners were quick to press their advantage here. They complained that the authorities were not keeping their promise of letting the minorities settle their own affairs; they were interfering between the slave-owners and their property. "What would you say if we enticed away your cattle and refused to return them because they came on their own legs?"

The *ganbu* tried to steady the situation by advising the slaves not to run away and at the same time launched the slogan "unity, production, progress". This last addition—"progress"—was aimed at getting the slave-owners to treat their slaves better and stop beating and maltreating them.

More slaves ran away and reports spread that they had got away with it. Feeling a new wind blowing, commoners became lax with the payment of feudal duties. Fat wedding pigs failed to turn up. Things were manifestly slipping.

There was an increase in banditry—always plentiful in the Cool Mountains. As a means to keep the allegiance of their slaves and to create difficulties for the *ganbu*, some slave-owners took their slaves and commoners on looting expeditions. "If you follow me," said one, according to a slave, "you will get property you will never finish carrying and food you will never finish eating."

These raids came to nothing, and often boomeranged. One big noble slave-owner took a band of slaves and commoners looting, ran into an armed escort and was roundly defeated. His angry followers revenged themselves on him by killing his sheep and refusing to do farmwork. He dared not do anything about it and this strengthened the feeling that slave-owners could be opposed.

By 1956 the trickle of runaway slaves had become appreciably heavier. I had several interviews with women slaves who had run away at that time—formerly woman slaves never did this, preferring to commit suicide. Precisely because they did not try to escape female slaves were more expensive than men.

A talk with Ashi Vugan provided an insight into the feelings at the time she escaped—June 1956. She was, I would say, a typical house-slave, unbelievably lacking in knowledge. It took a long time to get her to answer very simple questions. She was machining cotton-padded winter clothes in the Ninglang Handicrafts Co-operative when I called to see her early in 1958.

Ashi Vugan had no clear idea of her background. At first she said she was a Han who had been abducted as a child, then corrected this to say that her parents had been abducted Hans and she herself born in slavery. She had been sent to accompany her mistress to her husband's house. Her master, Buyu Tierz, owned thirty slaves.

Like many slaves, she planted a tiny patch of opium to sell and buy clothes and a little extra food. Two of her fellow slaves died of starvation, another had died in the course of a ferocious flogging. Vugan herself had tried to commit suicide once by eating opium but succeeded only in making herself very ill, for which she had been hung by her wrists and whipped.

In June 1956 she and another slave had been beaten almost to death. "Blood came out of the other woman's mouth," said Ashi Vugan. It was after this that the two girls—Ashi Vugan was only a little over twenty—discussed whether to run away to Ninglang, which was one day's walk away.

With the greatest difficulty I got her to answer such abstract questions as why she had felt that in June 1956 she could succeed in getting away. There was a long rigmarole about meeting another slave who said that in Ninglang people were saying all slaves would soon be free. This slave had said he was going to run to Ninglang and get *Gongzo* to help him. The Communists were stronger than any Norsu clan, he said. This slave had told them where *Gongzo* was— just by the new store.

As soon as the master and mistress were asleep a few nights later, the two girls had gone out, saying to the other slaves that one was going for firewood and the other to relieve herself. They fled, running as fast as possible for a long way and in the morning reached Ninglang.

They went to a building which turned out to be the county government where they explained their plight. "We were very scared," said Ashi Vugan, "because there were some people there who looked like nobles, looking at us all the time." The clerk told them in a loud voice that they ought to return to their master and gave them each a big piece of corn bread.

They left despondently, not knowing what to do next and another clerk came out behind them. He passed them and said, "Follow me." They went with him into another building where he announced that he was a Communist. This man said it would be better if they left the Cool Mountains for a time and arranged for them to go to Li Chiang to study. After a year learning to read the Han language and arithmetic, Ashi Vugan came back. Her district had already been reformed and she was free to take a job in the producer co-operative. Her old master,

Buyu Tierz, was now working for the county government and by a twist of coincidence she took her meals in the same government-run canteen every day.

"Are you friendly with him now?" I asked. For the only time during our talk she showed animation. Her eyes narrowed, and she said, "We never talk to each other."

If people like Ashi Vugan were running away, things must be getting very difficult for the slave-owners to control. But there were other horrifying reasons why slaves were now more willing to take the ultimate risk of flight and recapture. Slave-owners, sitting by their fires debating the probabilities of reform, were discussing what to do about it in the hearing of their slaves; and some favoured a general massacre of the slaves.

Two young and relatively articulate ex-girl-slaves who ran away and now work in the Ninglang hospital told me of a conversation they overheard between their master and his wife. Both agreed that with all this talk of reform it seemed very unlikely that the slaves would be their property much longer. He had talked with other members of his clan and they were fearful of what would follow the freeing of thousands of slaves who had plenty of reason for exacting the most terrible vengeance. They had decided to consult their friends and see what feeling could be found for a concerted mass murder of the slaves.

It was a blood and bone-chilling picture that Abi Jaja and Abi Vugan drew of the house-slaves in their wattle outhouse, sitting round a wooden trough on the floor to sup their thin gruel and wild vegetables, discussing this murder plot in whispers and planning how to run away. Six of them fled, were chased on horseback and fired at but got away to Ninglang safely. They warned the authorities, who took care to let the slave-owners quietly know that the plan was no longer secret.

From these two girls, as from all slaves, I gleaned a little more about their conditions of life. There was the usual tale of coarse gritty siftings of flour and wild vegetables for food and very little salt. "Often no salt for many days," said Abi Jaja. Goitre abounds in this area. "Mistress prepared the food and the salt was kept locked up. Impossible to get any."

"What happened if you stole some?" I asked.

"We couldn't sit where we wanted to sit. Couldn't go near the place of the master."

"But if you stole?"

"Severe flogging. You might even die from it. Some people who

B

stole were killed right out as soon as the things were got back. That depended on what they stole."

"How were they killed?"

"Beaten to death in front of all the other slaves to stop us doing the same."

"Wasn't it silly to kill valuable property like slaves?"

"They could buy more."

To approach their master, they had to creep sideways in a crouch with head averted and hidden in the crook of the left arm. Then they must pass whatever he wanted with the right hand under the left armpit and stay in that crouching posture until dismissed either verbally or with a kick. Generally it would be a grunt of dismissal but when guests were around, more often a kick. They must leave in the same posture. A slave's eyes must not meet those of the master.

Hu Tan happened to be present at this interview and watched my expression with his usual grin, wide-eyed and snub-nosed, looking far too young for a man who ten years ago was old enough to be entrusted with his delicate task. "To our eyes slave society seems very cruel," he said, "and changing it is not simple. If we came in here with the idea of transplanting the experiences of other places, and if we tried to measure Norsu standards of morality by others, we should only have caused confusion, and increased our difficulties."

Slaves are not regarded as people, and the slave-owners were only reacting as slave-owners, with a slave-owner's conception of what is right and a slave-owner's fears of a society without slaves. Plato and Aristotle themselves could not imagine a Greek society without slaves. Those fears were described by Zeku Alu, who owned twenty-four slaves.

"All sorts of rumours were spread," said Zeku Alu. "They said that all nobles were to be annihilated, their children fried and the rest also killed. When the slaves were freed, it was said, all noblewomen would be given to the male house-slaves as wives. People might not believe all these things but they were worried."

As the years passed and the Communist Party workers insisted that reform could only be carried out by the Norsu people and in agreement with the upper-class Norsu, fears had subsided, only to rise again when the slaves started to run away and rumours came in of the land reform. According to Zeku Alu, the prospect of losing their slaves and their privileges caused the slave-owners the least of their worries. They heard that the land-reform had been a great revolutionary movement in which the Chinese peasants had themselves struck the power from the hands of the landlords. Norsu nobles feared indignity more than anything—that they might be stood up in front of their slaves and commoners in great "speak-bitterness" meetings, that they might be "struggled" against, struck, spat upon and forced to work.

"They could not distinguish that there was a policy of peaceful reform for the minority peoples which was quite different from the struggles between Han landlords and Han peasants," said Zeku Alu in fluent Han, nursing his thin knee in long bony hands. "It's hard for a man who has beaten Han slaves to realise that it was not a matter of revenge, for we are great believers in revenge." His ascetic-looking face and sincere eyes, amazing in one of the Norsu's most-feared warriors, shone with simple integrity. I found these nobles always frank; they scorned to be otherwise. Opponents of abolition never hesitated to speak their mind to me in front of the *ganbu*. But they always implied that they had never beaten slaves, whatever others might have done.

"Some people picked up a smattering of knowledge and tried to turn it upside down," Zeku Alu said. "Some argued: 'Communists say that society had to pass through a period of slavery. This was a process of history. So why should it be tampered with in the Cool Mountains?'

"People thought slave-society good because they never saw any other and feared change. They had periods of hunger and poverty, always clan disputes, no security, but these things they understood. What would new things bring? I had the advantage of visiting Peking and it was very moving to see the government leaders clapping the minority peoples as they marched in the procession on National Day. I saw the new factories and began to understand that the future would be good for everyone who took part.

"Others had no chance to go to Peking. They thought of the future with minds in the past and their fears were the main thing. They said: 'Slaves are no good at managing things. Brainless. Have to be told to do this or that. It's madness to think they can run their own lives.' But when they actually saw that slaves could manage things they got even more nervous and said: 'Now the Communist Party will forget us and rely only on the slaves.'

"Slave-owners never worked, and feared what would happen if they lost their slaves. But even this was a minor worry. Mostly they said that they could live by their own efforts if they had to and if everyone else had to. Really what they feared was scoldings and beatings. They said: 'Peaceful reform, that's the story now. But will it be peaceful to the very end?'

"They believed that talk of peaceful reform was only to disarm us. Then in the end we should be at the mercy of the slaves."

A slave's-eye view of reform was also circumscribed by the past. They went through their own mental turmoil in that period of ferment that led inevitably to the abolition of slavery. A slave could think of himself only in relation to what he knew—slavery. His most golden daydream could only be of becoming a slave-owner. Norsu society seemed to him natural, original and immutable. It seemed sacrilegious to think of abolishing slavery. If that were done, how could anyone survive?

Most slaves wanted freedom within the confines of a slave system, others blankly refused—or were unable—to take any standpoint, still others took the position of the slave-owners as their own, but a very few were active abolitionists who swiftly came to the political front. Some slave women thought they would have to wear trousers like Han girls. Though they might have been Han children, stolen and later tattooed by their mistresses with the hallmark of Norsu women— black spots on the backs of their hands—they still feared being reduced from the dizzy heights of being slave-of-a-Norsu to the abysmal status of a "cheap-bone" free-Han. Those who had never had any real clothes feared having to make their own, feared emerging into a strange world and feared that they would be sought out and killed by their former owners. But however they thought, or said they thought, more slaves constantly ran away.

It had quickly become clear that there was no way to improve the situation in Ninglang county while slavery and servitude remained. Hu Tan said that the Communist Party Working Committee had concluded that both slavery and feudal privilege had to go but the main question was slavery. "Their relations with their masters cause slaves to be uninterested in production, slave-owners occupy the best land and almost all of the land. But privilege, usury and other exploitation of the so-called free people causes bankruptcies and new enslavements," he said.

Han-Norsu tension had somewhat relaxed. Reform had moved into its place as the prime issue. But these positions could rapidly be reversed once more if the political workers made any error in their work. Everything depended on allies. To win allies for the abolition of slavery required the most exact estimation of the caste and class interests of the various strata of people involved and the working out of a policy that would deprive the noble rulers of any opportunity to influence a decisive section of the Norsu people to oppose it.

In preparation for this moment, a thorough investigation into the total actual situation, similar to the Racecourse survey, had been steadily compiled by the work-teams, which operated at the lowest possible level—the villages. This survey had to produce the answers to such questions as: If slavery were abolished, who would gain and who would lose and to what extent? If feudal privilege were also abolished, would common slave-owners on the whole gain more than they lost? What would be the effect of wiping out usury? of dividing the land among those who tilled it? What changes had to be made to win an overwhelming majority to support reform and paralyse the opposition?

Failure to estimate all the forces and interests with the greatest accuracy would provide the opponents of reform with allies and—because of traditional feeling against the Han—jeopardise the entire process.

Every fact had to be verified by the patient work-teams. Gradually the figures were compiled. Surprisingly they showed that the conditions found at Racecourse were approximately accurate for the whole Norsu people. They were:

Nobility
Owning 10 slaves or
   more . . . $2\frac{1}{2}$%
Owning 1 to 9 slaves . $2\frac{1}{2}$%....5% Total slave-owning
(Few nobles owned no ——   nobles
   slaves)

                                                       owning
Free commoners   slaves
Owning 10 slaves or   33%
   more . . . 3%
Owning 1 to 9 slaves 25%....28% Total slave-owning
                ——   commoners
Owning no slaves 20%
Separate-slaves . 33%
(Owning very few   owning
   slaves)   no slaves
House-slaves . 14%....67% Total poor com-   67%
                ——   moners and slaves

Abolition of slavery by itself would be opposed by the 5 per cent. of nobles and 28 per cent. of slave-owning commoners. The 20 per cent. of poor commoners without slaves would be neutral or might support the retention of slavery for traditional reasons.

But if the abolition of slavery were coupled with the abolition of feudal privilege, at least 67 per cent. would find this an unmixed advantage—the slaves and poor commoners. A large part of the common slave-owners would also stand to gain as well as lose, since possession of a slave or two by no means removed a person from the danger of bankruptcy and consequent enslavement through failure to pay privilege dues.

If the abolition of usury were also included, this would cause a further polarisation of interests.

Whatever proportions might be involved, it was obvious that the 28 per cent. of slave-owning bondsmen were decisive. Failure to win this group would bring into question whether the abolition of slavery could be carried out at all. If they could be won as allies, the absolute majority of the population was won and success within reach. And if at the same time the nobility could be split, abolition was virtually achieved.

I choose the case of Yaze Bimor and his little slave-boy as typifying Norsu society, its hazards for the "free" and the possibilities of winning this group of slave-owners for the abolition.

Yaze's father owned two house-slaves and in keeping with Norsu custom, gave one of them to Yaze when he married. I met them in the adobe building of the Bolo work-team and the little slave-boy listened to his former master as we sat round a huge wood fire burning in the middle of the room on slabs of rock. Yaze, with the emaciation of an opium addict, hawk nose and great sorrowful eyes, was dressed in thin black cotton like his ex-slave and also wore no shoes.

Complex relations existed between Yaze and the nobility. His overlord was a Buyu, who not very long ago had been defeated in a battle with a member of the Loho clan. This Loho had claimed Yaze as his serf in part settlement but this was disputed by his Buyu overlord. Since this issue had never been settled, Yaze owed feudal dues to both noble families.

He rented thirteen acres of land from still another nobleman, of the Lomhm clan, for six hundredweight of grain and two ounces of opium a year.

His feudal dues were heavy but erratic, depending to the usual extent on the births, marriages and deaths in his two overlord families. He used his own little slave to herd animals (not Yaze's own) and later to do farm work.

Yaze got steadily into debt, began planting opium to clear it, ended by smoking it to cheer himself up and succeeded, as all opium addicts, merely in reducing his own labour power.

He remembered only two years in his life when he had enough to eat. Always he borrowed to live, "but those loans were nothing to worry about, as I got them from relatives".

What had to be worried about was back rent and debts accruing from failure to render feudal dues—three ingots of silver and three bushels of grain. These debts had been long outstanding and the time was approaching when the debtor must pay up or become a slave.

"Last year things were getting serious," Yaze Bimor said. "My landlord was demanding one slave, my Buyu overlord wanted one slave, and my new Loho overlord wanted four. I have three sons and one daughter but six slaves were demanded. So my wife and I would have become slaves too. All for three ingots and three bushels. Abolition was just in time to save us."

"So why not sell one child," I asked, "and use the money to pay the debt? You could have got ten ingots for the girl."

He at once launched into a long talk about usurious interest rates of 300 per cent. so that in three years one ingot became twenty-seven. There were so many debts and obligations and no way out. He could not name an actual sum that he owed other than the original figure. "If they said you owed this much, then you owed this much. It was useless to argue. They were the masters."

It was the abolition that saved him and his children, Yaze said, though he felt thàt the presence of the work-team had prevented his being enslaved several years before. "When *Gongzo* was here the landlord didn't press so hard and creditors felt less able to cause trouble over loans. Last New Year, before the reform, I was not asked for the customary pig by either of my masters."

Had he felt sorry at having to set his own slave free? I asked.

He smiled a long-toothed smile, passed a long dirty hand over his thin face and said: "Of course not. I lost one small slave and look what I gained: debts cancelled, no more payments to my two former masters, now my thirteen acres of land is rent-free. My wife and son work the land while I make wooden ladles and sell them to the state trading company. What was the use of my one slave when ten slaves would not have covered my debts? Now I could be well-off but for my own faults; I like liquor and opium.[1] But I'm cutting opium down and later I'll cut down on liquor. Then we'll be well off."

Yaze went off while I talked to his little ex-slave, who was as glad to see the back of slavery as his master had been over his twelfth-hour rescue. Yaze had shown every sign of affection for the little boy during our talk, but his ex-slave—said to be fifteen and looking more like thirteen—soon put the record right when he had gone, by saying he had been beaten nearly every day by Yaze. "I never had enough to eat. My father was sold by Yaze Bimor's father. He was worked to death and died of starvation. My mother was sold to another place and died soon after of cold and hunger. I was told these things by other slaves, I don't remember myself."

An example of the life cycle of a "first-class slave" or free bondsmen was provided by a wizened little man called Tiho Chiurlhu, who said, with unusual accuracy for a Norsu, that his age was sixty-two. Tiho's face was like a bit of smoked crêpe paper, lined with countless wrinkles; his foot-wide shoulders stuck up sharply inside a thin cotton jacket and his thighs were not much thicker than my forearm.

Tiho was born in debt. His father had borrowed to get married and then died, leaving poor Tiho to clear off the already inflated cost of his own arrival in the world.

"When I was twenty-three, this debt had become 250 ingots, though I had paid off a good deal. My father had originally borrowed one ingot and some grain, he told me. So I became a slave. Luckily my master had plenty of ground he didn't use and I planted opium in different

[1] Opium growing has been wiped out in most of China: in all places where Hans are in the majority and in most national minority areas. It is the policy of the central authorities, while doing everything to discourage it, to leave such matters to the voluntary decision of the national minorities themselves. As a result, the poppy can still be found in remote pockets where the transition from primitive, slave and feudal society is still going forward. In these areas, too, addicts realise that the habit is bad, frowned on by the government and soon to disappear. But the habit dies hard, especially since opium growing was commonly the only way open for the poorest people to make both ends of the harvest meet. Abolition of opium other than voluntarily and after secure alternative cash crops exist would make these people feel nervous. Thus to make the poppy illegal in those areas would be an act of political stupidity—merely adding new problems to those already difficult to solve, and presenting allies to those who want to stem the flow of progress. Its continuation has disadvantages since opium encroaches on the best arable land, emaciates its users, reduces labour power. It needs four times as much attention as buckwheat. However, since it is mainly grown by non-addicts as a cash crop, other cash crops can be substituted, while the market itself dies out as a result of the reform. I met poor people in such places as the Cool Mountains for whom opium was the only solace from the lash or from poverty and who are now painfully breaking the habit by daily reductions; they say that death is better than its sudden removal.

places. Opium sells for one ingot an ounce and in twelve years I had buried 250 ingots of silver and could buy my freedom."

Tiho had then set about finding a wife, had run into debt and repeated the old process. In 1952 his thirteen-year-old son had been taken as a slave, to clear off the accumulated interest on Tiho's marriage payment. When I met Tiho his son had just been released from slavery and was back helping his father on his four acres of issued land.

Slavery kept the productive method backward and backwardness ensured constant recruits to slavery. Jivu Lanu, a twenty-year-old poor commoner said that he, his mother, three brothers and sister had rented three acres of land which produced enough for six months food. For the rest they cut firewood. When their debts reached four ingots of silver his younger brother went as a slave. Later his elder brother was demanded for debts of ten ingots and a sack of oats. Their feudal lords had already notified them that the sister was required to accompany a bride to her husband's home and she was not to be disposed of in any other way.

"We had just reached the point of running away from our Buyu overlord and trying to get protection from the Wadja when the reform came," said Lanu.

It was in many ways better for slaves to be born into that condition than to have it thrust upon them later in life. A "genuine Norsu" slave, born into slavery and owned by a nobleman—the highest grade of slave—was certainly better off than many a "free" commoner.

Arlul Zeda, mentioned earlier, was one such: a separate-slave, son of a family who proudly traced their enslavement back through three previous generations of slavery—real Norsu, with good bone. Zeda owned two slaves: one said to be of Sifan nationality, whom he had bought at the age of four at a price of four ingots ($£6$). When this boy had reached the age of fifteen, Zeda bought an eighteen-year-old woman. This woman had been newly captured, but she was strong and big—so her price was high. Zeda had taken a bit of a risk in sinking ten ingots in a girl who would be a lot of trouble to break in, he said. However, he was assured that she had come from very far away at night, over the ridges and could certainly never find her way back.

Zeda at once mated his two slaves, neither of whom at that time could understand a single word spoken by the other, and as soon as the girl was obviously pregnant, Zeda could afford to relax his vigilance.

"Once they have a child they don't often try to escape," he said, with the wisdom of an old-hand slave.

Why, I asked, had he sunk so much capital in slaves? Wasn't one enough to take his place doing the master's work and enable him to do things for himself?

"I envied my master," he said. "He had many slaves and many animals. Owning slaves is good. Owning slaves *was* good," he corrected. "With these two slaves I could breed, sell, maybe get more slaves. These two allowed me and my wife to work at our own things and make money. Later we might get rich and buy our whole family out, but that is not so easy. Still we lived better than many folk."

Like all slave-owners, Zeda the slave denied that he beat his own slaves. But I never met a slave who was not constantly beaten. Zeda said: "I told them: 'If we work, we eat; if we don't we starve.' During the day they worked for my master and worked for me in the early morning and evening. My master gave me his orders when he got up, then I told my slaves what to do. I did practically nothing for my master and worked six acres of land for myself. I got along all right. I had my bad years and interest on loans was high. But I was not a freeman and so owed no feudal dues."

His children had all been taken away to the homes of his master's children.

"It seems you did fairly well as a slave," I said, posing the obvious question, "so you are probably worse off after the abolition?"

I received a look filled with patient tolerance of benighted ignorance. "Of course not. My sons and daughters are all back with me and their families, with plenty of land and labour-power. We're doing fine. Of course the reform came late, after spring sowing, so there wasn't much difference this year. Next year will be much better."

His two former slaves had remained in his household after the abolition, he added. "They eat the same food, but not with me. They and I have put one acre into joint farming."

I saw his former male slave who confirmed these things and also said he had been regularly and severely beaten by Zeda. Then why stay with him? He said he had been nervous at the thought of moving away and fending for himself. Zeda was experienced and, as there was to be no more beating and cursing, and more to eat, he decided to continue living in the same place and do some work with Zeda. "We have enough now, my wife and I. Nobody can use us, beat us or sell us. We have four acres, one draught animal, two cows and five sheep from the work-team. We are doing fine."

He went off with his tall wife, to whom he had been slave-married while he was still a boy. She must have been at least five inches taller than the shrivelled creature he had now become. I wondered how long their strange relationship could last with the man who had flogged them in the past and who most likely was cheating them in the present.

CHAPTER SEVEN

WHY THE SLAVE-OWNERS GAVE WAY

Slave-owners complain—Climax approaches—"Reform by peaceful negotiation"—Something for everyone—Two principles—Preparing the abolition—"Slave-owners" and "Working People"—Land and usury—Isolating the biggest slave-owners—Buyu Heipo flees—Stages in the abolition—Peace face-to-face, struggle back-to-back—Jobs and subsidies for ex-slave-owners

BY mid-way through 1956 the Cool Mountains seethed with discontent and anxiety. The former uneasy balance of forces had been disturbed but no new one had been established. News from the rest of China was of vast momentous change: land reform, the ending of private capitalism, peasants flocking into co-operatives, talk of the national minorities going together with the rest of China into socialism.

Efforts to raise production while keeping the slave system mainly intact had failed. Irreconcilable conflict of interest existed between the slaves and their owners, as between the bondsmen and their overlords. What one consumed the other could not consume. Norsu slave society must either smash or change into something else.

Noble slave-owners went to see the Communist Party Working Committee to complain that promises had not been kept. They demanded that all runaway slaves be returned to their former owners and the old situation be restored. They were told that it was not the job of the government or the Communist Party to interfere in minority affairs nor to help the Norsu nobles oppress their slaves and commoners.

"We have co-operated with the Norsu leaders, and we want to continue to co-operate with them. Now you ask us to return the slaves. Suppose the slaves, and there are more of them, ask us to destroy the slave-owners? We don't intend to do either.

"Our work here is to help with advice and aid and to mediate disputes. You Norsu must settle your own affairs. We genuinely want long-term co-operation but we don't like slavery or exploitation and we think it is backward. Unless it is reformed it is certain to be overthrown by the people themselves. It would be better if such a change came peacefully. Our advice is that you agree with the peoples' proper demands and we would try to help by working out the best ways—the most just ways—and provide subsidies if there are any hardships."

For several years the slave-owners had known that the abolition of slavery was only a matter of time and form, and they had been told that "reform by peaceful negotiation" was an unchangeable principle for the minority peoples. Now the crucial moment had arrived when the issue could not be put off any longer.

I asked a dyed-in-the-wool noble slave-owner, Buyu Heipo, who still makes no pretence about his hatred of reform, what he had thought at that time. He was the old noble who told me what I would have been worth as a slave-curiosity if I had entered the Cool Mountains in the old days.

"We slave-owners were all getting to the point where we welcomed a showdown," he said. "The Communists used to argue with us all the time. I never was much of a talker. They told us that up here we had slavery and down in Yung Sheng there was feudalism. You know, I used to think that the difference was that we were Norsu and they were Hans.

"I listened to their talk. They said the Communist Party didn't want to tell us how to run our affairs, but buying and selling men was out of date. Slavery was not a good system, they said. Ordinary workers in factories are better off than rich slave-owners, they said. But we didn't have any factories, I told them.

"I said to them: 'I am an old man and I don't want to change. If my slaves go, how can I live? I can't work.' They said it wasn't a matter of taking away my slaves. We Norsu should talk it all out and decide how everything should be done."

If diehards like Buyu Heipo felt that a showdown was welcome, this meant that the slave-owners as a whole realised that a new stage had been reached. It was palpably unrealistic for them to demand the return of their runaway slaves and they did not expect this to happen. It was a means of bringing pressure on the *ganbu*. They could see that more slaves would flee and could not be replaced. Control of the bondsmen was slipping. Any attempt to use open force to deal with the situation would be difficult in view of the presence of the army.

In every slave-owner's mind the question burned: was there a way out? What was meant by "reform through peaceful negotiation"? Was this a genuine process of co-operation or was it merely a way to keep the rulers in retreat until the appropriate moment to destroy them?

I asked Hu Tan to describe what was meant by peaceful reform, and I give the answer in his words.

"It is a movement from above to below," he said. "The upper and lower class negotiate and agree on reform measures which are to be carried out on a voluntary basis. We help and advise.

"No force is used, there is no bloodshed, no indignities, no mass accusations, no arrests or executions for past actions. The upper class retain their rights as citizens, they are not deprived of political rights. That's in general.

"In particular, here in the Cool Mountains, the slaves are released, the land is taken over and divided up, feudal privileges are abolished and usurious debts cancelled. Subsidies are paid to ensure that there is no hardship due to a fall in living standards."

Put like that in Hu Tan's dry unstressed manner it seemed that the slave-owners got nothing out of the deal at all. "Why should they agree to it?" I asked.

"They gain a great deal," he said. "They get subsidies, keep their face, have political prestige and salaries as leaders and members of local governments, committees and organisations. The Norsu representative to the National People's Congress is Buyu Wani, a noble. They keep their houses, grain, hoarded wealth and personal property. They get a slightly larger share of land in the land reform, for everyone is allowed to keep gardens and orchards over and above the per capita share of farmland. This also they can choose for themselves and so keep the best land.

"As to why they agree, there are many reasons. They realise that the changes in China are vast and far-reaching—not like the old dynastic changes or the corruption of the Kuomintang. China's general progress has its impact here and favours reform. And we have done a lot of explaining. They know slave-owning is backward; in a way they are rather ashamed of it.

"We have told them no lies and have kept our word," Hu Tan went on. "They respect frankness. And a way has been kept open for them to keep their dignity and enable them to bridge the gap between slave-owning and getting a living after abolition."

Hu Tan then described the "two unalterable principles" in peaceful reform. "Make no mistake about it", he said, "reform means rousing the people. One aspect of it is peaceful, the other aspect revolutionary. We teach that the old ways are bad, that living on the labour of other men is bad, and where to draw the line between work and exploitation. The people are aroused to the point where they can be relied on to free themselves and guarantee that the programme is carried through. It is a very complicated process which has to be both peaceful and revolutionary. Those are the two unalterable principles."

He added: "I should say that peaceful reform is out of the question without the Communist Party to advise and lead. The main thing is scientific leadership by our Central Committee, and the prestige of the Party among the people."

Direct preparations for reform began in the summer of 1956, taking the form of meetings with all strata of the Norsu people, leading up to a conference which opened early in September that year.

There was no central organ of the nobility capable of representing them. Each clan throws up its own leaders whose qualities are wealth, eloquence, fighting ability or command of many armed retainers. Even less had the commoners or slaves any organisations.

At the meeting which gathered in Ninglang in September 1956 were 400 or so of the best talkers and fighters of the nobility, the wealthiest common slave-owners, sorcerers, commoners and slaves who had come to the front in preparing for reform and others who had run away and now returned, some able to read and write; with Communist Party officials present in an advisory capacity.

The talks went on without break for six weeks, hammering out a basis for reform which could be accepted by slave-owners, commoners and slaves. In the end, agreement on a plan of reform was unanimous because everything had been talked right out and nobody had any alternative proposals to offer or opposing arguments left.

A People's Congress of the County was then convened which ratified the reform plan as law, elected a People's Council to remain in permanent session as the local government and formally established the area as the Norsu Autonomous County of Ninglang.

Put in simple terms, the reform plan decided that all slavery and all feudal privilege would be abolished area by area. People who possessed slaves would be divided into two categories: "Slave-owners" and "Working People". Four main criteria were used to differentiate these groups.

"Slave-owners" were those who: owned ten or more slaves; took no part in basic production work; owned more than ten acres of land for each member of the family; derived upwards of 70 per cent. of their annual income from the labour of others.

All others who possessed slaves would be classified as "Working People".

Those in the class of "Slave-owners", in addition to losing slaves and rights over the bondsmen, would have all land confiscated above the normal share distributed to everyone during the land reform, and would also lose all claim to outstanding usurious debts. Nothing else would be confiscated and there would be no loss of political rights.

These criteria, key to success for the whole reform plan, were carefully worked out on the basis of the overall investigations made by the work-teams, consolidated into a fairly accurate census of the slave-owning, feudal privilege and usury situation in the Cool Mountains. They emphasise the last point stressed by Hu Tan, that the reform would not have been possible without scientific guidance.

For these criteria are accurately calculated to isolate the decisive five per cent. of the wealthiest slave-owners. This was composed of about half nobles and half commoners who owned many slaves. At the same time the nobility was split into two almost equal groups—those owning fewer and those owning more than ten slaves to each household. The plan simultaneously united the slaves, free-bondsmen who owned no slaves and the smaller slave-owners (both noble and common, now classified as "Working People") in support of the reform plan.

Any error in evaluating the lines of demarcation necessary to meet popular needs and isolate the most powerful group of "Slave-owners" could have presented the nobles and rich commoners with allies, caused a potentially dangerous cleavage at a different point of Norsu society and turned the peaceful reform into a prolonged and wasteful struggle.

It was the estimation of the *ganbu* that almost 90 per cent. of the Norsu could support this policy and that only 5 per cent. had reason to oppose. With such a preponderance—combined with a dignified line of retreat, cushioned by subsidies—only rabid diehards were likely to reject reform out of hand and take the only remaining alternative of physical opposition.

Buyu Heipo himself, a typical diehard, on being told the terms of the reform as decided at the conference, grabbed his rifle and fled to the hills to oppose the whole business. But like many a Norsu noble before him, he reckoned without his women. A party of some twenty people, including his wife, daughter, cousin and nephew, with Buyu Wani, went into the hills to get him back.

"They sent the —— women up the hill so that I wouldn't shoot," he complained blimpishly to me. "Buyu Wani was there saying that we didn't have to worry, there would be no rough stuff, no insults and no killing. They said they would be responsible for my safety and guaranteed that if I wanted to leave again I could. They said it was all agreed and all promises would be kept.

"Well, I let myself be talked into it. I'm really a bit old for that sort of thing anyway, and rheumaticky. When I got back the *ganbu* were very friendly and pretended nothing had happened. I was not victimised in any way, though I reckon I didn't do so well as some others from the reform."

Once the plan had been agreed in principle, the Communist Party advised against trying to operate it everywhere at once. It looked all right in theory, they said, but faults might emerge in practice. Reform work began in three test rural districts on October 24, 1956. Leading people were concentrated in these districts to ensure that the principles would be properly observed and to accumulate experience before spreading the reform wider.

There were five steps in the abolition: 1. Election of representatives to a District Reform Committee; 2. Exact investigation into the local ownership of slaves and land, and liberation of the slaves; 3. Continuation of the survey and classification into "Slave-owners" and "Working People"; 4. Formation of a District Labour Association; 5. Distribution of the land and settlement of outstanding problems.

Members of all classes and castes sat on the District Reform Committees, meeting frequently to discuss questions coming up in the reform. These committees played the chief part in securing the acquiescence of the upper class locally. All adults except "Slave-owners" were admitted to the Labour Associations.

Locally, as on the county level, there must be agreement if the reform was to be peaceful and so there must be channels for securing agreement. These organisations provided such channels and also a means whereby the *ganbu* could keep their fingers on the pulse of the reform and deal with situations arising from past hates and servility.

Negotiation during the reform is almost continuous. Nobody wants to be classified as a "Slave-owner". Even when all the four criteria are fulfilled in the most obvious way there have to be many discussions before the person concerned agrees to be so classified. It takes an enormous amount of time but the *ganbu* insist that this is time well spent. It helps to make everyone clear about the policy of reform and

F

even more important, they say, because the slaves and commoners take part in it, they learn for the first time how to exercise democratic rights. Formerly, only the nobles and slave-owners had freedom of speech in differing degrees dependent on their caste. Slaves could not have different views from those of their masters nor do they find it easy after the abolition to contradict the men who formerly had the power of life and death over them.

Cases classified "Slave-owner" by the Reform Committees are sent to the District People's Congress (the local government) where they are discussed with the persons concerned present. This body refers its opinion both to the local Labour Association and to the County Reform Committee.

"It's not so simple as it seems," said a work-team member to me. "That's only the negotiating side. The other side is struggle. Because it's all done by voluntary agreement, the slave-owners use their position to cheat and bribe the slaves and commoners to tell lies and help them to sneak into the 'Working People' class. They also go in for sabotage, threaten to kill slaves, commoners and even nobles who are active in the reform. Of course it has to be made clear that force will be met with force.

"There are no mass 'accusation meetings' but sometimes when a person absolutely refuses to admit that he belongs to the group of 'Slave-owners', we may advise that he meets his slaves and commoners with others round a table to talk things out till he is left without arguments. That is a rare and last resort. In most cases there is no such open confrontation and the struggle is not face to face but, as you might say, back to back."

Hardest work of all, according to the Bolo work-team leader, was winning the acquiescence of the local upper-class people and keeping their co-operation. "They stick to their old ideas and don't want to accept the new ones," Chinluan Denze said. "Unless the poor people are roused and active, the nobles won't give up their privileges. But once the people are roused, the upper class gets scared and starts to panic. Then we have to steady them down and help them past their fears.

"Time and again we have to explain our policies and what they may expect in the future. In the end they feel reassured and start to get cocky again and backslide."

It is stipulated that no more than 5 per cent. of families may be classified as "Slave-owners". This is to prevent excessive enthusiasm in putting this label on people and thus scaring the large group of persons owning one to nine slaves.

I was also told by leading Communists in Ninglang that the Central Committee of the Chinese Communist Party had directed that the living conditions and political status of the "Slave-owners" must not be reduced as a result of the reform. "Some of them occupy a very high position among the Norsu and speak for many thousands of people. They have their appropriate place," said one official.

He cited a number of nobles occupying high positions: the county head and his deputies, members of the County People's Congress, vice-chairman of the Political Consultative Conference. "This is not only a prestige question or a matter of expediency. They have jobs and in the course of the work begin to have a deeper understanding of things."

Subsidies play perhaps the dominant part in securing the acquiescence of the "Slave-owners" in the peaceful reform. A large number of "Working People" also need subsidising because the loss of slaves and feudal privileges would otherwise have reduced their living standards. This is another fundamental difference from the policies in other parts of China, where the landlords had to live by their own labour immediately after the land reform as well as losing political rights.

I was interested to find out what was meant by "standard of living". Did it mean that the government provided funds to enable people to carry on, as Buyu Wani once had, having 300 cattle sacrificed in one year to cure his rheumatism? Did it mean that they could still entertain as in the old days, drink, smoke opium and squander?

Apparently there had been some differences of view about this. Some thought that subsidies should replace all the lost income of the former owners of slaves, should continue at least during their lifetime, or for as long as sixty years, and should include liquor and entertainment. This was a field of argument across which the struggle raged strongly. Majority feeling was that subsidies should be paid on the principle of ensuring no fall in the normal daily living standard and should be provided for a period calculated to bridge the gap between the reform and that time when the former slave-owner was able to adapt himself to live in a new way and work for a living. Old and disabled people have special consideration, being kept for life.

Naturally the ex-slave-owner tries to get the subsidy fixed as high as possible and for as long as possible. He names his figure to the District Reform Committee and then it is discussed. His proposal and the Reform Committee's counter-proposal are passed to the Labour Association and discussed by the "masses", who know the man's past situation. Then a plan for his subsidy and placement in a job are passed to the District People's Congress and up to the Ninglang County People's Congress which is the government of the Cool Mountains.

Most subsidies are provisionally fixed for three to five years. In amount they run as low as 40 yuan a year and as high as 700 yuan (over £100), a large sum in this area. This is in addition to salaries from official jobs.

"Slave-owners" land is automatically confiscated and divided, that of "Working People" is retained by them except in a few districts where there is a shortage of land and they have a surplus. Confiscated land is shared equally, the "Slave-owner" having the right to choose his own share. It works out at a little less than two acres per head for every man, woman and child in most areas. The permitted retention of orchards and gardens also gives the former wealthy some small advantage and helps to cushion the blow.

No grain or animals are taken from the rich and they are left with a surplus of these, having no slaves to feed and no large tracts of land to plough, while everyone else is short of grain and draught animals. At the same time, without slaves, there is nobody to tend the cattle.

To provide for the people, Reform Committees may buy surplus grain and cattle at the market price, and if the owner refuses—this may be a compulsory sale, subject to approval by the county government. To save the cattle, permission is given to hire ex-slaves, at wages, to tend the herds, and fodder is supplied by the government if necessary. For the same reason, pasture land is not confiscated along with arable.

These rules were introduced after the test reform because slave-owners tried to commit sabotage by slaughtering their animals and then offering the excuse that they had no fodder or people to herd them.

Bereft of slaves, former masters, especially nobles, are helpless as new-born puppies—their previous labour having been limited to fighting or flogging slaves for real or imagined faults in their work. Now, faced with the need to get water and firewood and mill grain, the indispensable tasks of Norsu society, quite apart from farming, slave-owning families do not know how to start.

This is a rod that slavery has made for their backs. When labour cost nothing, slaves could walk ten miles to cut firewood and carry it home, fetch water in barrels from far away, spend their evenings turning tiny hand-mills. Only the most primitive methods are suitable for slave society and no incentive exists to improve them.

Actually most of these jobs can be done better by horses and other means within the reach of the well-to-do. A horse can carry more firewood than a man, can grind corn and raise water. Work-teams have to teach such elementary lessons.

One very rich clan leader was so tickled at having constant running water brought to his house from a nearby stream by the up-to-date method of hollowed tree trunks that he was heard to say it was almost worth the reform.

Buyu Wani himself, who used to own about fifty slaves and now has none, regards himself as most advanced technically because the local *ganbu* showed him how to build a horse-driven flour-mill. I had many talks with Buyu Wani, whose slaves were among the first to be freed and at his own request.

He draws no subsidy because his monthly wage as county chief, 50 yuan, and as National Congressman, 195 yuan—over £35—is adequate. He also has two sons both drawing salaries. "In spite of my seven grandchildren we have plenty to live on," he said.

How did his fellow slave-owners feel about having their slaves freed? I asked him. "Some are worried, some disagree, some try to sabotage the reform, some are squandering their wealth, and thinking that these things will not be theirs very long, and a few can see further than their noses and they agree that reform was necessary. But you can't say their minds in general are very settled.

"That was to be expected," Buyu Wani said. "The young folk don't think like that though. They see aeroplanes sometimes, and pictures of motor-cars and railways and they say all we Norsu have is horses. They want to be able to do the things they see in the cinema."

It was Christmas Day, 1957 when I had my longest talk with this charming, modest and progressive slave-owner (I never had the courage to ask him whether he flogged his slaves, but I suppose he did). Since Christmas was my "national celebration", he and Hu Tan gave a feast. There was chicken, Yunnan ham, lotus root, pork, various vegetable dishes and gigantic Ninglang potatoes boiled in their jackets and eaten with yak-butter, great pancakes, noodles in soup, lashings of red pepper in everything and quantities of corn whisky.

Hu Tan passed the county chief a chicken head to demonstrate how the Norsu tell fortunes by the tendons of the lower jaw. So I showed him how the British do the same thing with wishbones and he was very happy that we had this superstition in common. Both wives of his second son, he said, had died because unfavourable pig-signs had been ignored. At the bethrothal ceremony, the sacrificial pig was found to have no gall-bladder, a very bad omen. "But the families were old friends and we went ahead." The wife died. His son then became betrothed to her sister and the same thing occurred. Still they went ahead, married, and the girl died. "We should have known better," said Buyu Wani.

Measuring my height, he remarked that while he was in Peking he had noticed how much taller foreigners were. I said it might be a matter of diet, more milk and meat. In Britain, I said, rich people were fewer and bigger than poor people. He pondered that and remarked: "Yes. Slaves are generally smaller than we nobles. And I am smaller than you. I suppose under socialism we shall all be the same size."

Buyu Wani was not a typical noble. For all that he took his pipe of opium, he was abstemious in drink and much concerned with social problems—very quiet and thoughtful. As he indicated, most nobles accepted the way out of slave-society with less than pleasure and because no other way existed than that abortively tried by Buyu Heipo, who very clearly resented the whole thing. Heipo's counterparts are to be found all over the world—relics of what was once the ruling caste—bemoaning the march of history and failing to understand it.

"Other people got better treatment than I," said Buyu Heipo, looking down his aristocratic nose. "My salary of 78 yuan monthly as a member of the County Consultative Conference is hardly enough to keep me in liquor. I used to drink a couple of bottles of corn spirit a day and now it's down to one. Just can't afford it."

Buyu Heipo used to own fifty slaves and said that now his old wife had to carry the water and firewood on her back. "I pay 48 yuan a year for a worker but he isn't much good, so I've asked the county to give me a personal messenger boy. Also my house is very bad and I've asked for another to be built. When I get the house and the messenger, things will be easier."

How did he feel about the abolition of slavery, I asked. "Ah, yes. That was a bad thing," he said. "I buy you, you buy me. That's not good. A man is a man, big or small. I used to have to feed and clothe all those slaves. Now I get less but it's all mine."

Under the classification of "Working People" came a wide disparity of slave-owners, ranging from those who owned more than ten slaves and failed to fulfil the other criteria, through the less wealthy nobles, to people like Yaze Bimor, himself on the verge of slavery. Most were commoners who worked and owed feudal duties to the nobility. They formed a middle section which was both exploited and exploited others. Generally they were short of land and either in danger of enslavement or having to watch their families enslaved for debt.

In the reform, "Working People" fell into three groups: the majority who gained more than they lost; those whose gains and losses approximately balanced and the few who lost more than they gained. Most of this last group could also support the reform because they gained politically. However rich they might be, they remained bondsmen of the nobles, second-class citizens. On this basis they had common ground with the poor commoners and slaves, while their desire to retain their land and recover their loans split them from the "Slave-owners".

During the reform movement, much time is devoted to calculating in detail what this or that group gains or loses, so that they can see beyond the mere matter of losing slaves. But because ownership of slaves itself carried prestige, care is taken to ensure that "Working People" have their due proportion of seats in government bodies and the various committees. Noisy condemnation of "Working People" is prevented as much as possible and the freeing of their slaves is referred to as "separation" not "liberation". Face is thus saved and this key group encouraged to co-operate.

In the area where slavery had been abolished by the end of 1957—twenty-seven rural districts—"Working People" numbered 9,442 out of a total population of 31,805, or 29·69 per cent. Considering that this, almost one-third of the people, are comparatively well-to-do, armed and capable fighters and control large numbers of slaves who can be mobilised, the importance of winning their support for the reform needs no stressing.

And it might be said that for the nobles, their Achilles heel was the large number of bondsmen who owned slaves. The support of the "Working People"—the overwhelmingly majority of whom were common bondsmen—decided everything, and the nobles lost that support.

CHAPTER EIGHT

SLAVES' CHARTER

THIS chapter contains two documents giving the measures for the peaceful reform of slavery and aristocratic privilege in the Cool Mountains.

MEASURES ADOPTED BY THE PEOPLE'S CONGRESS OF THE NORSU AUTONOMOUS COUNTY OF NINGLANG, YUNNAN PROVINCE, FOR DEMOCRATIC REFORM BY PEACEFUL NEGOTIATION.

The purpose is to: develop production, consolidate the unity of the nationalities, develop political, economic and cultural establishments, improve living conditions in the Norsu areas and gradually achieve the transition to socialism.

These measures, while taking into consideration the actual conditions that exist in Hsiao Liang Shan (Lesser Cool Mountains), are enacted in the spirit of the Constitution of the Chinese People's Republic.

Section One: General Principles

Article 1:

The slave system is to be abolished. The slaves, bondsmen and great mass of working people are to be liberated. Personal liberty and political equality are to be guaranteed.

These steps are needed to set free the productive power of the people, gradually improve their living conditions, develop mutual aid and co-operation and create the conditions necessary for the gradual transition to socialism.

Democratic reform by peaceful negotiation is in the interests of all classes of the working people. Persistence, patience and education are therefore needed to ensure the unity of the public leaders. The method of peaceful negotiation from above must be adhered to. There must be no resort to beatings, struggle or killing, no arrests other than of persons who commit crimes at the present time. United efforts may thus be brought to bear on the enormous task of carrying through the democratic reform.

Section Two: Liberation of the slaves and settlement of the various classes

Article 2:

The slave system is to be abolished, the slaves freed and personal liberty and political equality are to be guaranteed. The system of land monopoly by the slave-owners is to be abolished and land ownership by those who till substituted.

Arrears in rents and privilege dues dating from before the reform are to be cancelled without exception. The system of special privileges pertaining to the slave system, together with slave-owners' usury, is to be abolished.

Article 3:

In areas where the reform has not yet taken place it is prohibited to kill, maltreat, abduct, sell or give slaves in dowry.

Article 4:

During the reform, the houses, cattle, farming implements, food stocks, ingot silver and other money belonging to the slave-owners are to be preserved intact.

In cases where the livelihood of slave-owners is reduced as a result of the reform, the government is to take appropriate measures to make up the deficiency.

Article 5:

In the case of those persons who work and also possess slaves—some 30 per cent. of the total families—it is necessary to give them patient explanations as to their actual losses and gains resulting from the reform.

If any are short of labour as a result of the release of the slaves, the government shall make an appropriate settlement so as to maintain their living conditions and enhance their inclination to support the reform.

Article 6:

Liberated slaves have low productive power. Patient education, careful arrangements and a long period of nurturing in work are therefore necessary after their living conditions have been settled.

(a) The authorities shall give adequate help to freed slaves and bondsmen who have difficulty in making a living.

(b) When house-slaves are freed they are to take nothing from their owner's house except articles owned by themselves. Means to enable them to produce and live better than before are to be arranged entirely by the authorities.

(c) In arranging the means for house-slaves to produce and live better, attention must be paid to the following:

Those with homes should be helped to return to them;

Those who have parents, husbands, wives, brothers, sisters or other kin should be helped to rejoin them;

Those without home or kin should be encouraged to join with others on a voluntary basis to produce a living.

Article 7:

Regardless of class, those who are too old to work will be taken care of by the government for life.

Juveniles are to be looked after until they are able to live independently.

Those who are incapacitated are to be given appropriate help.

During the process of liberation and settlement in the various rural districts, these people must be well cared for so that they are never without a place to be.

Section Three: Differentiation of Classes

Article 8:

When differentiating classes during the reform, the only distinction required is that between Slave-owners and Working People. No further distinction need be made between slaves, bondsmen and Working People.

Article 9:

Slave-owners should not exceed 5 per cent. of the total households. This accords with the spirit of the decisions of the State Council concerning the class-differentiation of the peasantry, and takes into account the actual conditions in this County, the number of slaves owned, area of land occupied, whether or not labour is performed, the degree of exploitation and so on. These actual facts should form the data for analysis to achieve a fundamentally satisfactory demarcation.

Article 10:

In differentiating classes, data should be carefully gathered so that negotiations may be thorough. Results of the negotiations should be sent to the Rural District People's Congress for approval. They should then be publicly discussed and the results reported to the County for approval. If negotiations at Rural District level do not reach a satisfactory conclusion, they should be referred to the County.

Section Four: Confiscation and Distribution of Land

Article 11:

Land owned by the Slave-owners is to be confiscated and distributed to those who work. Slave-owners, including those who oppose the reform, shall receive an equal share.

Article 12:

The principles of land distribution:

(*a*) Taking the Rural District as a unit, productive capacity should be appraised and land distributed on the basis of what land is actually under cultivation each year.

(*b*) Generally no change should be made in the landholdings of Working People if the land requirements of those with no land or inadequate land can otherwise be satisfied. If a change is necessary it may be only on the principle of not reducing the income of the original holder and only with County approval.

(*c*) The land should be distributed on an individual basis. A single person should get two shares and a household with two persons three shares.

(*d*) Those who have sacrificed their lives in the revolution, members of the militia and persons working in public office should be included in the census for land distribution—each to receive one share.

(*e*) Mountain forests and pasture land are to be devoted to public use after confiscation and will not be distributed or used as arable.

(*f*) All customs and religious beliefs of the nationalities must be be respected, cemeteries and cremation grounds preserved and orchards, etc., protected.

(*g*) Land that will be needed for communications and construction should be set aside at the time of the distribution on the understanding that it may be used until it is needed.

Article 13:

Certain matters concerning Slave-owners that arise during the distribution shall be dealt with as follows:

(*a*) In negotiating the compulsory sale of excess draught cattle from Slave-owners, the price must be just and reasonable. There must be no forcing down of prices.

(*b*) To protect the herds and encourage the development of cattle-breeding, existing agreements under which cattle are tended should remain valid. Flocks of sheep are to be protected and no dispersal allowed. Herdsmen who were formerly the property of the Slave-owners should remain herdsmen if they are willing, being paid wages and having political equality. If Slave-owners find difficulty in paying such wages they shall be paid by the authorities.

(*c*) Firearms owned by Slave-owners should be delivered to the authorities in negotiations conducted by special representatives of the County. Compensation will be paid.

(*d*) In special cases where Slave-owners have a labour-deficient family, they should be permitted to hire wage-labour so long as this is done with the free will of the persons concerned.

Article 14:

Certain matters that arise concerning Working People during the distribution shall be dealt with as follows:

(*a*) Existing land-holding agreements of the Working People remain unaltered. Any anomalies should be settled by negotiations in a spirit of unity and for mutual benefit. During the distribution no land may be disposed of as gifts.

(*b*) Debts outstanding to Working People shall not be cancelled.

(*c*) Firearms possessed by Working People shall be assigned for use by the Home Guard.

(*d*) Working People deficient in labour power may hire labour or invite people to join their households on an equal footing to work and eat together with them.

Section Five: Organisations to Direct the Democratic Reform

Article 17:

County or Rural District People's Congresses, People's Councils, Reform Committees are the legal executive organs for the Democratic Reform.

Article 18:

Reform Committees are to be established in the County, in each Area and in each Rural District, to unite all available forces and ensure the success of the task. These are to be composed of competent persons recommended by the Rural District People's Congresses, or appointed by People's Councils of the next higher level. They carry out negotiations and deal with all matters affecting the reform.

Article 19:

Labour Associations are the voluntary organisations of the Working People, having the prime duty of organising and educating the Working People to carry out the policy of Democratic Reform by Peaceful Negotiation.

Section Six: Addenda

Article 20:

The above provisions are to apply to all areas of this County where the slave system exists.

Article 21:

These measures have been discussed and adopted by the First Session of the First People's Congress of the Norsu Autonomous County of Ninglang and are to be issued and put into force after reference to the higher authorities.

————————

SUPPLEMENTARY MEASURES FOR THE DIFFERENTIATION OF CLASS STATUS DURING DEMOCRATIC REFORM BY PEACEFUL NEGOTIATION
(Sealed) February 24, 1957

Two standards of class-differentiation are defined according to the nature of the two differing social systems: the slave system and manorial feudal[1] system. A person's class status is defined as it was on January 1, 1956, provided that it had not undergone change during the three years prior to that date.

Only two classes shall be differentiated—Slave-owner and Working People. The criteria for a Slave-owner are:

(*a*) Able-bodied but either taking no part in work or in main productive work.

(*b*) Possessing (as a household) ten slaves or more, equivalent to three house-slaves and above three households of separate-slaves.

(*c*) Occupying more than ten acres of tillable land for each member of the family.

(*d*) If engaged in auxiliary labour, nevertheless deriving more than 70 per cent. of annual income from exploiting the labour of others (by special privilege, land rent, usury, etc.).

Regardless of the above stipulations, the class of Slave-owners may still include persons having the following qualifications:

(*a*) While owning fewer than ten slaves, having a particularly large area of tillable land, drawing a high proportion of income from exploitation, able-bodied but not working.

(*b*) Living alone, possessing more than five slaves, able-bodied but not working, plus other above-mentioned conditions.

(*c*) Taking part in auxiliary work, income more than 70 per cent. from exploitation, plus other conditions mentioned above.

(*d*) Having little tillable land but an especially large number of slaves, privilege rights, degree of exploitation and able-bodied but not working.

(*e*) Owning no land but renting extensive land, able-bodied but not working, plus other above-mentioned conditions.

(*f*) Owning ten or more house-slaves and no separate-slaves, with other above-mentioned conditions.

Sample cases of above qualifications:

(i) Family of six, some able to work but not working, owning nine slaves (five house-slaves and one household of separate-slaves), having about 70 acres of land under own farming and 50 acres rented out to others.   Classified as Slave-owner.

---

[1] The articles pertaining to feudal areas have been deleted by the author as not being relevant to the subject.

(ii) A person living alone, able-bodied but not working, owning five house-slaves, 50 acres under own farming, credits of 320 silver dollars bringing in 320 dollars annual interest.

Classified as Slave-owner.

(iii) Eleven persons in family of whom five do some auxiliary work, owning thirteen house-slaves, twenty-five separate-slaves (in five households), 115 acres of land under own cultivation, 350 acres for renting out, interest on loans 350 silver dollars.

Classified as Slave-owner.

(iv) Ten persons in family, some able to work but not working, owning seven house-slaves and twenty-eight separate-slaves (in eight households), 12 acres of own farming, 16 acres rented out, 33 acres tilled by bondsmen, controlling thirty households of common bondsmen.

Classified as Slave-owner.

(v) Family of six, able to work but not working, owning three house-slaves, fourteen separate-slaves (four households), no land farmed by family but tenant-tilled land of 66 acres and sub-tenant-tilled land of 8 acres. Interest on loans of 120 silver dollars yearly.

Classified as Slave-owner.

(vi) Family of ten persons, some able to work but not working, owning ten house-slaves, 30 acres under own farming 20 acres tenant-tilled, 120 acres rented out, owning seven oxen, two horses, twenty-eight sheep, controlling twenty-eight households of common bondsmen.

Classified as Slave-owner.

Families possessing more than the stipulated number of slaves but not to be classified as Slave-owners include:

(a) Owning a few more than ten separate-slaves but no house-slaves.

(b) Owning a few more than ten separate-slaves, taking part in work, with less than 70 per cent. of exploitation in the annual income.

(c) Widowed or single persons unable to work, owning a few more than five slaves.

(d) Working, owning no land or privilege rights, more than ten slaves.

Sample cases having the above qualifications:

(i) Five members in family, no house-slaves, twelve separate-slaves (in three households), renting out 21 acres of land.

Classified as Working People.

(ii) Nine members in family, four able to work and doing auxiliary work, owning one house-slave, twelve separate-slaves (in two households) 28 acres of tenant-tilled land, 5 acres sublet.

Classified as Working People.

(iii) Single male, aged sixty, unable to work, owning eight house-slaves, tenant of 21 acres, owning two oxen and one sheep.

Classified as Working Person.

(iv) Nine members in family, three working, owning three house-slaves, ten separate-slaves (in two households), no land farmed by self, rent out 26 acres, income from interest on loans 40 silver dollars yearly, owning eleven oxen, seventy-five sheep, no privilege.

Classified as Working People.

CHAPTER NINE

PROBLEMS OF FREEDOM

*Jingu Hushe becomes rural district head—How the slaves "came out"—
Bargain honoured—First days of freedom—Artificial families—Slave's
view of liberty—Squandermania—Longing for revenge—Ex-slaves tell
their stories—Women more intelligent—Reunion of Ashi Chesa's family—
Aristocrats learn to work—Errors and corrections*

I GOT the seat where the family ghosts do not attack when I called
on Jingu Hushe—behind the fire on the same side as the door
hinges. "Pay no attention to his high nose," the local work-team leader
remarked. "He comes from Peking and he is against slavery. He's all
right." This caused some serious nods and also some titters from the
girls, easing the polite atmosphere. I accepted a bowl of parched barley
flour, poured a little tea in and proceeded to get it stuck all over my
fingers. Then we had a drop of corn whisky and things got more free
and easy.

It was an ordinary Norsu house of split-bamboo matting, built in
a single day as custom requires and offering little protection from the
cold upland winds. A perpetual wood fire was burning between three
stones supporting a shallow cast-iron cauldron like an upturned watch-
glass three feet across. Smoke filled the room; the rafters gleamed black
with smoke varnish. Everything was the best available, barley *tsamba*,
oat trenchers and even a pinch of tea baking in a little earthenware jug
which was then filled with a sizzle and handed to the guest. Ex-slave
Jingu Hushe was now the Yen Shan rural district head and was
behaving appropriately. We had brought biscuits, sweets and cigarettes.
Neighbours kept coming in to see what was the fuss and stayed to
listen or talk. Everyone had been a slave, for this was a separate-slave
village, recently liberated.

Before the abolition, Jingu Hushe's wife had been half his property
and half the property of his master, who had originally arranged the
match. Now Jingu either owns all of her or none of her, depending on
which way it is seen, for she is free. She sat nursing her seventh child,
handsome, independent looking, and frequently interrupting her mild
husband to enlarge on some statement. She had been a very expensive
slave—worth fourteen ingots.

Yen Shan Rural District was formed on June 29, 1957. That was the date when all the house-slaves came out, separate-slaves were freed, privilege and usury cancelled. Encouraged by his dynamic wife, Jingu Hushe had been an "activist" in the six months preparation for reform and this had later led to his election as district head. He told me about the whole process, with interpolations from the ex-slaves standing and squatting all round. It was January. In six months the ex-slaves had certainly found their voices.

Separate-slaves already had their houses, but homes had to be built in advance of the actual liberation for the house-slaves. For the first time in the Cool Mountains, these were not of the customary bamboo wicker but solid houses of rammed-earth adobe, wind-proof and windowless—glass is a rare and costly thing in the Cool Mountains. Food for the slaves had to be accumulated and stored, ready for the day when the master no longer fed them. To supply the freed slaves, Yen Shan and the other three Rural Districts that make up Racecourse Area, needed 415 tons of rice, all of which had to be carried on the backs of pack-animals or men along the high mountain trail I had traversed.

"For most of the six months before reform it was meetings, meetings and then meetings," said Jingu Hushe. "There were talks and explanations about policy: there must be no killings, beatings or struggle. We discussed it till everyone understood—masters, freemen and slaves."

"My own master," he said in answer to my question, "didn't like the reform at heart, but what could he do? He dared not oppose it. At the meetings the masters could see our strength. They were out-powered and could only agree or run away, so they stayed and agreed.

"Some masters made the best of a bad job and lent a hand to help build the new houses, just to show that they were heart and soul in the reform. We knew better and we still keep a very strict patrol with the new Home Guard. In the end both sides kept their bargain. There was no fighting, no trouble, a few little quarrels.

"At eleven in the morning on the 29th, all the house-slaves walked out and their masters went along with them to their new houses to signify that they left by agreement. All the slaves had places in various houses settled beforehand. Then there were speeches and presents. All very nice, no bad feeling shown. That night there was another meeting mainly to get the house-slaves talking about their new life. How to depend on themselves."

That was indeed the problem, according to every *ganbu* in Cool Mountains—far more difficult than dealing with the slave-owners.

House-slaves leave their masters' homes innocent of all belongings, clad in a patchwork of tattered felt and bits of rag stitched with string, to enter a chaotic world of adjustment and readjustment.

Some can still recall their family ties and can return to rejoin parents, husbands, wives, brothers, sisters. Some make that hopeful journey only to find bereavement. Those who can remember from whence they were abducted and ask to return, leave the Cool Mountains for other parts of China, but unless the request is made, no encouragement is given to this because in any other society an ex-slave is a pitiable, disoriented thing, not able even to speak his local tongue.

Families cannot be united all at once, even if their whereabouts is known or guessed, because the reform takes place in stages.

Separate-slaves are also poverty-stricken, but they have homes, kin and—most important—some farming experience. All they need is food, tools, cloth, loans or gifts of cattle and help in reuniting their families. Where house-slaves are able to return to their former families, they too present no problem.

Otherwise house-slaves are helpless. The fundamental problem is that they have always been under the direct orders of the master or his major-domo and have no idea of the productive process, or of the connection between work and food.

When they leave the masters' houses, they are organised into households, through some members of which the *ganbu* can guide them in productive work and in organising their lives. These households are largely artificial and remain unstable for a long time, but the alternative of still bigger units would require more preparation, more direct leadership by the *ganbu* and might defer the time when the slaves can stand alone. Experiments in larger scale organising are taking place, but the standard method at the time of the abolition is separate households.

Households average seven to nine members and are of various kinds. Where husband, wife and children have all been separated and can reunite, these households are called "reunion of kin" and are stable. It is sometimes possible to add an orphan or a disabled person to such a household, because one of the aims is to spread round the people of low labour-ability. A similar sort of household, and quite common, is formed when a male and female slave decide to get married during the course of the reform. In such a case, the total household might consist of the married couple, two more people of full labour-power and two of half-labour power. This is called a "husband and wife household". They are next in stability.

A third type is the "voluntary household", when slaves who have been friendly before, or have worked together, decide to pool their land, live and eat together and form a household. Without the steadying factor of a married pair, these households are less stable, and are usually less willing to accept a share of the old and weak.

Last and biggest headache for the *ganbu* are the "residual households", formed from the poor remnants of slaves after friends have elected to be together, stronger have rejected being saddled with weaker, married have said they don't want single people, and young people in their prime have refused the old. Half of these "residual households" in one district of Racecourse Area were still unstable six months after the reform.

In most of these various households, some leading figure usually emerges quickly and naturally as a person best able to get things done. Sometimes the most apt person is also a bully or dishonest. But there seems to be no realistic alternative to forming households and encouraging the former house-slaves to produce for themselves. To create the conditions that will make this possible, the authorities have to supply everything needed for living and production during the transitional period until they can stand on their own feet.

"Two rules that make the reform possible," said one *ganbu*, "are that the slaves get enough to live on and gradually start to produce, while slave-owners get enough to maintain their original living standards." In each Rural District, he said, the average cost at the time of reform was 15,000 yuan (£2,200) in fulfilling these two principles. The cost for every house-slave freed was about 80 yuan (£11 10s.). These costs are borne by the Yunnan provincial authorities.

All materials for the rammed earth houses—rafters, shingles, doors, formers—are supplied by the authorities, but the work is done voluntarily by the people, even the slave-owners doing a token stint. For each household the following were supplied as a minimum: cast-iron cauldron, bread steamer, cooking spatula, big spoon, kitchen chopper, plough-frame and share, grain basket, one milch cow, two sheep, one pig, a few chickens, seeds. One draught animal is supplied for each three households.

Each person gets: eight months supply of grain, one or two complete outfits of clothes (a woman's dress takes 12 yards), a large and small bowl, kitchen knife, wooden basin, 5 lb. of salt, a length of rope. Each person who labours gets an axe, hoe, mattock and sickle. A blanket is issued for each two persons.

Such is the abysmal poverty of this area that I met well-to-do slave-owners who envied the ex-slaves their complete set of equipment.

To provide the means to work is one thing, a practical matter, but to provide the incentive, desire and knowledge of how to work is much harder. A slave's conception of life is bound up in what he has experienced. He did what the master ordered and was fed by the master. This was an unbridgeable gap, and he sees no connection between the labour he did and the food which the master gave him. A slave exists to work and the master feeds him. That is life. In their masters' houses many slaves did nothing but some simple task; getting firewood, carrying water, digging, all under orders. Almost none knew the whole picture of elementary farming. The mental gap between a house-slave and a self-supporting person was seriously underestimated by the *ganbu*.

And abolition of slavery was not understood by the house-slaves. It was regarded as a change of master: the new master obviously should feed the slaves and give them their orders.

Another point was: who were the *ganbu* anyway? Here were people willing to sit with slaves and eat with them, when it was well known that freemen and slaves do not mix together. These *ganbu*, therefore, must be the over-slaves of the more powerful and more benevolent master who had suddenly given them houses and pots and food.

So the *ganbu* quite misjudged house-slave mentality in thinking that the food they issued would be made to last somewhere near the stipulated time and that the animals would be used for breeding and establishing farms. Formerly half-starved house-slaves who suddenly get their hands on several bushels of grain cook it in great masses—as much as the cauldrons will hold at a time—and what they cannot stuff into themselves they feed to the animals. Big Ninglang potatoes, some of the best I ever tasted, they cook in their jackets, break in half, take a bite from each side and throw the rest to the pigs. One family, having received one hundredweight of rice on Monday, came for more on Tuesday. They had cooked the lot and fed it to their animals.

Remonstrances about this sort of behaviour got the response: "If you don't want us to eat it, why give it to us? Then give us each time how much we should eat." Which would have left the *ganbu* with very little time for anything else.

It was similar with the livestock. Norsu noble custom dictates scores of fixed occasions when cattle, sheep, pigs and chickens should be sacrificed. There are also plenty of emergency occasions when someone is sick, dies, gets married or plaits her hair for the first time. So at the earliest opportunity the cattle issued by the government were killed. In some cases the *ganbu*, to save the issued sheep, would provide the money to buy a sheep for special ceremonial occasions, but the County Working Committee of the Communist Party issued a directive that pandering to superstition must stop.

It took the total efforts of the Bolo work-team and my own pleas, arguing for the best part of an hour, to dissuade old Ashi Chesa from killing a government issue sheep to entertain the high-nosed friend of *Gongzo* who had come all the way from Peking to see him.

Ex-slaves have carried over other ideas from their ex-masters. To a house-slave, freedom means idleness—to be like his master. When told that they were free the slaves' reaction was to lie around all day, eating and smoking, never doubting that the wherewithal to do this would come from the same unknown source from which slave-owners derived their own ability to live without work.

They got confused when the *ganbu* said: "Now you are free and should work hard for yourselves." It hardened their conviction that they were really only working for the *ganbu* or the *ganbu's* master and were still slaves. They carried on as before, doing what they were directly ordered to do, sleeping and eating as much as possible, and had no idea that what they were planting was for themselves.

Other matters cropped up that sounded ominous but were relatively easy to cope with. Some slaves, when they realised that their former owners had lost their power, wanted to reverse the situation and kill or enslave them. They also wanted to take the noble women. One former house-slave told the *ganbu* that his master had tried to bribe him into making false declarations at the time of the class differentiation by promising to marry his noble daughter to the slave—an unheard of thing, as the slave knew. "Of course I didn't believe him," the ex-slave said, "but there's nothing now to stop me going and grabbing the aristocratic ——!"

The *ganbu*, while showing sympathy with their bitterness, pointed out that there were many reasons why these things were bad for everyone. First, agreement had been reached that no force would be used. If the slaves used force their ex-masters would be entitled to do so. Second, killing always led to more killing—so it was better to stop killing altogether. Third, freedom for oneself was only possible on the basis of freedom for all. Slavery must be wiped out and that had been agreed. Fourth, working people needed working wives, not aristocratic lazy-bones.

Fear of the slaves turning round and taking revenge had been one of the slave-owners' most powerful arguments against reform. In fact, it came to nothing. Slaves are conditioned to obey orders. If the *ganbu* found difficulty in convincing them, it was necessary only to issue orders and they obeyed. Eventually they would understand.

The Chinese Communist Party's practice of testing everything in a small way at first, then discussing it before proceeding to wider application, turned out to be valuable also for the slaves' understanding. Ex-slaves found that their crops were actually intended for them and were distributed to them when harvested. News of this spread like yeast and changed the situation at bottom. Where trepidation had previously existed about "coming out", now the problem became how to prevent them all coming out without preparation, which would have caused chaos.

Work-teams found by experience that it was better to form production units of about ten households each and put one member of the team in direct charge of each to lead the household heads and, through them, the slaves. Work-teams are the lowest Communist Party organisations in these circumstances and work under the instructions of the local Communist Party committees. Their job is to interpret policy at the lowest level, do anything from building houses, settling feuds, planning irrigation projects, inoculating babies and performing minor surgery. Whatever mistakes they make—and mistakes are no doubt plentiful—these teams require courage, persistence, flexibility, unusual devotion, to settle in those dark, hostile hills, relying on nothing but their ability to convince, half a day's march from their nearest little team of equally isolated colleagues, and work year after year for the slow change of which they are the catalyst. And if their mistakes were at all serious, they would be the first to pay the penalty —for life in these parts offers little quarter.

I found the work-teams knew every inch of their areas and everyone in them. It was only necessary for me to ask to meet an ex-slave formerly owning two slaves, and himself owned by a commoner, not a noble, for someone almost instantly to say: "Ah, yes, So-and-so. About two miles from here. Has five children but only four have come back yet."

One ingenious work-team member, living with ex-slaves and getting daily more uncomfortable, finally showed them how to dispose of lice. He boiled and dried their clothes and his own, cropped everyone's head and scrubbed them, and for a week there was comfort. This news spread rapidly and led to a greater interest in hygiene. So far it is mainly interest, rare washings do not extend beyond the wrists and cheeks. But that is not confined to slaves; their masters never washed either, except at birth and marriage.

New villages, quite unlike the wattle-hut settlements of the Norsu, came into existence with the freeing of the house-slaves. Both for mutual comfort and the feeling of security it gives, house-slaves like to be together in the journey from chattel to yeoman. Their new adobe villages—spaced about half a day's walk apart—are usually ringed with a high wall, topped with twigs to render climbing more difficult. They have little confidence in the promises of their ex-masters and maintain constant patrols of armed Home Guards, shadowy figures in black turbans, cloaks and wide short trousers. They flanked our journey all the way, and when our tiny cavalcade of teetering pack-horses and bored riding animals stopped for a breather, a few such guards would materialise to join us in a smoke. Except for these ubiquitous armed figures, the bitterness behind that closely controlled clash of forces, peaceful, but still a clash going to the roots of human relationships, would never have been apparent.

Inside the villages, newly-freed slaves loll patiently around waiting for the next meal, lying in the sun; only women with babies seeming to have any avocation. Now and again apathy disappears with the announcement of a new issue of cloth, grain, tools or a meeting to discuss work. In this early phase[1] of liberty, the ex-slaves mostly looked bewildered and lost, except the youngsters, giggling girls and naughty boys who behave like their counterparts anywhere. Though at Bolo, where the outer wall of the new village was not yet built, I noticed the young people joining in just as earnestly as the adults in compacting it. Inside the walls there are more than an average number of morons, deaf, lame and halt, a few babies to whom liberation has come in good time, and a few old folk with work-stiffened fingers for whom it has come almost too late.

In Racecourse Village, centre of the area, was a more settled air of community life. Already it was necessary to make an appointment to

---

[1] I was asked not to press my request to see the actual process of release in a village since it was felt that the presence of a foreigner would add to the *ganbu's* problems.

see any particular slave, because a casual visit might find them all in the fields at work. This is partly because Racecourse was reformed a little earlier, but even more because the ex-slave leadership there was of a better calibre than in most places I visited.

Alin Niha was quite exceptional: a former bondsman, taken into slavery at seven for a debt of 400 lb. of rice. His father had originally borrowed 40 lb. At eighteen Niha ran away, was chased, shot at, and finally made his way over the ridges to Li Chiang, living on wild plants and a little stolen barley. That was in 1950, when the Chinese army had just driven the Kuomintang out of Li Chiang. Niha joined the militia, then the army, finally the Communist Party—one of its rare Norsu members. On demobilisation he opted to return to Racecourse Village to help in the reform.

Another local figure is the twenty-two-year-old girl Lulrl Duve who, like Niha, works full time for the work-team at a monthly wage of 18 yuan (£2 15s.). She leaves four yuan with the team to accumulate for clothes and I imagine she needs all that, for when I met her she was quite the best-dressed Norsu girl I saw—noble, common or slave—with a white felt cloak, silver ear-rings and, above all, was sparkling clean, having learned to wash. This wage is low for China but high for the district, where an average farm worker's wage is three or four yuan monthly plus keep. People doing public work can eat at the work-team canteen where an all-in-diet costs four, five, six, seven or eight yuan monthly depending on choice. Dishes vary and rice is *ad lib.*

Jin Mo, though only twenty, is a member of the Racecourse Rural District People's Council. She was formerly a shepherdess, abducted into slavery at the age of six or seven. Jilu Dehor, vice-Head of the Rural District, is a twenty-six-year-old born-slave who played a very active part in the abolition movement and risked his life to denounce a plot by his master to sabotage the cattle.

Perhaps the most striking of the slave leaders of this village was old Budia Aniu, who was abducted forty-four years ago at the age of twelve. She was a Nashi girl and very beautiful as well as clever, so that she became her master's permanent house-slave, and therefore unmarried. She bore one son by a man brought in for the purpose and never seen again. Her son died eight years ago. "He was never strong because the master ill-treated him and beat him as much as three times a day. Once he was put in water with a big stone to hold him there. Once they tortured him with thorns in front of me. I couldn't bear to watch."

Tears ran down the handsome old face, now coloured and lined like a walnut shell. Several neighbours standing in the shadows were quietly weeping with her. I offered her a cigarette which she split open with a gnarled thumb and stuffed into a wooden pipe.

Budia Aniu had gleaned the opium fields, saved a little money and bought a goat which later had twelve kids. Her master ate all the goats because he said falsely that she had failed to repay a loan. After much stinting she bought a cow and two sheep, then her son fell sick. Her master persuaded her to sacrifice the two sheep to save him. Everyone ate the sheep but the boy died. Then her master made her sacrifice the cow to provide her son's spirit with expenses to go away so that he would not trouble the living. I asked what happened about other slaves who had no cows. Normally, she said, the master would adopt a cheaper method, driving two nails into the heels of the corpse to prevent the ghost walking back to the master's family and haunting them.

Now Budia Aniu is the head of a household of six ex-slaves—two young men, two young women and her own small grandson. Her son's widow is somewhere else.

This ex-slave village has twenty-eight households, twenty-eight cattle, twenty-eight sheep and thirty pigs which they regard as collective property—not to be sacrificed. All the households are in a single mutual-aid team, Jilu Dehor said. Work-points are remembered by the heads of households, since they cannot write. Was it hard to remember, I asked. Not at all, said Jilu Dehor. "Anyway, the amount of labour each does is not important, but of course smaller people need less to eat."

He had actually been as far as Kunming and spent a month visiting and talking with people in co-operatives. He thought co-operatives better than mutual-aid. "But we are not advanced enough yet to have a co-op," he said. "We are still living on government grain because we haven't started production yet."

His household was typical of many. It contained one old man, Dehor himself and his mother, his elder brother and newly-married wife, a young man, and the "natural" daughter by someone else of his brother's wife. His mother was the household head.

Women, in fact, generally seem to be more intelligent and active than the men and less obsequious. Male slaves had always been fewer than female and since 1952 the best men had fled. Women could seldom flee. Also it seems that women's traditionally high position among the Norsu nobles is reflected in the other social groups.

Unlike the helpless house-slaves, separate-slaves need mainly subsidies and relief which are settled through the Labour Association. Other than this they need help and money to travel and seek their children and additional housing if the reunited family overcrowds the old house. Ashi Chesa had two new and very large adobe houses built for his brood of fourteen, including in-laws and grandchildren.

Having overheard his ex-master talking of killing the slaves, Ashi Chesa's second son escaped with his wife and three children, picked up his younger brother and ran to the old man's place. But they were being chased and had to leave. Soon the reform made their escapes "legal" and one son went to help Ashi Aniu, his sister, to escape in a district the reform had not yet reached. That accounted for them all, except a daughter whose whereabouts is still unknown and his eldest son, killed long ago for attempted escape. Ashi Chesa's wife and lame daughter made up the brood, now all together in Bolo.

If among the former house-slaves the joy of freedom was blended with apprehension and bewilderment, among reunited separate-slaves it was pure happiness. Even at this distance in time and place it is hard to recall that smokey house in Bolo without a tear. It is a terrible thing to see such simple human happiness telling of the misery that lay behind. After his abortive attempt to kill a sheep for his guests, Ashi Chesa sat baking a little pot of tea leaves, wiping his eye occasionally while his son told the story. All around the big room, lit by a fire of pine logs, ex-slaves sat, stood and leaned, old and young, straight and crippled, militiamen with rifles on their cloaked shoulders, listening to the familiar horrors told again. Behind me under the loft a pig snored, a cow champed and roosting fowls made little protests.

Ashi Aniu had been dragged from her mother at the age of eight and was first put on herding animals. I asked her: "Did you cry when you were taken away?" She nodded—she was crying now—and said: "I cried for days and nights and when I cried they beat me. I had to cry quietly. After a while I was able to stop crying when master or mistress came round."

Her father broke in to cheer things up a bit. "We've got 13 acres of land now, mostly good land, and we have a mutual-aid team of twelve households with a *ganbu* helping us. Things are pretty good now.

"Of course this year can't be very good, we got most of the land after the planting." Their total harvest for fourteen people had been

50 lb. beans, 50 lb. corn, 350 lb. wheat, 1,200 lb. oats, and 1,500 lb. potatoes. "We can do better next year," the old man said, "and in the meantime we can borrow from *Gongzo* or sell an animal. My son gets his wage from the rural district. We can get by fine."

This was a common tale; most ex-separate-slaves and commoners said they had to rely on help for six months of the year until they got production going better. Either land reform came too late for the sowing, or draught animals were too few or, as one young commoner said: "We just ran around playing for a time and didn't get busy." For him, like many another poor commoner, reform had meant the lifting of feudal privilege and no more fear of enslavement.

One anomaly was that people who owed money to a classified "Slave-owner" had their debts wiped out, while others still had to honour them. That was a matter of chance, and one reason why the struggle over classification was so acute was that debtors tried to ensure that their creditors were classified "Slave-owner", which would cancel their debts, while the creditors fought to avoid this. In an average rural district, the annual saving in privilege was about 10,000 yuan, and a similar amount in interest on usurious debt. But debts could no longer mean enslavement and debtors could borrow from the authorities to repay capital and thus evade usurious interest rates.

In Racecourse Area the cancelled debts, owed to classified Slave-owners, amounted to 4,165 yuan, and those owed to Working People and not liquidated were 4,878 yuan.

Fortunately for the *ganbu*, separate-slaves far outnumbered house-slaves. By January 1958, figures were available for twenty-seven rural districts where slavery had been abolished.

| Classification | House-holds | Number of People | | | |
		Male	Female	Total	%
Slave-owners	. 299	808	908	1,716	5·39
Working People	. 2,208	4,545	4,897	9,442	29·69
Poor Commoners	. 1,875	3,992	4,026	8,018	25·21
Separate-slaves .	. 2,144	4,293	4,757	9,050	28·45
House-slaves .	. 859	1,644	1,935	3,579	11·26
Total . .	. 7,385	15,282	16,523	31,805	100·00

It would need a long stay in Ninglang to discover how the former slave-owners are liking the reform. A few, like Buyu Wani and Zeku Alu are genuine progressives who are glad to pay the price in their own personal power for the general advance of their people and recognise that the way out has been made very smooth for the slave-owners. Others pay lip service to the reform, but it is easy to see hatred and opposition below the surface. Many are squandering their family wealth in a reckless last binge of a dying order. They can be met travelling with escorts of commoners and hangers-on who still cling to the old ways, still expecting to be treated as Black-Bone Aristocrats, still quick to take offence but withal carrying a subdued air.

But most nobles are trying to learn how to work as local officials, how to plough, get firewood, carry water. Jingu Hushe said that the ex-slave-owners in Yen Shan now approached him and the Rural Council to discuss problems. These slave-owners were commoners, not nobles, but this was still regarded as quite amazing. Hushe could not forbear the remark: "They used to say 'Slaves can't manage affairs any more than a plough-frame can ride a horse'. Well, now the plough-frame is riding the horse." Most members and heads of Rural District Councils are poor commoners and ex-slaves.

I asked Hu Tan what he thought the main errors had been in carrying out the reform, and this is what he said:

"Reform of a slave society by peaceful negotiation is new, our understanding of the situation was poor and time for investigation inadequate. So we went in a rather zigzag fashion.

"On the one side negotiation is a very important point and there was some wavering between Left and Right trends. Some failed to see the necessity to arouse the people—couldn't see the reform's revolutionary aspect. This led to excessive compromise with the slave-owners. It caused a diversion and more work because the commoners and slaves did not see their place as masters of the situation and when the work-team left the people didn't know how to manage.

"On the other side there was the error of transplanting to this place the experiences of the Land Reform from the inland feudal areas, paying too little attention to the aspect of peaceful negotiation, raising demands too high and not striving enough to win the support of the slave-owners.

"Slave society cannot avoid being cruel. If the standards of judgement applicable in other places were thoughtlessly applied here there would be chaos. Then even a person with one sheep or one slave would begin to worry and confusion would set in.

"Such errors were quickly corrected though they still appear in isolated places. Ninglang is a complicated place and the level of our *ganbu* is not uniformly high." Hu Tan went on to the next point. Like many Chinese *ganbu* he seemed to carry a mental notebook which kept his thinking in very ordered channels.

"We made some mistakes over grain. Our first idea was that the slaves should take some grain with them when they left the master. After all, they had grown it. Then we decided that this would complicate things and that little grain was involved.

"But when the slaves came out we found that it was quite serious. We had to bring in 2,000 tons to last six months and this was not enough. After the abolition there has to be organisation, land division, planting and waiting for the harvest. It all takes time. Nothing much can really be expected till 1958.

"The Provincial Committee [of the Communist Party-A.W.] and ourselves quickly discovered this error, and with the freeing of the third batch of slaves we instituted the compulsory sale of part of their grain by the slave-owners. That original 2,000 tons is still coming in on pack animals and I reckon we could have bought half of it from the slave-owners.

"Lastly, I would say, we didn't accurately estimate the difficulties that would follow the freeing of the slaves. It took us half a year of study and getting experience before we could draw up a set of regulations governing this. There are still problems, such as the residual households. In some places 10 per cent. of those still have difficulties. If it isn't settled this will hold up progress because these households contain many of the most revolutionary elements."

These were the main errors according to Hu Tan. Owing to the careful area-by-area handling, and within areas, group-by-group, control was kept and very few excesses had occurred on either side. There were cases of slave-owners killing slaves and of slaves killing their masters, but they were exceptional.

CHAPTER TEN

FEELING THE WAY

*Hopes and calamity on Happy Stone Mountain—Backwardness and waste
—Remnants of primitive life—Work groups, factories, experimental farm—
Four-hour day—Medicine and the sorcerers—"Learning to read is worse
than slavery"*

HAPPY STONE MOUNTAIN was one of the first rural districts to complete the abolition of slavery in November 1956. In the fourteen months from then until my visit, in December 1957, it demonstrated the trials that face the ex-slaves and the work-teams and also pointed to possible lines of development into a new order. This place is almost 10,000 feet above sea-level and its entire population consists of Norsu.

In the enthusiasm after liberation, spring cultivation in 1957 went well and there were soaring hopes of an excellent harvest. Then came a frost of unheard-of severity in August, wiping out the buckwheat and killing most of the potatoes. Optimism turned to despair. People who hoped to be well-to-do found themselves with less than six months' food. It was a deadly blow economically, but psychologically even more. Apathy took over. People talked of leaving this alpine desert.

During the reform, slave-owners, wolves, leopards, sacrifices and lack of winter fodder had made colossal inroads into the livestock. Only three families out of thirty-eight composed of ex-house-slaves were without serious problems. Thirty-one of these needed food for at least six months. Some had sold their issued equipment. Six people, unable to face the prospect of independent life, had returned to their former masters. There were complaints against the work-team and the trading group. The latter was said to be high-handed in its dealings with people who brought herbs and furs to sell and its members to be on bad terms with each other.

A team of investigators, checking on the results of the reform, made a report which was at once gloomy and optimistic. At the same time it produced a plan to reverse the rot.

Happy Stone Mountain, like much of the Cool Mountains, has tremendous potentialities for farming, livestock breeding, hunting, handicrafts and various occupations like collecting wild herbs. There is also scope for industry. Its altitude is offset by its southerly position. But its remoteness, background and primitive productive methods make the realisation of these possibilities "no easy task", as the investigators said, with notable understatement.

First necessity was to assist those in need and stabilise the situation. For this they proposed a number of minimum requirements:

Animals: Enough draught animals to provide one for each two families and enough pigs to make up the number to one for each family.

Winter Clothes: Twenty families and twenty-three incapacitated people needed full sets of winter clothes.

Farm Tools and Utensils: Mattocks, hoes, sickles, ploughs, harrows, cauldrons, tongs, winnowers, mills to re-equip every family to the basic level.

Sustenance: One and a quarter pounds of rice per head daily for six months for most of the families.

This made a subsidy of 28·7 yuan per head, which the investigators reckoned would fall to 7·4 yuan for the years 1958 and 1959, and to 2 yuan for 1960.

So backward is this district, the investigators said, that the soil is ploughed only 2 inches deep and buckwheat is sown on unturned soil. Almost no fertiliser is used. A farmer commonly spends only about 100 days a year in tilling because the ground is frozen most of the time. Despite poverty, waste is rife. Good grain is fed to animals. One example cited is that owing to the lack of wood-working tools other than the axe, each plank is chopped from a solid tree, wasting nine-tenths of the wood.

Beyond this gloom lay bright prospects: gigantic virgin forests, excellent pastures, fertile soil, enormous stocks of leaf-mould from the woods, valuable medicinal herbs and minerals. Means of exploiting all these resources would turn this area from a wilderness to a garden. Tools were needed for carpenters and blacksmiths, equipment for setting up small factories, experts to teach the local people how to distinguish valuable herbs and a switch-over made to tested hardy seeds, which should be supplied from other areas in China with a similar climate. Detailed plans were drawn up, including the opening of a gunpowder factory, clinic and school in this little district.

Once the people got free of their masters they turned naturally to mutual aid. One reason was the shortage of large farming tools and draught animals. But it also has its origin in Norsu tradition. As the Norsu system of marriage and consanguinity retains strong traces of an earlier form, so the custom of co-operative working, common to primitive societies, persisted in an attenuated form long after the slave and feudal systems rendered it anachronistic.

In four villages in Happy Stone Mountain, after the abolition, the people spontaneously formed seven mutual-aid groups, consisting of thirty-six families. One of these groups was composed of Working People who had formerly owned slaves, the rest were made up of house-slaves, separate-slaves and poor commoners who had worked together in a similar way previously. They exchanged labour for labour, regardless of skill, strength or age.

Astonishingly, the local work-team, which was severely criticised by the investigators, had tried to discourage this form of activity on the grounds that such teams had little or no value and if enthusiasm were aroused and the teams failed, their disintegration would lower morale. But people went ahead and formed more groups. In Abolition Village, three teams had been formed, of which two had advanced to the point of using work records for each member, and these had proved successful, although most members were not able to calculate themselves.

The leader of one of these "advanced" teams told me that mutual-aid teams united people to help and care for each other, saved labour and enabled work to be allocated according to skill—a very vital issue for house-slaves who frequently can only do one simple task.

A movement has now been started to stimulate such groups there, first in the elementary form of work-for-work, moving on to division of labour and accounting. A tentative plan was made to broach the question of changing some or all of them into co-operatives in the spring of 1959.

All *ganbu* were instructed to study farming and take part in farm work as the quickest method of ending "planning in generalities" and to discover the real wealth potentials of the various districts. The line of development in Happy Stone Mountain is more clearly marked than in places liberated later, in spite of 1957's tragic harvest failure, and that line is towards eventual co-operatives based on mutual-aid groups formed voluntarily among the households.

Another line of development, entirely untested while I was in the Cool Mountains, would enable the house-slaves to pass directly from slavery to socialist forms of organisation. That is the large-scale farm.

H

About two hours march from Ninglang lies a tract of lovely country, deserted for forty years. Some fifty families used to live there "who all became very rich" according to local tradition, until they fled during the upheavals that accompanied the Chinese revolution of 1911.

This is the site of Honeybee Rock Farm where a large body of ex-house-slaves and a few others are taking part in an experiment that may have wide repercussions in Ninglang County.

At dawn on a crisp morning in December 1957 it was the scene of bustle and laughter as upwards of 100 former slaves scurried up and down wooden ramps carrying earth to build the walls of their main farm buildings. Women were working alongside the men, running up bouncing ramps with baskets, their ground-length flounced skirts threatening to trip them up. I never saw such energy and good humour displayed by other ex-slaves in the Cool Mountains.

Some of the responsible officials in Ninglang are convinced that large-scale farms will solve many of the problems of organising house-slaves, but it was felt necessary, as usual, to test it experimentally before any general application. Arguments in favour of this type of farm are very convincing.

House-slaves, freed and given tools, food and land, then run into many difficulties which would take a long time to overcome while they are organised as separate households. But they are accustomed to collective work and have a rather strong collective spirit, rendered necessary in self-defence against their masters.

Large-scale farms, permitting a division of labour, would enable their narrow, specialised skills to be brought to bear and, by developing distribution of the product according to work days, would increase the interest in work, which is naturally low among slaves. At the same time, the limited number of *ganbu* would be more economically employed in leading larger organisations rather than the scattered and helpless families which are largely artificial.

The urgent need to fix farm-land and put an end to wasteful, inefficient slash-burn cultivation would be facilitated by this type of farm, making possible an immediate wide extension of arable land and the planned planting of greater areas of high-yielding crops, including paddy rice. Irrigation would also be possible on a wider scale by the use of collective labour, as in the rest of China.

Centralised catering would stop the waste of food, and monthly payments from their work-day dues would permit the slaves to escape their present hand-to-mouth way of living and become accustomed to adjusting their expenditure according to income, while common ownership of animals would prevent sacrifices. Sanitation, medical care and the promotion of leaders from the ex-slaves' own ranks would be speeded up.

I gathered that there was no opposition from the higher authorities to the proposed experiment, but the ex-slaves were by no means without qualms. Accustomed to a clannish mode of life, they felt that a large, heterogeneous collection of people would squabble and that theft would be encouraged.

Another problem was opium. Not realising that the reform itself would immediately reduce the use of opium and its value as a cash crop, and soon wipe it out, the former slaves feared the possible loss of this main source of income above their barest subsistence, which it was before. Traditionally the growing of opium, which few slaves smoked, was their hope of occasional meat, tobacco, essential dress and possible freedom.

Explanations about the possibilities of a much higher income from the farm went right over their heads. On the other hand, no fears were expressed about the complexities of running a farm, presumably because they had no idea that it was complicated.

What won most of them to support the idea was the desire to be led rather than to have to lead themselves.

Opinions of this sort were thrashed out at meetings called by the work-team of the New Barracks (a garrison village built by the Kuomintang) Rural District, in whose area the Honeybee Rock Farm is situated. Leader of this team is a twenty-two-year-old girl named Hsia Cheng-yu, who insisted on giving up her bed for me when I stayed the night in New Barracks—having first removed her service rifle from it. Her work-team called the family elders of the former house-slaves together and many meetings were held to try to explain the advantages of the plan.

Finally, most families wanted to join. On the critical issue of the poppy, it was agreed that pocket money should be paid out monthly during the formative stage of the farm and that no opium should be planted on farm ground. The few ex-slaves addicted to the drug should grow it only on waste land and must gradually break the habit.

At the time of the abolition there had been 264 house-slaves in New Barracks Rural District. Of these, forty-seven had gone to find their families, had married commoners or been adopted as sons and daughters.

When the registration for the farm was made, the following decided to join in the venture:

House-slaves	.	.	152	37 households (newly formed)
Separate-slaves	.	.	15	4 households
Poor Commoners		.	3	1 household
			170	

The sixty-five house-slaves who decided against joining were mostly people who had some skill, or had grown much opium in the past. Some were waiting to find out about relatives and expected to move away.

The ex-slaves elected a committee of nine members to run the farm, all people who had been active in the reform. This committee co-opted the chairman of the Labour Association and two *ganbu* allocated by the work-team, one of whom was the farm accountant. As its first work the committee drafted a detailed plan for 1958 and a general Five-Year Plan.

Main Headings of the 1958 Plan

Investments by the authorities		Yuan
Four months' grain for 170 people (about 10 tons) . .		1,530
Seed for 158 acres		993
Farm tools, etc.		950
Handicrafts: Three sets of carpenter's tools . . 150		
One set of stonemason's tools . . 20		170
Animals		3,940
Administration		200
		7,783

Income (Estimated)		
Nett estimated crop of rice, oats, soya, broad beans and early spring crops, allowing for 10% loss due to weather, etc. 6,395		
Less seed 993		5,402
Handicrafts production and two water mills . . .		585
Animal husbandry		3,732
		9,719

Deductions for new capital outlay

	Animals	.	.	.	1,187	
	Farm Implements	.	.	972	
	Construction	.	.	972	
Reserve	. . . .				758	3,889
	Nett income for 1958	.	.	.	.	5,830

This works out an annual income for every adult and child of 34·3 yuan and this is reckoned to be higher than the average per capita income of the nobility. However, no figures exist to prove that assertion. A not-too-accurate survey of the same families' incomes per head gave 13·6 yuan for 1957, the year after abolition—10·5 yuan from crops and the rest from side occupations.

No mention is made in the two plans of repaying the original investment and presumably the authorities intend to write it off. Administration costs are for the half-time work of the two *ganbu*. The sum marked for reserve appears to be intended for welfare, education and so forth.

An average work-day of four hours for the able-bodied is estimated at the beginning, rising to six hours. There is no mention of an eight-hour day. Nor is this surprising. Yunnan is a province not remarkable for hard work and the Norsu are not its hardest working people. Shops in Kunming open as late as possible—usually a little before noon—and close early. In journeying through this most delightful of all China's provinces I found it hard to arrange my affairs so that a full day's work was possible. The natural indolence of the minority peoples, many of whom have only to reach into a tree for wild bananas and other fruits, or throw seeds into untilled land and smoke a bamboo pipe while they grow, seems to affect even the hardworking Hans once they reach Yunnan.

Nobody was more indolent than the Norsu slave-owner, sitting by the fire till almost noon when the world was warm and then spending the rest of the day, eating, drinking and smoking opium, when not feuding and flogging slaves. And slaves tell the *ganbu* who urge them to work in their own interests: "Oh, you Hans. Always fussing. Here we are, just out of slavery, and you come worrying us again about working."

In the hope of increasing the zest for work, the farm sets aside a little money each month to present as awards to the hardest working of the ex-slaves when the monthly pay-out of foodstuffs and pocket money is made.

A draft Five-Year Plan envisages that by 1962 there will be 615 people on the farm, tilling 500 acres of dry land and 160 acres of wet paddy. Fruit trees planted in 1958 will be bearing, and other sources of income will have risen. In the last year of the plan, 1961-2, the net income, after deducting 40 per cent. for accumulation, will be 55,650 yuan or 90·5 yuan per head. This plan was considered somewhat conservative at the time I left the Cool Mountains. If it works out like that, which seems very probable, this would be a great step in solving all problems of the house-slaves.

The argument that large-scale farms would more rapidly solve educational and medical problems is a forceful one. And the medical problem is related to production and consumption, since most sacrifices of animals are to cure sickness. There is little faith in sacrificing— though the feasting is enjoyable—and not much trust in the sorcerers, for whom it is a trade; but in the absence of an alternative, a sick person will do the traditional thing.

I was able to trace eighteen different customs requiring sacrifices. Norsu superstition is animistic—everything with its ghost, which will go away if it gets what it wants. What ghosts want are animals— especially cattle—according to the sorcerers, who get the choicest parts of each animal killed. The rest is eaten by owner, guests and relatives. Buyu Wani was ordered by sorcerers to sacrifice 300 cattle in one year—and still had rheumatism. Other reasons for sacrifice range from betrothal to killing any ewe which is still suckling last year's lamb when this year's is born.

Equally soaked in superstition, but never formerly having enough cattle to sacrifice, the ex-slaves and poor commoners at first regarded the government issue animals as a glorious opportunity for a religious splurge. Even pigs suckling their young were killed, so that suckling pigs were often reared at the breasts of the women.

Spreading confidence in modern medicine and collective ownership of the animals are the twin lines for saving livestock. But China's overall shortage of doctors renders the development slower than the *ganbu* would like.

Modern medicine never had a footing in the Cool Mountains. During the days of the Kuomintang, one "western-trained" doctor set up in Ninglang with a small case of blunt hypodermic syringes and a few of the "latest" drugs, charging "the price of a good horse" for a dubious injection. His patients ran grave risks.

Now there is a hospital in Ninglang, with operating theatre, a health centre for women and children, seven clinics, one mobile medical team and two midwifery centres. The fifteen doctors and thirty-five other staff include Abi Vugan and Abi Jaja, the two runaway slave-girls, training as nurses. Between 1953 and October 1957, 236,000 yuan had been spent and the number of cases treated had reached 372,934. Smallpox is already under control.

In education, so decisive for the future of the Norsu people, no big break has yet been made. While I was having a midday meal at Clear Water River, a child came panting in from Yangping and flung himself at his mother. "Sitting there learning to write is worse than being in Zeku Dehor's house," he wailed. Zeku Dehor had been his owner. But his mother gave the boy a beating and sent him back the 15 miles to school without a meal.

Yangping Primary School was the first to be opened in the Norsu areas, in 1951. Now there are sixteen other schools and 3,979 pupils. Most nobles will not allow their children to go to school, having had bad experiences with Han schools under the Kuomintang, who used schools as a means to get hostages for the future penetration of the Cool Mountains. To prevent this, the nobles ordered their commoners to send children as part of corvée obligations, but all these schools collapsed.

No fees are charged for the new schools and subsidies are paid. Tuition starts with hygiene and goes on to the three R's. Teachers use the standard text books until books in the newly devised Norsu written language are ready.

There is also one middle school near Ninglang, which mainly trains Norsu people working for the authorities in literacy and accounting. Sixteen more primary schools were scheduled to be opened by the spring of 1958.

Aristocratic Zeku Alu once said to me: "My only real use was to settle disputes. In the old days people died every day in clan battles. Now most of the feuding has stopped. What use am I? I cannot even read and my brain is no good at learning." Education, it seemed to me, was the way to better farming, industry and full independence of outside help; but educating slaves from their condition of blank ignorance must be a long and heartbreaking task.

CHAPTER ELEVEN

TRANSITION

From owned to owner—The future of the slave-owners—Subsidies, enlightenment, social pressure—No private industry or commerce—The Cool Mountains could be wealthy—Roads and airlines soon—No tears need be shed

B Y the time I left the Cool Mountains in January 1958, it was yet too early to draw a detailed picture of the next stage after the still incomplete abolition of slavery, though the general lines were being sketched as new experiences were garnered.

Its broadest strokes were roughed out by the law passed at the first People's Congress meeting in Ninglang, where the aim of the reform was set down: "To develop production, consolidate the unity of the nationalities, develop political, economic and cultural establishments, improve living conditions in the Norsu areas and gradually achieve the transition to socialism."

How far these aims are being achieved I have tried to describe, rather than interpret.

Socialism, in its simplest terms can be taken to mean the public or collective ownership of the means of production—in this case land, tools, minerals, industry, trade and commerce—and reward according to the quantity and quality of work performed.

Seen in this light, the situation in the Cool Mountains has gone a very little way and not uniformly. When slaves and bondsmen are freed, they cease to *be* property and *acquire* property instead. The land is distributed and becomes the property of the commoners and slaves. Cattle are owned by households or groups of households.

Many of these individual owners of land, partly of necessity and party for traditional reasons, combine their land in various ways. Mutual-aid or production teams, where they are formed, also work the land jointly in varied ways, but as yet the private ownership, both of land and produce, remains. Mutual-aid is a step before co-operation and collective ownership of the land.

Possibly, if the Honeybee Rock Farm is successful, and there seems no reason why it should not prove superior to individual farming, the house-slaves, that absolutely propertyless group with literally "nothing to lose but their chains", may pass directly into socialist organisations more quickly than the property-conscious separate-slaves and commoners. It is not unlikely that this most supremely oppressed group will set the pace for the rest.

Slave-owners appear to present a problem less economic than ideological. The wealthiest of them were not rich by comparison with the ordinary factory worker elsewhere in China, and a rise in general living standards could rapidly overtake their petty wealth and make a Honeybee Rock Farmer better off than the average slave-owner in a few years. But the nobility among the slave-owners are sharply set apart by their historic caste position and deep-rooted contempt for work. Subsidies, propaganda and social pressure seem to be the only means to change their way of thinking. If they reject progress they can only become pauperised anachronisms. Experience with former capitalists in China generally would indicate that most slave-owners will learn how to change.

No private industry or commerce ever existed in the Cool Mountains. Hand-woven cloth and hand-felted cloaks are made in the home for personal use and few are sold. There was no division of labour even between farming and handicraft. Consequently the way was absolutely clear for publicly owned industry and commerce from the beginning. Already there are the state banks, trading companies, retail stores and the Ninglang Handicrafts Co-operatives, making clothes, shoes and light metal goods.

Looking to the future, there is no doubt that the Cool Mountains has enormous potential wealth. Though high, it is southerly with a hot-house climate, and excellent yields have already been cropped by modern farming methods. Officials are convinced that the present food deficiencies due to backward methods will be turned into a surplus by 1960. Meat, butter, potatoes and other produce will exceed local demands to a growing extent and a big "export" market in skins, valuable herbs, musk, wool and other local goods will be easy to build.

Preliminary surveys show that the Cool Mountains possess a wide range of minerals, including coal. Plans for exploiting these and setting up factories are being prepared. Since I left the area, a number of small factories have been established. Many mountain streams exist suitable for driving small power plants to supply electricity for homes and farming, but bigger plants will have to wait until a road is built.

Transport, in fact, seemed to be the one major difficulty in making progress there and would become a still greater one if production rose, and spending power with it. A survey was completed for a road to Ninglang which would be ready in 1959 and there was talk of an air service, for the town stands on a flat plain several miles long. My old pack-horses, Little Flower, Date-coloured Cow and Shorty will then, no doubt, be relegated to local transport.

I left the Cool Mountains with the single regret that I was not able to stay for as long as might be necessary to follow this historic transition right through from ancient to modern—though even as I write this, the total end of slavery has already been achieved there.

I was able to see that political equality existed and that the people were able to exercise their democratic rights because they had taken part in the processes that broke—albeit peacefully—the power of the slave-owning nobility. Imperfect as they yet are, the new Rural District People's Congresses are stable and undoubtedly operating as the organs of government power. And all this complex and delicate change was effected without throwing the 30 per cent. of slave-owning commoners into support of the slave-owning nobility and causing untold loss and destruction, in which the slaves would probably have been the first to suffer. It would be difficult not to admire the skill, courage and patience of the *ganbu* whose leadership made this possible, and especially of the work-teams who operated at the lowest level.

Leaving the Cool Mountains it must needs be said that all the imagined romance of this by-passed pocket of slave society disappeared at close quarters, leaving only squalor. Nature dispensed wealth generously on those lovely fertile uplands but men, organised in a rigidly conservative slave system, could do little but waste and destroy it. Although it was not their fault, for the Norsu rulers were also imprisoned by their slave system and oppressed by the Chinese imperial rulers, they left no beautiful buildings, art, culture or even handicrafts to atone to the human race for the sufferings inseparable from slave society. And only incurable sentimentalists or worse could regret its passing.

Part II

THE WA

CHAPTER TWELVE

HEADHUNTERS OF THE BURMA BORDER

The unconquered Wa—Another pocket of human history—Hazardous for visitors—Dragon Mountain—Jungle warfare—Sacrifices take time— Headhunting as an aid to farming—Primitive democracy—Beware red pepper and feathers—Slavery had just begun

FEW enough places remain on this globe untrodden by the restless feet of journalists and their ilk. I had just left one such place and now— impelled by that urge to go where others have not been—made plans to visit another. This was the most south-westerly tip of China, a little region of mountainous jungle straddling the still unmapped section of the China-Burma border east of the Salween River, where the Wa hillmen live.

Visiting the Wa tribes—a small group of primitive people who have remained almost entirely unaffected by outside influence—was always reckoned a pretty hazardous undertaking. Living in isolation in a mountainous pocket of territory surrounded by virgin jungle, they were well able to protect themselves from the British in Burma, and the imperial, warlord and Kuomintang régimes in China—which was one reason why the China-Burma border in this region remained undemarcated. On some British maps the area is erroneously labelled "The Wa States"; anything less like "states" could hardly be imagined.

It is interesting to note that under "Wa", the first word in the "W" section of the *Encyclopædia Britannica*,[1] reference is made to material no later than the *Gazetteer of Upper Burma, 1900*—almost sixty years ago. But the Encyclopædia's note on the Wa—full of inaccuracies as I was later to discover—was certainly enough to make anyone's feet itch to get there and find out what was happening now. "They are popularly divided into wild and tame," the Encyclopædia asserts. "The wild Wa are headhunters. Outside every village is an avenue of huge oaks. Along one side is a line of posts facing towards the path with skulls fitted into niches. . . . Skulls must be added annually if the crops are to be good; those of distinguished and pious men are the most efficacious, and headhunting (q.v.) takes place

---

[1] *Encyclopædia Britannica*, 1953 Edition, printed in Great Britain.

during the sowing season. Villages are high on the slopes of hills, usually on a knoll or spur. The only entrance is through a tunnel 30 to 100 yards long, of which there are usually two at opposite sides of the village, about 5 feet high, and so narrow that two people cannot pass freely, sometimes winding slightly to prevent gunfire; the path is studded with pegs to prevent a rush."

What I had learned in the Cool Mountains and on more up-to-date authority was that a very early form of slavery also existed among the Wa, but that owing to the very different, primitive conditions there, quite different methods were being used to bring about its abolition.

From the Cool Mountains to the south-west tip of China is little more than an hour by plane, but fourteen long days of travel by foot and motor. We toiled all the weary way back to the Upper Yangtse and somehow managed to clamber up the perpendicular side of Twelve Barrier Mountain, and down again in twelve hours. The tiny cobbled town of Li Chiang seemed such a big city now, and as we turned the corner on to the motor road I involuntarily shouted to Li Ping-tai: "Look, a bus!"

From there we drove down to Tali and back on to the Burma Road, through the dizzy coils of the road section called "Nest of Wire", past a big new electric power station and cement factory to where Kunming lies balmy and blooming by its lovely lake, 6,400 feet above the sea.

Until recently, a visit to the Wa involved weeks of horseback or foot travel over very difficult country, mountainous, slashed by rivers, inhabitated by a dozen different peoples, from the exotic Flowery Miao to the song-loving Hani, the "tiger-eating" Lahu and the slender Chinese Tai. The motor road used to end at Sze Mao, 300 miles from Wa country, but now a new highway runs right up to the Burma border. It was opened on October 1, 1956 and is a very serviceable road, though one of the most mountainous I was ever on.

People used to say: "Marry off your wife if you mean to cross Sze Mao basin",[1] that low-lying, mosquito-plagued malarial incubator. This saying well illustrates why the upland people seldom crossed the tropic lowlands.

Forty years ago Sze Mao was a thriving trade centre with 70,000 inhabitants. Then it was struck by bubonic plague followed by malaria. When the Chinese People's Liberation Army entered it in

[1] Yao guo Sze Mao ba
Xien ba laopou jia.

1950 there were only 3,000 people living among the rotting houses, with a 90 per cent. incidence of malaria. I did not see a single mosquito and malaria is down to 3 per cent.; but even so, I felt safer under a mosquito net.

On this one-time adventurous journey to the Wa area, the biggest hazard I ran was at Sze Mao—a spectacular meal composed of all the delicacies found in the jungles around the town: bear paws, elephant, deer sinews, venison, a boned wild bird of some sort stuffed with rice and truffles, fresh bamboo, not to mention the usual dishes—pork, fish and vegetables. These were pressed on me, one after another in a most alarming manner, until I ate myself right out of good manners and had to refuse the last two or three courses.

All down the road, the effects of co-operative farming were now very visible. People were working in the fields in groups and a solitary farmer was rare. Water conservancy operations on a major scale were going on everywhere, often causing detours. Several times we drove round great new lakes, several miles long, with former roads disappearing into them and trees sticking above the surface until the deeper water covered their topmost twigs. Old men, who in former times would have been a burden on their families, were busy on the road collecting animal droppings with little scoops and baskets, to swell the co-operative stocks of manure for the spring sowing. One bearded old peasant gleefully nipped a bit of dung from almost under the wheels of our Land Rover and saved our squashing it into the dust. Incidentally I found the Land Rover an ideal vehicle for journeys of this sort, but possessing one drawback: long descents in gear caused oiling up of the plugs and constant cleaning was necessary. If this vehicle had an engine more suitable for mountains it would command a ready market in China.

The new road crosses the warm upper reaches of the Mekong River at a ferry, where Tai girls flirt and take their baths—deftly manipulating sarongs as they wriggle out of them and into the river to bathe in the nude. Now there are palms, bananas to be had for the picking, sugar cane, close packed rice paddies and such fertility on the lowlands that the peasants used to burn rice for fuel while other parts of China were stricken with famine because of poor transport.

Beyond the upper Mekong, on the last lap to the Burma border, the road shoots up, and instead of lush paddy land there is inefficient slash-burn farming with fields rising 45 degrees or more from the horizontal. People are few as the road climbs into high plateau and bleak rocky mountains, and soon it crosses a wild desolate ridge about 20 miles long with deep bare valleys on either side—a natural no-man's-land separating the Wa people from their less primitive neighbours. Once over that ridge, the road winds down deep into a virgin jungle of thick bamboo where old trees fight for life against a pall of vines, living and dead intertwined, and emerald dragonflies dart among steamy sunbeams.

Up again, and from the top of the last range can be seen Hsimeng, "capital" of the Wa country, sitting on the tip of Dragon Mountain—only about 8 miles away as the crow flies but reached by a gigantic horseshoe of zigzag road 44 miles long. I found later that this long detour had been made necessary by the primitive democracy of the Wa. To go direct, the road would have to pass through Jung-ke, where most people wanted it; but a few members of Wa clans in the area objected. Important matters among the Wa can be settled only by absolute unanimity of view and a single opposing vote is enough to quash a proposal. Bowing to local custom, the authorities sent the road round through territory occupied by willing clans. Now the capricious Jung-ke people all want a road, but that is a costly business.

A few Wa can be seen along this part of the road, swarthy people of short stature, burned purple-brown by the upland sun, with wide black turbans, wide short trousers, long swords, broad and heavy at the end for slashing bamboo, carrying cap-firing muzzle-loaders, some of them with six-foot barrels, and pistol stocks 8 inches long, inlaid with silver.

Hsimeng, on the peak of Dragon Mountain, was originally a group of mud and wattle huts, where people met to trade. No Wa people lived there; they preferred the jungle. Now it is the political centre of the area, where the Chinese Communist Party Working Committee for Hsimeng County has built offices and dwellings, opened a general store and trading centre, a hospital and schools. I was met by Ping Fu-chang, secretary of the committee, four Wa headmen and a member of their brother nationality, the Lahu. Curiously, this Lahu family are the hereditary titular heads of the Wa people. I could not discover the actual reason why the Wa should have accepted a Lahu as their leader. There are very few Lahu in their own area, though many nearby. Legend has it that a man called Asa Jauvong came to the area 100 years ago and appointed new officials, one of whom was a forebear of this Lahu whose name is Jabuei. I can only say that he was universally recognised by the Wa wherever we went and greatly respected as a demon fighter, although a plump young man of twenty-seven with a good-natured manner.

This region was never under even nominal control by Chiang Kai-shek or previous Chinese rulers, but because it is remote and marches with the north Burma jungle, large numbers of Kuomintang soldiers fled here as the People's Liberation Army pressed down from the north and east in 1948 and 1949. Jabuei, the Lahu leader of the Wa, spent most of his time in those years organising the Wa people to fight and destroy these remnants, disorganised troops who hid in the jungles and made raids on the Wa villages for food, women, liquor and opium. He led the Wa in battles that wiped out hundreds of them until the Kuomintang forces in the area were reduced to fewer than 100 men.

"At that time," said Jabuei, the faint cast in his dark brown eyes accentuating his naturally shy appearance, "I was moving from village to village, not living anywhere. It was a life and death struggle. They had already destroyed my house in Hsimeng and they robbed, burned, looted and raped. All Wa fighters were in arms, with sentries everywhere and people taking weapons to work in the fields. We gave the Kuomintang no rest. Our Wa people are good fighters."

In 1950 the People's Liberation Army contacted Jabuei and other Wa leaders, who went down to the Mekong[1] and had a meeting. "They said they were against the Kuomintang and so we listened to them, although they were Hans," Jabuei said. "They told us that once the Kuomintang was driven out, there would be no more oppression of the minority peoples by the Hans. We should be masters of our own lives and they would co-operate with the headmen to bring a better life to all the Wa people. Instead of stealing from our people they would bring gifts and new doctrines that would help the Wa to grow rich like the Hans."

Jabuei and several other headmen went back into the jungle but it was not until two years later that the People's Liberation Army entered the area. By that time something, but very little, had been done to overcome the Wa hatred of the Hans. When the army came in it was because the personal guarantees of Jabuei, Aikan and other big Wa headmen had been given that they were disciplined troops and would not take anything from the Wa.

They distinguished the grey-green PLA soldiers from the Kuomintang by calling them "Jiefang". This is still the name used by all the

[1] In China the Mekong is called the Lantsang River.

I

Wa to describe the new system and its representatives—army, Communist Party, government functionaries, medical workers, traders, work-teams and the rest. It has no meaning in the Wa language but is taken from the Han-Chinese *Zhongguo Renmin Jiefang Jun*—Chinese People's Liberation Army. *Jiefang* in the Han language means "Liberation".

What the army found was a poverty-stricken people whose children of both sexes went nude up to eleven or twelve years of age, and whose adults commonly wore nothing but a strip of cloth. Almost everyone was half-starved and living on the jungle for the best part of the year.

Farming was, and remains, of the most primitive kind. An area of jungle is burned off and the land scratched a little before the seed of dry upland rice is scattered by hand. No fertiliser is used and when the soil is worked out, a new patch is cleared. Animals are not used for farming at all. Instead, most of the people's wealth and a good part of their time goes in sacrificing cattle, pigs and chickens to the ghosts. If a leopard is killed, a village will spend five or six days feasting and sacrificing and the same time is taken if a blood feud is successfully avenged by the cutting off of an enemy head. When a house burns down—a common enough thing with light bamboo houses, thatched roofs and no chimneys—there are three days for sacrificing, and the same time for a man wounded in battle. For customary festivals, if a woman dies in childbirth, to prevent hail, for the first rain, for personal taboos and special clan and tribal occasions, two or three days are taken up in ceremony and animals die. In general the Wa people are far too busy to waste much time in farmwork.

On certain occasions, these cattle sacrifices are a test of courage and skill as well as a method of paying off old scores. For these "tail-cuttings" the men whet their broad-ended swords all day till they will cut a falling feather. The young men especially are out to make a good showing before the girls, and excitement reaches climax when the sorcerer cuts off the tail of the tethered water buffalo to signal the start. In a matter of moments the animal is dead and in pieces, sliced by the razor-keen blades of the surging crowd of men struggling to grab a piece of the twitching flesh and cut it off. Failure to get a piece of the meat is a sign of cowardice. Groups sometimes work in concert according to a plan, as in a football scrum, one getting into a favourable position to cut meat and passing it out through the legs of the others to friends. When cut, the meat is still fair game to be grabbed by someone else until it is run to the women, who sit with waiting skewers of pointed bamboo. Once on a skewer, the meat is safe. Accidental cuts on arms and shoulders are the least risk run. Old enmities can be "accidentally" paid off among those flashing blades.

The Wa people live on the jungle hilltops in fortified villages of bamboo, thatched houses built on stilts and entered by an inclined wooden ramp. In the space below live pigs and chickens. The clans and tribes have headmen chosen partly by heredity and partly by democratic vote. Village heads are similarly appointed, and all such public leaders can be deposed if incompetent and new ones chosen. Sorcerers, the only other important figures, mainly proceed from father to son. They deal with the ghosts, big and small, and are also the only repositories of Wa history. When a human head is cut off for religious or clan reasons, a sorcerer will usually be found in the background as instigator.

This custom of decapitation appears to be a hangover from an earlier, purely superstitious form, and is now largely a method of settling clan or village blood-feuds. In this it differs little from any other form of feuding, but the tradition still persists of placing the head for one or two years in a basket on a tall bamboo near the hut where the great wooden drum is kept. This is believed to ensure good rice crops. It is not correct that the heads of foreigners, or pious or distinguished Wa are more efficacious than others. On the contrary, the heads of sorcerers or other leading figures are more or less immune.

One Wa legend says that decapitation all began with a trick played on the Wa by Chu Ko-liang, the famous Han military leader at the time of the Three Kingdoms (A.D. 220—A.D. 280). Chu Ko-liang is said to have given the Wa boiled rice to plant. Of course it did not grow. Then he told them that rice would grow only if they sacrificed human beings and cut off their heads. After they had taken his advice, Chu Ko-liang gave them proper rice seed which grew. This tale is remarkable in demonstrating the terrific reputation of this Han military leader, even in so remote a place, and is a manifestation of the bitter anti-Han feeling of the Wa.

There is no Wa central administration, no army, no permanent organisation, no State. All male Wa of the appropriate age are fighters, called together by village, clan or tribe as occasion requires, when a temporary command is appointed. After the battle everyone disperses. Essential messages are in a universally understood code: sugar cane, honeycomb, salt, tea, tobacco are signs of friendship; bullets, red pepper are signs of enmity and if a chicken feather is included, instant war is signified. A decision to go to war requires the unanimous agreement of the people concerned.

It is said by the elders that slavery began among the Wa only about sixty years ago. Certainly it is still in a very undeveloped form, slaves consisting exclusively of Wa people and comprising less than 5 per cent. of the population. One very credible reason advanced for this is that the level of production is so low that slaves can produce only a very small surplus above their own subsistence level, and then only if put to work on the very little good, fixed farmland that exists.

Estimations by the people now working in Hsimeng vary as to the nature of Wa society. Predominant is the view that the Wa are in the last stage of primitive society passing into a patriarchial slave system. Some say that they are in no clearly defined stage but, due to outside influences, have become a mixed society containing slave, feudal and capitalist elements (wage labour), superimposed on a primitive base. There seems to be a measure of truth in both theories, which are not mutually exclusive.

All these different social forms also exist among the Norsu, though theirs was predominantly a slave society. What I was anxious to find out was where lay the differences which decided that a different policy should be applied among the Wa and what that other policy would be.

CHAPTER THIRTEEN

UNWEDDED BONDAGE—MARRIED FREEDOM

Impenetrable village defences—Biggest Wa slave-owner—Between sobriety and drunkenness, business—Primitive basis of usury—From debt to enslavement—Wa slaves have social equality—Freedom on marriage— No class of slave-owners—First Communists in Wa jungles

TO get into any Wa village you must fight or be invited. Urnu village, a few hours horse-ride from Hsimeng, is no exception. Half a mile from the village the path through shoulder-high undergrowth enters a narrow tunnel, where dense jungle overgrows a boulder strewn mountain stream and it is necessary to dismount and clamber down. This steep slippery tunnel debouched on to a thread of path running along steep precipices to the village entrance.

Like all Wa villages, Urnu is surrounded by a high growth of dense thornwood between 15 and 20 yards thick, with dead and living thorn intertwined to form an impenetrable natural barbed-wire barrier. At opposite ends of the village two tunnels are cut through the barrier, closed on the inside by massive doors hacked out of large trees— hinges, door and bolt slots all cut from a single piece of hardwood— giving the villagers an advantage over attackers in the tunnel.

Sorcerer Aisung[1] met us at the gate. Jabuei and Aikan, the most important Wa leaders, and Ping Fu-chang, the local Communist Party secretary, kept me company. Among the curious villagers was the biggest Wa slave-owner of all, Aiga, headman of Urnu village. He bobbed about, very much on edge, and obviously uneasy in his mind as to what this strange *Jiefang* visitor might portend. We all walked up through the village of thatched bamboo huts where women sat suckling babies and old men dozed in the shade of tall bamboo. Outside the hut of the resident work-team, built of mud and wattle and far superior to the draughty woven slats of the Wa houses, was the community platform and meeting place, also of bamboo, as almost everything is.

As far as eyes could see, below us lay the mist-hollowed jungle, mostly denuded by wasteful slash-burn tillage, with patches of virgin

[1] All Wa male names begin Ai, and all female names Na.

forest on the hilltops—a gigantic piece of green chenille carelessly flung down.

Sorcerer Aisung presented me with two sticks of young sugar-cane as a sign of welcome and said, "Let us talk of peace. No quarrels." Then he went to a huge bamboo cylinder where millet beer was brewing, stuck in a flexible tube of bamboo and syphoned it out by sucking with his mouth to create a vacuum. He came towards me with a mug of the creamy tingling beer holding about one and a half pints. Having had several "dry runs" I knew what to do. Aisung said "Aha" and I said "Aha" holding out my hand. He took a sip, wiped the side of the mug with his hand and gave it to me. I took a sip and did the same, handing it to the next person and so it went round, everyone taking a sip including Napai, one of Aiga's slaves, then Aiga, and so it came back to me still almost full. Traditionally the guest must now knock it back in one swig. Here was one advantage conferred by a lifetime of steady beer-drinking and I poured the pleasantly sharp milky beer down without taking a breath. This was clearly most satisfactory and the mug circulated again until everyone had plenty of millet beer sloshing round inside, with chasers of fiery rice spirit which I had brought as my offering.

Among the Wa it is traditional that you cannot settle anything without a drink and you cannot settle anything when you are drunk. This leaves a remarkably small margin of time when anything can be settled. It is always easier to start a feud than to end one.

As we drank we ate boiled sweet potatoes, a crop grown for the first time in 1957 on these hills, and everyone passed the inevitable betel-tobacco-lime concoction that blackens teeth, browns lips and puts a mahogany gloss on dirt-encrusted feet where the bright red saliva splashes and dries over the years.

Headman and slave-owner Aiga, for all his wealth, was unshod like his slave, no cleaner and not much better dressed. He seemed to be going out of his way to be pleasant to the slave-girl Napai, whom I had requested to meet; handing her bits of pancake and empty glass bottles, much prized among the Wa who have virtually no handicrafts that cannot be achieved with bamboo and blade. Napai seemed to be embarrassed by these unusual attentions of her owner, whose blowsy new wife kept a sharp eye on him from under the eaves of the hut. From the first moment, Aiga's behaviour gave me the strongest impression that slavery had already achieved a degree of social odium. Perhaps it always had been odious to the Wa, for their social system is more communal than individualist, and slavery is a new growth.

As usual among primitive peoples, there is a form of joint farming in which families get together to clear land, contribute seed and till. There are no rules about how much work any person should do; they go along with each other as much for the company as for anything else and on the principle that many hands make light work. Distribution is therefore on an equalitarian basis with no distinction between skill or quantity of labour. Every person involved gets an equal share of the crop—man, woman and child.

Apart from their belief that this method is natural, there would be little possibility of distributing the produce according to calculations of the work done, because the Wa cannot calculate. They do not write and have little ability to count. A Wa selling bananas at so much for six cannot sell fifteen of them, and if three were left over he would eat them or carry them home.

If they run out of food they call around on each other, eating what others have until none have anything, and then go into the jungle hunting, getting wild fruits and vegetables, cutting firewood and selling it, doing day labour or borrowing. Debts and interest are fairly new developments. In the past, people who borrowed did not particularly regard this as a debt. Even if the principal was returnable, no question of interest was involved. Everyone was at times "in debt" to everyone else, but since the relations were simple human relations unaffected by thoughts of gain or loss, no debts existed—or if they did, nobody really bothered about it.

Among the Wa new ideas began to sprout within the past century, though they have not yet fully taken hold. The idea of private ownership in land is fairly well established. Good land, near the villages, is mainly fixed and privately owned. More distant, poorer land is usually clan or village property and may be used with the agreement of the headmen. The renting and even the sale of particularly desirable land exist, but are not important. Land can be had for the trouble of burning it off, so its value cannot be high; except in the case of irrigated paddy land, which is small in area and limited by taboo.

Political privilege is not great. A headman traditionally gets three or four pounds of meat from any animal sacrificed, can ask for a little unpaid labour, sometimes acts as a middleman in sales or disputes and charges a commission. A sorcerer does rather better on the whole, getting more meat from each sacrifice and charging between 25 cents and 5 dollars (the old Yunnan silver dollar) for officiating at "small ghost" or "big ghost" affairs. These privileges and the right that exists for headmen to settle questions of land usage, so that the best land tends to get into their hands, have been enough to set them a little above the rest of the Wa economically, though not enough to enable them to live without working.

Usury began to develop on this basis, according to the older folk, about sixty to 100 years ago, the first usurers probably being the better-off headmen and sorcerers, with others following suit until borrowing became impossible without payment of interest. Any usury led straight to slavery as the only ultimate way of collecting a debt. Usury is now general, and normal interest rates are 100 per cent. to 200 per cent. at simple interest. Usury is said to have increased sharply with the development of the opium trade when Kuomintang officials entered the district thirty years ago.

Usury spread very rapidly, and swiftly created new social relations. In Urnu village, almost every family was in debt, mainly to Aiga. In another village, Mandegor, I found that seventy-seven families out of about 100 were in debt, some of them paying 60 per cent. of their income in interest and some able to keep nothing of their income at all but having to borrow to live all the time.

Loans are needed first of all for food, especially grain—other things being available in the jungle. Next in urgency is the need to borrow to buy animals for the customary sacrifice. Animals for "statutory" sacrifices have to be supplied in rotation, family by family, and this is socially obligatory. A third reason is to pay marriage gifts to the families of girls. A fairly common cause of borrowing is to pay fines imposed by clan or village for theft or some breach of traditional law. Failure to pay leads to the culprit's house being sacked or to worse punishments, including slavery or death.

Usury, although new, is harsh as well as widespread. Debts are passed on to the children of the debtor and if there are no direct descendants, to the next of kin.

If a debt is not repaid in three to five years, the creditor will take the debtor's children as slaves, or if there are no children, some juvenile relative or—in rare cases—the adult himself.

Napai's case was typical. She was enslaved by Aiga at the age of ten, four years before I met her, and is now a very pretty young woman. Her old widowed mother Nahung told me her story because Napai, either through shyness or fear of her master, said not one word during the whole talk, though Aiga was not present at that time. Napai was dressed in the red sarong skirt adopted by most Wa women, with a crossover of only about 3 inches, a patched jacket that must have been given by a *ganbu* and a many-stranded necklace of beads. Round the tops of her calves she wore the usual thin bangles of black polished rattan and her long, unwashed and uncombed hair was kept out of her eyes by a white tiara of bone. She took cigarettes when offered, but did not smoke them; they disappeared, with sweets and biscuits, by what seemed to be sleight of hand. Her teeth were quite black from betel, though she was still a mere girl.

Napai's brother had wanted to get married and had borrowed cattle and a pig from Aiga for this purpose, as well as incurring other debts in another village. Time passed, the debt was not repaid and Aiga demanded a slave. "My son being grown up, my daughter Napai had to go, and a little later my other younger girl was taken to the other village," Nahung said. "Aiga has many slaves; seventeen others now. He used to have one more, but she died."

Females, being the main Wa labour power, are preferred as slaves, and they are also considered more obedient and less prone to run away. Slaves are valuable. An adult costs three buffaloes or about 360 yuan (£53), and a child slave 50 yuan or one ox or a muzzle-loader. This is far more expensive than in the Cool Mountains.

Wa slaves are said to be lazy and disobedient. They are completely under their masters' power and can be bought, sold, exchanged and given as presents or killed. Their entire product belongs to the master, who returns only the minimum subsistence. Crimes, such as secretly selling labour elsewhere for a day, stealing food or opium are visited with severe punishment of which beating is the least. Female slaves (unless they belong to the same clan) have to be the bedfellows of any male in the master's family, and if children result they may be either kept as slaves or taken into the family.

In spite of the harshness of their conditions, it points to the newness of Wa slavery that in outside society slaves are equal. They take part in the village and clan superstitious ceremonies and other villagers do not discriminate against them. When I had finished talking to Napai, she went and sat with the rest and people moved up to let her sit down next to Aisung, sorcerer and village notable. On her other side was Nashang, a plump free girl, and they sat with their arms round each other, whispering. It was impossible from dress or behaviour to tell which was slave and which was free.

And there was another fundamental difference between Wa slavery and the far more developed form among the Norsu: Wa slaves mix with the other villagers, make love and marry free people or other slaves. As soon as a slave marries, the couple set up house separately and the master is traditionally bound to help them do this. A mean slave-owner who skimps this duty suffers social criticism.

After the slave's separation from the master, enslavement is fundamentally ended. Slave-owners retain the right only to the slave's market value, which the slaves can redeem with cash, animals or, in what I was told were extremely infrequent cases, their own children. Probably that is rare now, but it seems to contain the seeds of development into the life cycle of separate- and house-slaves as among the Norsu.

This separation ends the expropriation of the slave's labour product by the master, though he can still demand a small recognised amount of unpaid labour until the slave's value is repaid. It is understood that slave and master are "kinsfolk" and the slave still addresses the master as "father". When such an ex-slave has meat or wine, it is common for a little to be sent as a gift to the master and a return present is often made.

Until the repayment of the slave's price has been completed, those obligations remain and a slave is expected to help the master over any living difficulties and even maintain the master if necessary. If that occurs, the property of the master is inherited by the slave.

This release-on-marriage rule explains why children are preferred to adults when distraining for debts, though there are adult slaves—usually wives, who have been sold for food or given into slavery for debt when no children are available.

Children "adopted" by relatives when their parents die constitute a type of slave, though these often become free very quickly and at no cost. If they are seen to be obedient, good workers and an asset to clan or village, they may be adopted by a ceremony and have equality and freedom, after which they can only be resold with permission of the Big Ghost and the sacrifice of a cow.

As to how important slavery is in Wa life, I made an investigation into the situation of Yuesun area covering several villages. There were 407 families and 1,487 people. Of these, sixty-eight were slaves or 4·57 per cent. of the population.

These sixty-eight slaves were the property of forty-seven families, of which one owned four slaves and two owned three each. It is rare for a family of Wa to own more than one slave.

There were thirty-nine female slaves and twenty-nine males, in the following age distribution:

Age						Number of slaves
Below six years	.	.	.	.	.	13
Between 7—14	.	.	.	.	.	28
Above 14	.	.	.	.	.	27

Reasons for their original enslavement were given as:

i.	Distraint for debt	.	36
ii.	Lack of food (sale of wives or children)	. .	17
iii.	Theft or crime	. .	5
iv.	Other reasons, including adoption	. .	10

These proportions are reckoned, on the basis of wider surveys, to be roughly true for the whole of the 40,000 Wa who live in Hsimeng County—about 5 per cent. of them or less are enslaved and ownership of more than one slave is exceptional. Aiga with his eighteen slaves is phenomenal. But he might have indicated the shape of things to come. Aiga is a young man, less than thirty years old, and a slave-owner of a quite unusual type.

No stable class of Wa slave-owners exists. A slave-owner may lose his slave by marriage, or get into debt and not only have to sell his slave but become enslaved himself. Life is at such a low and precarious level, especially because of sacrifices, that a person can easily pass into slavery or from slavery to freedom, and most slaves are in any case juveniles who do not remain slaves all their lives. Headmen, sorcerers and usurers do not exist as a separate class of slave-owners owning a stable class of slaves.

Headmen represent the unity and democratic leadership of village, clan or tribe and are not the rulers. A headman can only keep his position and the perquisites and prestige that go with it if he serves his people well. The other elders of the tribe and the sorcerers keep him in check. Leadership is not on a purely hereditary basis, though this plays its part in the selection of headmen.

In contrast to Aiga, who is rich and owns so many slaves, the head-man of Little Masang village, an hour's walk away, owns no slaves and spends a great deal of his time doing day-work at the usual rate of 4 lb. of unhusked rice a day, or collecting firewood to sell for a living.

This headman, Ailun, was very tickled at the similarity of his name with mine, Alan, and toasted our kinship. Then he found that the Wa for "peas" is *apees*, for "jacket", *ja* and for "trousers", *cloh* (cloth), and started to toast the kinship of the British and Wa at such a rate that he had to spend the rest of the day sleeping it off. The Wa all drink as much as they can get, including the women.

Slaves would have no value at all if they did not produce a surplus for their masters and this is very difficult to calculate. After numerous cross-examinations in typical areas, I estimated that a slave can produce at most 200 lb. of grain annually more than he is allowed to consume. At day-wage rates, that represents fifty work days and therefore the major part of his time is spent in producing his own means of subsistence.

This surplus derives from several causes. A slave gets only the coarsest food—and not much of that—and has to work all the time, whereas most Wa, by custom and due to a low diet, are lazy and wasteful. Slaves cannot waste their grain making alcohol, or entertain and sacrifice as free people do; the master has everything. Slave-owners can use better land, if only for the reason that they can usually afford to give a bottle of liquor or a chicken to rent good land when they have none themselves. For similar reasons slave-owners frequently have better tools.

Ordinary Wa farmers produce no more than 700 or 800 lb. of rice per acre and the amount of land sown is limited by lack of seed, poor tools, too little labour power, taboo and indolence. Most Wa—the figure was put as high as 80 per cent.—live from hand to mouth for half of every year; in debt, "eating next year's harvest" and harried by the ghosts.

Even pottery making seems to be unknown to the Wa, hence the value of an empty bottle. Few handicrafts exist, other than whittling bamboo into household utensils and weaving. Markets are infrequent, distant and on a barter basis. Hygiene is unknown, washing done by nobody, infant mortality horrifying and disease rampant—for which the only cure is the expensive one of placating the appropriate ghosts.

Few of these things were known to the first political workers who went into the jungles where dark suspicious people peered at them from behind bamboo clumps; armed people with little respect for human life and none at all for the hated Hans.

Aikan, formerly a big sorcerer and still headman of the powerful Ayam clan, told me that his clansmen said many times to him: "Aikan, if these *Jiefang* Hans come here and cause trouble, after all your words, your head will go up in the basket." Aikan, small and lame, with a little grey wisp of walrus moustache, grinned at me and took another swig of rice whisky.

"Some of our Wa people wanted to fight *Jiefang* as well as the Kuomintang. They said there were no good Hans. Besides, the *Jiefang* soldiers had good rifles and machine-guns which they wanted to get. Some headmen encouraged them and it was very difficult for a time. Others felt like me. *Jiefang* seemed sincere and took nothing. They had doctrines. They said they would teach us doctrines that would make us rich. We could only try, and if they turned out badly, fight them as we fought Li Mi [a Kuomintang general who fled to these parts—A.W.]."

Under such protection Communist work-teams were able to live inside the barricades of a few selected villages, build houses and settle down under the sighing bamboo, far from any hope of succour if the word of the headman proved inadequate to stem old hatreds, especially when the wine was in and the sorcerer in a sarcastic frame of mind, goading the young men.

I talked with one of the first political workers to settle in a Wa village. He was only twenty-one at that time, a Han named Hsu Wen-ping. He said that two leading Wa brought the ears and nose of a Kuomintang commander to Lantsang (on the Mekong River) and asked the PLA to help destroy all Kuomintang remnant troops in the jungles. Hsu was one of six civilian workers who went with the army as interpreters because he knew the Lahu language. That was in December 1952.

"A little later a meeting of headmen was called and agreement was reached that the army should stay. But the air was alive with propaganda that the PLA would be worse than the Kuomintang. We would loot, rape and kill, tax them and make them collectivise their wives, and so forth. The people feared us. I was scared, too," said Hsu Wen-ping, who now speaks Wa better than he could speak Lahu.

"I went to Mowor village where a *jumi* (rich man) had offered to put up the work-team in his own guest room. That was very good for us because we could learn more things quicker.

"At that time it seemed impossible that these people could be brought to the point of understanding socialism. But that was the job we had to do and the only way was to start at the beginning.

"We had the same slogan here as in most of the national minority areas: 'Do good and make friends'," Hsu went on. "And that was hard enough.

"We went with them to the fields to guard against Kuomintang attacks, nursed their babies, gave them medicine, helped to cut and carry firewood, distributed free rice, cloth and salt and gradually learned the language.

"But they used to say these things were not gifts. This was just Han cunning. They said we wanted to keep the Wa on our side to destroy the Kuomintang and then we would be ready to deal with the Wa. 'Soon you will demand these things back,' one old Wa said to me. 'Then if we cannot return them you will take the younger people away and kill the old ones.' Some put these relief goods away so that they could return them if called upon," Hsu said.

"Time passed. We went on giving food, tools and clothes. Our entertainers came and did shows for them and they saw their first films. We learned their customs and were always very careful to observe them. This was very important.

"It is a deadly insult to touch the centre pole of a house, sit on the family bed, carry green leaves into a house or eat ginger there. If you arrive at a village when a cow is to be sacrificed, you have to stay several days. There are many things that may not be done, trees that may not be felled, places that may not be visited.

"I think that our care in not breaking their customs did a lot to convince the Wa that we were not the same as the Kuomintang. We showed them better ways to do things and how to get better crops. After some time people in villages where there were work-teams began to talk to other villages and boast about having *Jiefang* people in their village. So headmen went to the Working Committee to ask if they could have work-teams sent to their villages."

Those few original headmen who befriended *Jiefang* played a bigger part than they know. Work-teams were the yeast in that "point and area" method which I saw working so successfully in the Cool Mountains.

Villages like Mowor, Little Masang and Urnu were the "points" from which the work of "doing good and making friends" spread to wider "areas". As that occurred, the "point" villages were able to shift the emphasis to developing and testing new ways of life as prototypes for the eventual transformation of society throughout the Wa area.

CHAPTER FOURTEEN

OFF-THE-PEG MORALS DON'T FIT

Wa leaders are not despots—Plenty of land—Direct leap from primitive life—Usury the main obstacle—Preventing new enslavements—The head-hunting problem—Salaries for the headmen—Co-operatives the main vehicle of change—Wet fields annoy the ghosts—Bridging the harvest gap

IT is one of those contradictory facts of life that slavery is in some ways harder to abolish among the Wa because there is less of it. Slavery is not an important feature of Wa society, nor are the privileges owed to headmen and sorcerers heavy or irksome. No class has come into existence which rules by hereditary right or by reason of wealth. Everybody, even a slave, takes part in the democratic affairs of the village or clan and, as a consequence, Wa leaders command a respect which is directly derived from everybody's right to recall them if they are incompetent. Slavery, privilege and even usury are not issues which particularly interest the Wa people, and anybody who went among them trying to rouse them to oppose these things "on principle" would simply not be understood.

Similarities between the Wa and the Norsu social systems are super-ficial. Both are extremely backward in productive methods, but there the likeness ends. Slavery, privilege and usury had developed in each case to such markedly different stages that the differences were greater than the similarities. The Norsu rulers had become a separate, sharply differentiated class, living without work, whose interests lay in per-petuating slavery, privilege and usury. It was the estimation of the political workers in the Cool Mountains that no progress could be made without the liquidation of the slave class and the slave-owning class, and they adopted a line of approach to this which at the same time freed the intermediate class of commoners from the oppressive corvée system.

In Hsimeng the situation is very different. Possibly, if they were left alone to develop in laboratory conditions, men of the Aiga type would ultimately emerge as a ruling class of slave-owners. But this being the twentieth century, the question facing the political workers in Hsimeng was not academic or hypothetical.

They were concerned with what to do in such a situation in order to change it.

And I was concerned with finding out the differences in policy and its effects between the two areas. Much of my time in Hsimeng was spent in discussing this with members of the Communist Party Working Committee, and in the course of many conversations I achieved what I believe to be clarity on their aims and methods. With apologies in advance to the very helpful political workers in Hsimeng for any distortions I may have inadvertently introduced, I give my own summary of their estimation of the Wa situation and their policy.

For reasons that derive from the past, there is conflict between the Wa and the Hans and there are traditional conflicts among the Wa themselves. These conflicts have to be straightened out and relations improved, gradually and piecemeal, starting from small matters and proceeding to bigger ones. Better Wa-Han relations and peace among the clans and villages is the precondition for everything.

Among the Wa, the beginnings of exploitation and separation into classes are superimposed on strong remnants of primitive society.

Land is plentiful, is common property and can be made available rent-free for the mere trouble of clearing it. Irrigation and modern farming methods would lead immediately to a vast increase in available wealth.

The prime need of the Wa people is to produce more food and other means of life—to raise the general standard of living. In the process of raising production, by new methods, less fundamental problems such as usury, slavery and privilege, clan disputes and cutting off heads, can be gradually solved—village by village and area by area.

The transition to socialism in Hsimeng County should therefore be direct and gradual: direct, because there is no need for an intermediate stage of land reform with private ownership of the land; and gradual, because it will take the form of a general movement to develop production, leading to mutual-aid working of the land as a stage before producer co-operatives.

Usury, slavery and privilege will be dealt with—as it were—in passing. It is not regarded as necessary to solve these at one stroke. Where they manifest themselves as obstacles to increasing production and improving general relations, stop-gap solutions will be found.

K

First on the list is not slavery but usury, which affects a large number of people.

"The existence of usury on such a wide scale tends to keep production at its lowest level," Ping Fu-chang, secretary of the Communist Party Working Committee said to me. "People heavily in debt get passive and lazy and only want to get through their days. If they are single they don't want to marry and face the prospect of their children being taken as slaves. Forcible distraint for debt causes strife and battles between villages and clans and these sometimes develop into major disputes. All of this tends to perpetuate the low level of farming production."

There is no necessity for a frontal attack on usury and no popular demand for it. Eliminating usury gradually presents little difficulty because low-interest state loans can prevent new usury (who would borrow at 200 per cent. when loans without interest or at $2\frac{1}{2}$ per cent. can be had?), and such loans provide debtors with the possibility of borrowing state money to clear their existing usurious debts. State loans therefore, will soften up the usury situation, enable debts to be cleared and so strike a blow at the basic economic reason for enslavements.

No frontal assault on slavery is envisaged, merely because slavery is unpleasant. This would be political infantilism, since it would set many of the most respected and influential of the Wa people against all reform, without getting the support of the majority of the Wa, 95 per cent. of whom are not slaves and do not feel that slavery is immoral or anti-social.

What is immediately possible is to prevent new enslavements, by means of loans at negligible interest or even paying the debts of those about to be enslaved if the case is urgent. The Working Committee told me that they have taken a decision that not one new enslavement must be allowed to take place, but that they intend to maintain the greatest caution and flexibility to ensure that this is done by individual mediation of each case as it arises and not by any sweeping action. At the same time there will be no overt propaganda against slavery and no incitement of the slaves to run away. This is necessary to stabilise the leaders. On the other hand there will be no returning of slaves who seek sanctuary. In the meantime, there is propaganda and persuasion to prevent maltreatment of slaves and brutal punishments.

Privileges, which among the Wa have only developed to the point of giving the leg of a hunting quarry or sacrifice to the headman, two or three days of unpaid labour a year and income from the sorcerers' religious activities, have no appreciable effect on the main issues, once usury is made impossible.

Decapitation, which is mainly related to clan disputes, is also seen as something which can be readily eliminated in the general process of education and advance. Its superstitious aspect—that it improves rice crops—is hardly likely to stand up to modern methods of crop raising.

These were the general lines that had evolved since 1952. They might be summarised as: improving Wa-Han relations and relations among the Wa themselves, and developing production. "The clear course for the Wa people is transition directly to socialism under Communist leadership, using whatever methods may be best to settle questions of democratic reform," was the way Ping Fu-chang put it in one conversation.

Two main currents of work emerged: political and economic.

To provide a transitional form of Wa administration which could lay the foundations for an autonomous government of the region, local "United, Patriotic Production Committees" were formed, consisting of headmen, elders and influential people with *ganbu* advisers. These were a means to stabilise the leaders, maintain contact with the people, gradually change the balance of power between the leaders and the ordinary people and spread new methods of production. Ping Fu-chang summarised the work of these committees as: 1. Improving production; 2. Winning over the leaders; 3. Making contact with the people; and 4. Mediating disputes.

Now there is also a Preparatory Committee for the Wa Autonomous Region, which represents the next stage in the development of a Wa administration.

Towards the Wa leaders themselves the policy was defined as "unity, education and reform". They occupy high political positions on these new-type democratic organisations and receive salaries and subsidies and prestige in keeping with their position in Wa society.

One member of the Working Committee, in the presence of four big Wa headmen who all hold salaried positions on the Preparatory Committee for the Wa Autonomous Region and all speak the Han language, said to me: "Our method is to keep contact with the people through the village and clan leaders and rely on the mass movement of the people to educate the leaders. We must maintain a balance between these two aspects. Our final aim is to win over the leaders to support the direct transition to socialism."

He went on to say, with a frankness surprising in view of the company, that the Wa leaders were "already rather stable", partly because of the effect of the Chinese revolution in general—a good many Wa leaders had been taken on tours to other parts of China to see the developments—and partly "because of our policy of subsidising and buying out the leaders". Ping Fu-chang added to this: "The Wa people are very keen on the new production methods and what they call our 'doctrines'. Our work-teams help them by showing them how to do things in a better way—everything has to be by practical demonstration—and gradually they accept Communist Party leadership. In the same process, leaders of a new sort also emerge from among the ordinary Wa people."

Ping Fu-chang stressed: "The main thing is to create the necessary conditions for forming co-operatives everywhere. In this fundamental task we cannot be said to have got very far and we are still feeling our way."

Tradition and superstition have to be surmounted before any appreciable results can be got in farming. All that is known generally about agriculture is how to scatter the seed of dry upland rice on burned-off land which is abandoned when it is worked out. The other main crop is "little red grain", a sort of tare mostly used for brewing. Vegetables are usually gathered wild from the jungle.

Wet paddy farming of rice is the key both to raising output and fixing the fields, but it is hedged in by superstition. Only about 150 acres of wet paddy had existed in the whole county, all in the hands of "well-to-do" people. How those fields originally came to be opened I do not know, because among the Wa there is a belief that levelling and irrigating paddy fields irritates some very powerful land ghosts.

Work-teams themselves opened some 500 acres of wet-paddy, accepting on their own shoulders the anger of the ghosts, and to everybody's surprise they did not fall sick or come to any dreadful end. The sorcerers explained this by saying the ghosts were afraid of *Jiefang*, but that ordinary Wa people had better not run any risks by recklessly opening paddy land.

The use of cattle for ploughing and the use of manure, also taught by the work-teams, are having an effect. Ploughing and manuring help to fix the arable land, and the use of cattle for ploughing diminishes their waste in sacrifices.

In some villages now, early crops such as sweet potatoes, corn, wheat, peas and beans have been successfully introduced and these help to bridge the shortage period before the main harvest. Other villages are now asking to be given seed and shown how to plant these crops. In all cases, demonstration is the only way to convince people of the advantages of the "doctrines", under which title are placed all the ideas of the political workers.

Consistent farming depends very much on being able to bridge the pre-harvest shortage period, which is as long as six months for a great number of the Wa. If this is not done, the people have to spend their time trying to get a bare subsistence from the jungle and have still less time for proper cultivation. Food relief thus helps both their present living and makes possible more developed farming.

Since the first government and Communist Party people came to Hsimeng in December 1952, the total quantities of relief goods handed out up to August 1957 were:

Food and seed grains	740 tons
Farm tools	69,786 items
Machine woven cloth	719 bolts
Handwoven cloth	13,281 pieces
Suits of clothing	1,100
Relief salt	54 tons
Salt transport subsidy	102,101 yuan (£15,000 approx.)

The number of iron farm tools given away is really very large—averaging two for each person or several for each family. Very few iron tools existed in Hsimeng before and it is said that those were only introduced about twenty years ago. Bamboo tools are still in use.

I saw no Wa who was not fully clad. Six years ago a loincloth was as much as most wore, although the weather is quite cold in December and January. Now people wear clothes of machine-made cloth and I even saw a few young men wearing rubber sports shoes. Old Aisung, the sorcerer, wears a pair of zip-up women's rubber overshoes. The Wa are very hard on clothes; after two days wear a new wool serge coat and trousers seems to have been slept in for a year.

Although figures are not available, the work-teams make the reasonable claim that loans, relief and tools have cut down the time wasted in the jungle and have encouraged people to cultivate for themselves instead of doing day-work for others. This makes less labour power available for hire and shifts the balance of economic power away from the more well-to-do.

As to how deep these things had gone, I was told that there was not yet any fundamental change and that I could see for myself by going into the jungle.

CHAPTER FIFTEEN

BATTLE AGAINST PRIMITIVE DEMOCRACY

Progressive sorcerer—Co-operative's uneasy birth—Vote goes against the headman—Ghosts, wet fields and co-operatives—Slaves go on strike—Debtors prefer to pay—Aiga stops distraint by enslavement—Slave's mother sees hope—Reprieve of the buffaloes—Slave-owners' fears for the future

URNU VILLAGE is a social battleground. Although there are only twenty-six families, elements of five distinct social forms coexist: primitive communism, slavery, feudal privilege, wage-labour and the first Wa experimental co-operative society, formed in 1956. When it was decided that some experimental producer co-operatives should be developed among the Wa, in places where most work had been done to establish friendly Wa-Han relations, Urnu was a natural place to choose.

Aisung, the sorcerer, was known to be "progressive". He and his whole family worked in the fields and though they owned some of the best fixed land locally, had no slaves. On the other hand, Aiga, the village headman, was a slave-owner of an entirely new type who owned eighteen slaves—enough to enable him to live without working himself, if he had ever dreamed of such a thing. To fight out the issue of co-operative working in the village of the biggest Wa slave-owner had its obvious significance.

A meeting of the headmen and elders of several villages was called to discuss the purpose of co-operatives, and the Working Committee suggested that the leaders help to set up a test co-operative. Sorcerer Aisung immediately asked for Urnu to be the selected village and Aiga politely acquiesced. After the meeting Aiga privately told his friends that it would all be very simple—he would lead the way into the co-operative and everyone would join because he joined. There would be good pickings because the Working Committee had promised to subsidise the new venture. Under primitive democracy, if the headman joined, the other villagers would all join and the village would call itself a "co-operative" while remaining exactly as it was. This was by no means what the Communist Party workers had in mind.

It was a crucial issue for the whole future of co-operatives among the Wa and the first major battle had to be fought on whether or not Aiga should be admitted to the co-operative. This also would determine whether entrance into the co-operative would be democratic and voluntary in the modern sense.

When the *ganbu* arrived at the village to have a meeting and talk about the new co-operative they were met at the village tunnel entrance by Aiga and Aisung. Aiga threw a drinking party at which he told the political workers: "I call the people. You do the talking."

By the time everyone had had enough to drink, the work-team leader said "No need to settle things now", which always suits the Wa. After this, for several weeks the work-team members talked with the villagers, finding out how they felt about the co-operative and explaining how it worked. Poor people were more willing to give the co-operative a trial than the better-off, who were hesitant about pooling their land and receiving payment according to work done. Aiga was keen on joining because he wanted to keep control. He also feared that *Jiefang* would forsake him unless they had his help to get the co-operative started, and he had heard that the co-operative would make its members more prosperous. He wanted a share of the new prosperity.

On the other side the *ganbu* knew that almost all the people likely to join the co-operative voluntarily were heavily in debt, mostly to Aiga. If later on, as he must, he found the co-operative conflicting with his individual interests, he would be in a strong position to sabotage or even destroy it.

To those wishing to join, the work-team explained why co-operative members should be people who do not live on the labour of others, and pointed out the difficulties that their indebtedness would cause if Aiga joined. He would be the boss. To Aiga they explained that membership of the co-operative would be useless to him because income was only according to work done. He would lose by it. At the same time he was appointed to a leading position on the United Patriotic Production Committee, which allayed his fears a great deal and gave him prestige.

At the first co-operative meeting, restricted to those intending to join, a majority voted against Aiga's admission. Sorcerer Aisung, however, was admitted by majority vote. This was the first victory for modern democracy over the former primitive unanimity vote and settled in principle that headmen would not be admitted to co-operatives.

It was a victory, but considering how much depended on this first

Wa co-operative, it got off to a very unpropitious start. Its members, twelve households, fifty people, only pooled two-thirds of their land, partly because they had already done some work on it and partly because they were affected by the rumour that the co-operative was a Han trick to get grain taxes. They had little faith in being able to increase production and almost none at all in the system of distribution of the crops according to points given for work done.

Again, a bone of contention was opium. Opium growing here, as among the Norsu, had become the average person's only hope of getting out of debt. Creditors and debtors both were anxious over what would happen if they did not grow the poppy. The *ganbu* advised the new co-operators that debtors only should be allowed to plant it, not on co-operative land but only on their family fields. They should stop planting it as soon as they got out of debt and no co-operative members should smoke it. Even before all debts were cleared, it might be possible to find industrial crops to replace it.

But the opening of new wet-fields for rice, which at once doubles the yield from the same quantity of seed, caused much more serious disquiet. Even daring Aiswai, the co-operative chairman, was scared. Opening irrigated fields was universally said by sorcerers to annoy the ghosts, who would visit the people with sickness and prevent the crops growing. The leader of the Working Committee of the Communist Party personally gave his guarantee to Aiswai that nothing of the sort would happen, and in the end Aiswai agreed to convince the other members. But he made a special journey to Hsimeng to tell Ping Fu-chang: "If the rice doesn't ripen, or if people get sick—look out for your head." Ping Fu-chang grinned as he said this and patted his head. "It was a pretty tense business until the first rice crop was gathered, just the same. Now everyone is talking about how much better wet land is than dry, because the co-operative paddy land produced twice as much grain from the same seed as dry land would do. But they are still scared to open paddy themselves.

"Paddy land," he said, "is of the utmost importance in stabilising the co-operative. Being opened by collective work it is owned in common, so it cannot be taken out of the co-operative, and no land dividends are paid on it as on land put into the co-operative by the members. Every acre of paddy land opened by the co-operative increases the proportion of socialist ownership and makes it harder for members to leave the co-operative at the same time as it raises their living standards."

During the time I was at Urnu, Aiswai was absent at a distant meeting of co-operative and mutual-aid team leaders. But the co-operative's production team leader, Aikwai, confirmed that whereas dry land gave ten or at best fifteen times the quantity of seed, wet paddy average twenty-five times.

"And we get still more if we use manure as well," he said. "We never had this custom in the past. At first I told the work-team it was filthy—eating manure, it amounted to. But the work-team opened a paddy themselves and used it. When we saw the difference, and they did not seem any the worse, we used it last year [1957]." Aikwai had a strong intelligent face and spoke easily, without any shyness. He was dressed in a blue cotton "Sun Yat Sen" uniform, as worn by all the *ganbu*, and wore an old cap with a broken peak instead of the usual Wa turban. Later I found that he was heavily in debt to Aiga.

"We borrowed money from the work-team and *Jiefang* gave us things. Now we have seventeen cattle, eleven ploughs and many hand tools, as well as a threshing machine. Last year we did well and this year we'll open more paddy and do still better."

With us as we talked was the co-operative accountant, Airey, who said, when I asked his age, that he was ten. I took him to be about twenty-three. He can "count up to 5—or even 600, and do sums", having studied in Hsimeng. A work-team member who joined our talk helps him with the co-operative accounts. I asked for comparative figures of grain production before and after the co-operative was set up. Those for 1955 were estimated by the work-team, on the basis of land sown and average output, at 12,200 catties[1] for the twelve families in the co-operative. In 1956, this had doubled to 25,668 catties and rose in 1957 to 37,568 catties. In two years, income per head of the families of co-operative members had risen from 240 catties to 750 catties.

"But that's not counting the new crops which we never grew before," Aikwai broke in to say. "Now we grow peas, potatoes, sweet potatoes, soya, wheat, tea and vegetables. As production leader I went to meetings to study how to grow these things. They taught me how to plant in rows—not scattering—soaking seed in warm water before planting, trenching and planting the taller crops more closely. We learned how to use animals to plough. One buffalo can do the work of five men and do it better. That's why we bought so many buffaloes. We shall pay the loans back over a time. All these are things we didn't

[1] A catty is about 1 lb. 2 oz.

know before. Why, we even tried to use the harrow upside down with its teeth up in the air at first." He used the Han-language word for "harrow" and giggled as he said this.

Aiga, the headman, not being present, I asked how he was taking to all this. "Well, he doesn't like it but what can he do? In fact our headman can see which way the wind is blowing. He can't stop it so he's trying to keep what he can. He suggested that he should manage village affairs, Sorcerer Aisung should manage ghost affairs and our chairman, Aiswai, should manage production affairs. Now that shows that our co-operative has already got face."

Some of Aiga's slaves had become restless about not being able to enjoy the new prosperity, he said. They had quarrelled with their master and once had a sit-down strike. "Some of his slaves asked to be set free to join the co-op. But that's not good. They belong to Aiga. The work-team says that if we all produce more this can be settled slowly," Aikwai said.

Were all the co-operative members satisfied? I asked. "Oh, yes. And now others want to join. Our members say 'The co-op will run for ever and our road will always be wider. Our children will run the co-op after us.' But they don't want other people to join. They say that they took all the trouble to start it and other people would get the benefit. Our work-team says that more people will make the co-op richer and we should take in new members including slaves that are freed in the usual way. We haven't settled that yet."

A check round the twelve households in the co-operative showed that they still owed the following debts to richer people, mainly to Aiga:

> 460 Yunnan silver dollars
> 636 catties of grain
> 95 ounces of opium
> 14$\frac{1}{2}$ cattle

The total value of this was reckoned at 1,920 yuan. Every household was in debt, the largest sum owed by a single family being 550 yuan and the smallest 10 yuan.

Not one person I spoke to considered that these debts should be cancelled, so firmly has the new custom of usury taken hold. Aikan, the biggest debtor (not the Aikan who is vice-Chairman of the Preparatory Committee) told me that all he wanted was time to pay.

"If I tried to return all the debt at once," he said, "I couldn't do it,

I'd have nothing to eat and would have to borrow again. After the harvest I will return what I can and eat what is left. And do that every year till the debt is paid. If I don't pay, Aiga will come to trouble me every day. I will borrow no more in future. All I want is time."

Aiga himself, worried about his capital, has ceased to demand interest. He told me: "If my loans cannot be paid this year, then I am willing to have them back year by year as much as possible until they are paid." He has ceased to threaten distraint by enslavement. But Aiga's village is one of the concentration points in the "point and area" method, and he is clearly subject to growing social pressures. In other villages, creditors still demand both capital and interest and are still threatening to distrain for debt.

The political workers are not in favour of disturbing the equilibrium of the creditors—often the clan and village leaders—by proposals to cancel the debts. Nor do they favour payment of the debts by the authorities, since this would lead to a slackening of productive efforts. They regard the co-operative as the means to raise everyone's ability to pay. The co-operative could work out satisfactory instalment plans and so prevent new enslavements, thus becoming the focus of the policy to "solve all problems in the course of increasing production".

I asked the widowed mother of the girl-slave Napai if she wanted to buy her girl's freedom. She said she would do so if she had the means. Aiga treated Napai very badly, and she needed her girl because she was getting old. "Maybe if I join the co-operative it can be done," she said, and added that she had already applied to join.

When I asked the accountant, Airey, the man who can count, what they intended to do about admitting her to the co-operative, he was evasive. According to him, the leader Aiswai was away and the old widow had only applied for membership in the previous week. When he returned, they would discuss it, and if they agreed she would be allowed to join.

All decisions in the co-operative, he told me, were by majority vote and they would follow the majority in this matter. Several families had applied to join. He personally agreed with letting new families come in. There would be more people to open up new paddy fields.

Airey said that before he joined the co-operative, he worked land that only yielded 70 lb. of rice a year so he "had to work for others or visit other households to eat". When my he saw questioning look he added: "It's the custom here. If you go to a house at meal times you will get food to eat." Relatives, friends and strangers would all offer this hospitality—one of the hallmarks of primitive communal life.

Since joining the co-operative he has been to Hsimeng to learn to read and write and study arithmetic. He can add but not subtract and this is enough to register work points, so he became accountant to the co-operative.

Airey had two wives before but they both left him because of his poverty. His parents married him when he was very young and his wife ran away. Later he gave a cow to marry a wife of his own choice, but people jeered at him for his poverty and she ran away. In reply to my question: What did the doctrine of co-operation mean to him? he replied: "More food and clothes and to go into socialism." He was not clear on the meaning of socialism.

Other members said that they still lacked sufficient grain for the whole year but this could only be due to waste, debt and inability to calculate their needs. If properly spread over the year, 750 catties a head would be more than enough, with a surplus to sell and buy meat or other things.

But co-operative members are no different from other Wa in their custom of feasting and brewing when the grain is available, entertaining others until it is all gone and finding a big gap between plenty and poverty before the next harvest. In one respect they differ—cattle sacrifices. Cattle are now collective property and are no longer sacrificed by co-operative members, who find collectively the moral strength to resist tradition. Aikwai said: "We need all our cattle production. When we have more than enough for that, we may kill some for meat." One thing which helps to perpetuate sacrifices is the difficulty of preserving meat, especially in a place where salt is a luxury. When a large animal like a buffalo is killed—an event which often barely antedates its natural demise—the only way to dispose of so much meat is to eat it immediately. Sacrifices, being public or clan affairs, permit this. Doubtless, fifty members of the co-operative could cope with the meat from one buffalo, and beasts would be killed as needed rather than in accordance with the rulings of superstition and clan custom.

Aiga was not very frank and I found my talk with him provided little real information about his feelings. Most of the time I was in Urnu village he hovered on the outskirts of whatever was going on like a will-o'-the-wisp Uriah Heep, and whenever there were any drinks going he got very drunk. If he was not there an eye was kept on events by his shrewish-looking second wife—a coarse young woman covered in heavy silver trinkets as befitted the wife of the owner of eighteen slaves. Aiga spoke in generalities about *Jiefang* being the "mother and father of the Wa" and his own agreement with everything that was going on.

I therefore pumped Sorcerer Aisung for an opinion of how Aiga was feeling. He said: "Ga is a big *jumi* (a rich man) and full of fears. He knows that *Jiefang* is for the poor, though because of their doctrines they want to work in unity with the leaders of the Wa."

He counted off Aiga's fears on his fingers: "He fears being cut away from the villagers; he fears that the time will come when *Jiefang* can rely on the villagers and he will be neglected; he fears that *Jiefang* will look on him with contempt for being an owner of slaves; he fears that the work-team will 'give him a lesson'; he fears the loss of his wealth and he fears not being able to go on using his slaves to work." I caught what seemed to be the faintest trace of satisfaction in the old man's wrinkled, humorous face at the apprehensions of the young *jumi*.

We were sitting outside the sorcerer's own house, overlooking the shack where the giant wooden drum is housed. At its side, on tall bamboos, were three sinister little baskets containing the heads of men cut off in the past to secure better crops. "What about that?" I asked.

Sorcerer Aisung did not blink, but he did not answer. Instead he made a little speech. "Let us talk about peace, no quarrels. Peace is the best doctrine and we shall follow it. Because of the new doctrines, our life is better than before and by increasing production it will get still better. Now we are beginning to have knowledge.

"As to sacrificing to the ghosts, those parts that are bad for production will be stopped and those which are not bad will be kept up. Now we are learning new things such as opening paddies. All these doctrines are good." Although a sorcerer, Aisung supports the co-operative's "no sacrifices" rule.

Looking out from his house, the importance of fixed-fields was self-evident. For scores of miles the mountain ranges, once rich virgin forests, now had only a covering of head-high brush. Although only a tiny part is ever cultivated at one time, a few people in many years do this terrific destruction with slash-burn farming.

Aiga is not the only one with apprehensions. People who preferred to remain outside the co-operative developed bad relations with those inside because they felt that the work-team was favouring the members of the co-operative. This caused difficulties in spreading the knowledge of farming. Later, stress was put on more help from the work-team to non-co-operators.

In the first period, the work-team members were so concerned to ensure that the co-operative would be a success that they did work which the co-operative officials should have done for themselves, such as planning the day's task for the members and going round telling them what to do. This convinced some people, including co-operative members, that really they were working for the work-team. But this feeling was dispelled when the first vegetables were sold and the proceeds used to buy salt which was distributed to members according to work-points; this convinced them they were not "working for *Jiefang*", and acted as a starting point for their understanding of payment according to work done. They are still incapable of calculating their own work-points but are emphatic that if more people are admitted to membership, they shall include "no lazybones".

Women are the main Wa labour force, though by no means having equality of rights. This, too, is influenced by the work-point system, under which everyone wants to get more points and a bigger share. More men are doing farm work now instead of lazing round whittling bamboo. According to Nashang, a plump unmarried co-operative girl, the women now have meetings "where we talk about things like not quarrelling, how to run the co-operative well, washing, health and babies. Some women didn't want to go but now they like them."

Wa custom, as she said, "is not equal between men and women. A man can have many wives if he has wealth and he can sell them or give them away. If he puts away [I supposed it to mean divorce—A.W.] a wife, no other man can have her unless he pays the price. But if a wife leaves her husband he can still put her away and nobody can have anything to do with her." However, the co-operative members were not among those sufficiently well-to-do to be able to afford polygamy, and what will happen if they are later able to afford extra wives must wait to be seen.

This Urnu Co-operative is one of only three in the whole Wa region. It seemed to be firmly established and to be doing what its originators intended it to do. The other two co-operatives, I was told, were doing well, though not so well as Urnu.

In quite a large part of the Wa region, the political workers are still in the early stage of "doing good and making friends" but the success of the test co-operatives may speed up all processes. Many Wa eyes are fixed on these three co-operatives to see whether the "doctrines" are successful or whether the big ghosts will strike down these people who have recklessly challenged them by opening new rice paddy and added insult to injury by refusing the customary sacrifices.

CHAPTER SIXTEEN

CHAT WITH A HEADHUNTER

Why Aidong lost his head—Blood debt and rice crop—Woman's view of headhunting—"They egg each other on"—Do motor cars eat grass?— New headhunting theories—A negotiated peace—Sorcerers responsible— Headhunting has no future

A YOUNG man of Little Masang village had cut off the head of a man about two weeks before I visited the place and a storm of argument had been raging ever since. This news prompted me to go there and find out more about this Wa custom.

Little Masang is a very beautiful village, approached in both directions through tall forest. Outside the village entrance is a silent bamboo glade where a number of carved wooden posts like little totem poles, some new, some very old, were quietly rotting. I counted up to seventy of them—ceremonial posts, each showing where a human head had been buried. At some old villages there are as many as 700 such memorials of past trophies. According to Wa tradition, once the head has been placed in its little woven basket next to the sorcerer's drumhouse, with suitable ceremony, eating and drinking for several days, it should stay there a couple of years to ensure good crops. Then the head is removed and buried in the graveyard outside the village; an eerie place to pass through on the way to and from the fields in the twilight.

Things had been very quiet in the Little Masang area for a year or more, until people had got drunk at a feast and the village sorcerer made some provocative remarks to a group of young men. "The people of Gotgor village owe us a blood debt and you should go and collect it," he had said. "Look at the last rice crop. No good at all. And it never will be until a head gets cut. I don't know what has happened to the young men of today. In my day we would have known what to do."

A few days later a group of young men led by Aileh ambushed a Gotgor man and killed him, carrying the head home gleefully to Little Masang where it now swayed in its high basket above the drumhouse. But far from getting a hero's welcome, as he would have done

L

a year or two before, Aileh was astonished to find himself the centre of criticism and controversy.

A very ancient man in a dark blue woollen *ganbu* uniform was the only occupant of the village meeting platform when I arrived. He was smoking an enormous bamboo water-pipe which bubbled and whistled as he inhaled more noisily than he wheezed as he blew out the smoke. This was Aisor, a big clan leader who has long claimed to be ninety-nine years old. It was his duty to welcome the visitor with a ceremonial speech, but he immediately came out with what was on his mind.

"I hope that you have come to teach our young people some lessons," he started off bitterly. "A little time ago they cut off the head of a Gotgor man. Now it is said that Gotgor will join with Dalan village to retaliate. Our villagers can only go about together in large groups after this happening. It's a bad business. We had peace with Gotgor for a long time. Old hatreds were forgotten and grievances had been settled. We could go to Gotgor and drink with them. Now we are not welcomed."

As the old man talked others gathered round and sat on the bamboo platform, including a middle-aged man with a gentle, wily smile and enormous feet, almost as wide as the span of my fingers, the tops of which were pinkly shining with betel-spit and dirt. This was the sorcerer who had instigated the headhunting expedition. Through the bamboo clumps I could see the newly woven basket containing the head of Aidong, the murdered Gotgor man.

Wine came along as usual, and then more wine, and the more he drank, the more old Aisor talked. "Aiya! Now who knows where this matter will end? Just when everything had become peaceful again. There are people who should know better, but teach our young folk bad ways." He fixed his fluid, glittering old eye on the sorcerer, who paid no attention to him. "Crops grow if you look after them, without that head-cutting business," the old man added loudly, and repeated it louder so that all could hear.

Little Masang is a slightly larger village than Urnu but "not yet so advanced". It has two mutual-aid teams and some other villagers are considering forming teams. A group of people want to start a co-operative. Talking to the leading people of the village I saw why Urnu, rather than this village, had been chosen for the co-operative experiment. In Urnu, apart from the "progressive" sorcerer Aisung, there are several ordinary householders who are quite above average in intelligence; who seem to have some insight into what the "doctrines" mean. In Little Masang I had the sense—like something seen beyond the range of vision—that apart from old Aisor, the village elders, while saying the appropriate things, were enjoying some private understanding.

Several people I spoke to had various personal reasons for not joining mutual-aid teams. Aibili, son of old Aisor, said he was ill and could not join in 1957 but "I hope that next year everyone will be in mutual-aid teams." Yet another, Aikan, which is a very common name here, thought mutual-aid good and he would join later. He was trying to increase production on his family land. I asked him how.

"Not to quarrel and fight," he answered, "pull out weeds two or three times and use manure. Our work-team has helped me by opening a new paddy field. Now my family land can produce 600 catties for myself and my wife. This is more than others." He said it was enough food for nine months. For the rest: "I go to work for wages, sell firewood or go to eat with a Lahu family, or the government helps with money or rice. I do not borrow. The government gave me a hoe, salt, cloth, needles and thread and a loan of rice."

But Napu, outspoken wife of the first mutual-aid team leader in Little Masang, had plenty to say on any subject. Her husband was away at a meeting of mutual-aid team and co-operative leaders.

"Head-cutting is bad," she said. "It's better not to cut off heads. That's men's business and we women hate and fear it. The men hate and fear it too, but they egg each other on. Not many people do it, but because of those few we all have to go in fear. The new doctrines say that crops grow well if you look after them. After the mutual-aid team was started, we had a better crop this year. These doctrines are good. But head-cutting is bad. Still, it's men's business and we women can't do anything about it."

Napu, a handsome woman with a wide smile, black teeth and ear-lobes greatly lengthened by heavy silver rings, smoked and drank rice whisky as we talked. When offered biscuits she popped them into her big black turban for later use. She spoke quickly and clearly.

"Our mutual-aid team is good," Napu said. "It's better to get together and organise because then the government helps with hoes, cows and grain. *Jiefang* gave our mutual-aid team one buffalo, a plough, hoes, sickles, salt, cloth, rice and seeds for two kinds of peas, potatoes and wheat. Mutual-aid is good, but I think a co-operative is better."

A co-operative, she explained, could open more paddy land and breed cattle and do many things.

Mutual-aid teams have also discarded the method of primitive democracy according to Napu: "Everyone goes to the meeting and we vote by holding up our hands. We do what most people want. We try to persuade the others and make them understand."

We were talking in the house of the work-team where there was a Red Cross box and various instruments lying under gauze on a table. Napu said: "When we are sick we come here or go to the sorcerer. Here it costs nothing, so many people do both. But I fear injections. I am willing to eat pills, but no injections."

As she was leaving she stopped at the door, came back, thought for a moment, and said: "Chairman Mao is good and Communist doctrines are good. Organisation in farming is good. People are happier. We want more people in organised farming. Then we shall all be better off." I asked why she had come back to say this. "Some people say *Jiefang* will go away. I told you these things because we want *Jiefang* to stay here, and more people will learn the doctrines." She seemed to think as others did, that I was a high *Jiefang* official making an inspection.

Her brother-in-law, Aidwai, is also an enthusiast for mutual-aid and said he opposed head-cutting. "I know this Aileh who cut off Aidong's head and I think it wrong to do this. I will listen to the words of Chairman Mao and if others tell me to go and cut a head off, I personally would not go.

"I used to be lazy," he said, "and tilled only one small piece of land. Now I till three times as much, using manure and doing weeding. We use manure now and it keeps the village clean. This year my team will open new paddy land."

By opening new paddy land in common, the team will create collectively owned land, the produce of which is shared according to work done. This is a step to full co-operative working of the land, because as more irrigated land is opened the privately worked dry land will become of less value.

Aidwai preferred the new method of working. "We used to work in common before and divide the crop equally. So the family that did more work lost by it. If you get more of the crop by doing more work everyone will work harder and learn better ways.

"When we have a co-operative here all my land will go in," Aidwai said most emphatically.

The centre of the head-cutting controversy, Aileh, turned out to be a young man with a full, petulant mouth, good-looking, wearing a ragged pullover under his cotton coat, rubber shoes and a long dagger—or short sword—stuck horizontally through a belt across his stomach. He clearly felt the pressure of social opinion and was puzzled at all the fuss.

We chatted for a while about his family: his father had been rich but he was poor; he had not joined a mutual-aid team; the government had given him and his wife tools, grain, cloth and salt.

He was cheerfully eating biscuits during all these preliminaries, but he stopped in mid-bite when I mentioned Aidong's head.

"I was sick at the time Aidong's head was cut off," Aileh said quickly. "I was not there, though I know who was." Then he followed up, with entire lack of logic, "I won't do such a thing again." Ignoring both the denial and admission, I asked who started the idea. He said that old people get drunk and tease the young people about not being as brave as their parents. Anyway, Gotgor was always quarrelling with Little Masang.

"Gotgor has two clans and one is hostile to this village. That is Aidong's clan. We cut off a Gotgor head because they did this village wrong. Both sides have cut off heads. Now Gotgor is scared. If they are willing to stop quarrelling, we will. Before it happened we all talked and said: 'Gotgor owes us one head. Let's cut if off and then ask *Jiefang* to mediate.' The whole village was in on the talking, though some now say they disagree. But I will do no more of this."

At this point, Ping Fu-chang, who had listened to our talk, broke in with a little lecture which went like this:

"Aileh, when a head is cut off you can't put it back again. There is some danger now that your's will be cut off and then your wife and children will suffer. But this is a tradition of your people and nothing to do with *Jiefang*. You discuss it among yourselves and *Jiefang* will stand in the middle. It will not take sides. You should talk it over, whether more people think head-cutting is good or bad. But in talking about it you should be calm. No quarrelling."

The young headhunter broke in to say: "It's better for *Jiefang* to mediate. If Gotgor gets several villages to attack this one, many lives may be lost. That is not good."

Ping Fu-chang took up the point. "If we hear that Gotgor means to attack this village, we will try to persuade them not to do it. At the same time we will not interfere with your customs.

"But we also have our doctrines, as you have yours, and we think ours are better. If you want to have good rice harvests, that depends on hard work, opening wet fields, plenty of water, weeding often and manuring. Dead heads will not help. If you don't understand this, you should try to understand. Our foreign friend has come here to ask you questions so that he can understand your customs. Just as you ask questions about things you don't understand: such as, does a motor-car eat grass?

"In future you should respect our doctrines as we respect your doctrines."

Aileh said: "I hope you will mediate with Gotgor and we can make amends and visit each other."

"Well let's have a drink and a smoke and talk about it some other time," said Ping Fu-chang. I sympathised with Ping Fu-chang. He has to do so much drinking with the Wa and, like a good many Hans, dislikes alcohol which makes his face red and his head ache.

The job of mediating the case of Aidong's decapitation fell to old Aikan, clan headman, vice-chairman of the Preparatory Committee of the Wa Autonomous Region, who acts as tribal liaison officer. Aikan, short, wizened and lame, gave up being a sorcerer when he took up his present official position. He had a good record among his tribesmen as a fighter against the Kuomintang, and this helps him now in his mediation work. Everyone knows he is against disputes because of the "doctrines", not through cowardice.

He has his own theories about head-cutting. "I tell the people to do it less and if they have to use a head, use one from a person already dead. Some people think it would prevent disputes if they were to buy some lazybones and use his head. There's something in that. Leopards' heads will do as well, but they are hard to get. Some people use monkey heads but I don't agree with that. At Awaluei they use insects heads. Lazybones or thieves or other people doing wrong things could be used. I disagree with cutting off Aidong's head, and this matter must be settled or it will become a big quarrel.

"Both sides should come to Hsimeng and negotiate. A buffalo should be sacrificed and other things done to comfort Gotgor," the old man went on, sitting in his blue-wool *ganbu* uniform with the enamel badge of the county administration, and occasionally expectorating a great gob of scarlet betel saliva, which had browned the ends of his thin grey walrus moustache. I asked whether Aidong's widow and children should be compensated. He looked surprised at this question and said: "No."

Little Masang wanted Aikan to go with them to negotiate with Gotgor. "They will not be afraid if I go with them." Little Masang was willing to return Aidong's gun and come to Hsimeng next market day to negotiate. "I think Gotgor will agree and receive the gun. *Jiefang* can be there too, to see that no fighting starts." I asked Aikan whether Aileh should be punished. Again he looked surprised.

"No. This is a clan matter. Aileh did not cut off the head of a person of his own clan. He would be punished for that. But Aidong was of a different clan."

It happened as Aikan predicted. On the next market day both sides met in Hsimeng market and in that brief period between sobriety and drunkenness when matters can be settled, Little Masang made restitution, promised the necessary sacrifices and the dispute was ended. Aikan came back reeling drunk and was beaten up by his tough young wife for some actual or fancied offence. At the request of Ping Fuchang, I avoided the market place that day. The presence of a foreigner might have disturbed the delicate negotiations.

I noticed that throughout my talk with Aikan he did not once mention the supposed real purpose of head-cutting—to make the rice grow better. Nevertheless, he could not see past the custom itself and was arguing for a method that would retain the tradition and prevent clan warfare, by using it to punish vagabonds, thieves and other offenders.

I met nobody willing to make a public defence of the custom and plenty of people who denounced it. As Napu said: "The men hate and fear it too but they egg each other on." Sorcerers have the greatest vested interest in keeping up the tradition. They profit from the accompanying sacrifices and by their supposed intimacy with the ghosts that decide on such matters as good and bad harvests, health and the weather. My impression was that in Urnu—where there was a co-operative—the village would never again achieve unanimity over cutting off a head, and in Little Masang, Aidong's head would also be the last. Head-cutting was on its way out.

CHAPTER SEVENTEEN

MODERN SORCERY

Putting the ghosts in their places—Doctors in search of patients—New sorcerers win a victory—Atabrine as a political weapon—Leaders fear isolation—Impatience the worst mistake—Some disquiet—Not a single new slave

REGARDLESS of their intimacy with the ghosts, sorcerers fall ill. They also fail to cure people. A person who feels no better after sacrificing cattle and getting into debt to appease the ghosts will try to find some other way. Medical work in Hsimeng is therefore more than just a battle for people's health and lives, it is a battle against superstition, tradition, sacrifices and backwardness. As better farming methods constitute the easiest and surest road to wiping out slavery and headhunting, modern medicine is the most effective way of putting the ghosts in their places.

In Hsimeng County today there is one medical worker for every 950 people, a hospital in Hsimeng, right on top of Dragon Mountain, with ten beds, operating theatre, laboratory, dispensary and out-patients' department, administering four clinics in other parts of the jungle, a health centre for women and children, and travelling teams of medical workers.

It is difficult to get patients and at first was almost impossible. Sorcerers, fearful of losing both fees and prestige, used all their influence to prevent people going to see the new doctors—the *"Jiefang* sorcerers"*. Pills and injections were Han poisons of a very cunning type which would gradually destroy the Wa people. Very early in the hospital's history a patient died of a heart attack in the hospital and the news was spread round that this was due to an injection.

Two things made a break-through: one was atabrine, whose effect on malaria is readily demonstrable; and the other was a big sorcerer named Aimor who got his hand burned by gunpowder while officiating at the sacrifice of a cow. These old cap-firing muskets very often backfire through enlarged cap-nipples. Gangrene set in and all Aimor's ghost medicine was clearly not going to stop it spreading and killing him. He stubbornly fought against going to Hsimeng to see a doctor, realising that if a Wa sorcerer, of all people, had to go to a *"Jiefang*

sorcerer" it would have serious effects on his flock. Finally, in agony
and fear, he went to Hsimeng, but in the operating theatre he took
fright and went home again. After another night of pain and mumbo-
jumbo, he returned next day. His hand was in a bad state and amputa-
tion seemed the only way. On being told this he ran away again. Also
realising how much hung on this case, a doctor went after him and
promised to do the job by excising the gangrenous parts and saving
his hand by skin-grafting. The doctor knew the promise was a gamble,
owing to the thinness of the tissue. The sorcerer was assured, "No
pain", and watched the miracle of his flesh being cut out without his
feeling it, under local anaesthetic. When the skin grafts took, it was
hard to say whether the patient or the doctor was more pleased,
because this represented a real political breakthrough by means of
medicine.

Next they cured the son of Aikow, the Great Masang sorcerer, of
malaria, after his father had lavished every ghostly cure on the youth.
Next time his son had an attack, the old man again caught a chicken to
sacrifice and the son released it. There was a first-class family row,
ending in the son sending for a "*Jeifang* sorcerer". This son, who
would in the ordinary way have grown up to follow in father's foot-
steps, recently asked to be sent for training as a "*Jiefang* sorcerer" and
is now studying medicine.

Since malaria is very common and relatively easy to relieve and
cure, the faith of Wa people in atabrine grew quickly. As Napu
said: "I am willing to eat pills but no injections." Curative treatment
is one thing but there is still no understanding of the need for preventive medicine.

An elementary course in health work was opened in 1956, attended
by thirty young Wa people, and some of these were sent inland for
hospital training in Sze Mao. Village work-teams all have elementary
medical training.

All medical treatment is free and present plans are to build a new
hospital with twenty-five beds and to open two more clinics.

The hospital superintendent said that modern medicine has not yet
made any deep inroads, especially on the preventive side. People tend
to go to their own sorcerer first and then, if he fails to cure, to the
modern doctor.

But now the sorcerers are having to find plausible explanations for the
successes of the modern doctors. Some say: "We are best at controlling
'small ghosts' and the *Jiefang* sorcerers are best with 'big ghosts'." In

serious cases some of them advise patients to go to the doctors after sacrificing, to get the best of both worlds.

Another reason offered is that the ghosts are afraid of *Jiefang*. So it thus becomes all right to open up irrigated land and do other forbidden things, if a *Jiefang* work-team member starts the work and runs the risk of ghostly vengeance. Also sorcerers say, "*Jiefang* will not always be here. When they go you will still need us."

One work-team member said to me: "In this you can see the practical result of relying on the leaders to reach the people and the people to educate the leaders. If the leaders don't support things which are obviously beneficial, they will be isolated from the people. But the leaders are sensitive and don't allow things to reach the point of losing their influence or causing an open breach. They say: 'We leaders used to help you and now *Jiefang* helps you more. But when they go, we shall be needed to help you again.' "

There is now an idea of teaching suitable sorcerers some modern medicine and scientific knowledge.

Hsimeng now has two schools. One is a training class for people who are active in the new developments in their villages. This is called the Nationalities Training Class and has ninety-six students, of whom fifty-six are Wa. They get six months intensive training in farming technique, how to organise co-operatives and mutual-aid teams, education about socialism, general education, reading and writing,[1] national and international politics. The eight tutors include one Wa.

The Hsimeng Primary School has 160 pupils, ninety of them Wa and the rest mostly Lahu. All Wa children are supported, clothed and educated free of charge. This is a six-year course on the same curriculum as all Chinese primary schools. Here also the new Wa written language is being studied.

Other than this, when I was in Hsimeng I saw a new brick factory, established to supply bricks and tiles for permanent hospitals, stores, schools and offices, and a bank and post office in temporary buildings of mud and wattle. Since then I have heard that a number of small new factories have been built, including an iron foundry, pottery and textile mill.

On the eve of leaving Hsimeng, I was asked by Ping Fu-chang to attend a meeting and give my opinions and criticisms of the work of

[1] There is a Wa written language newly devised by the Chinese Academy of Sciences and at present being tested.

the Communist Party Working Committee. This is customary, for the Chinese *ganbu* have an insatiable thirst for criticism, which they regard as the best means to improve their work. It was a full-dress affair with several members of the Working Committee and half a dozen top Wa headmen present. As usual on such occasions, I found myself making a few platitudinous remarks in the course of which—more for something to say than out of conviction—I tentatively suggested that everything possible should be done to accelerate the abolition of head-hunting and slavery.

Ping Fu-chang said: "You may be sure that we are constantly reviewing this matter and the hope cannot be ruled out that we may be able to go faster—very much faster—as the situation becomes more expedient.

"Because of the complicated relations between the nationalities here we have followed the Communist Party directive that all the nationalities of China will go together into socialism by different methods that take account of their national characteristics.

"The worst error we could commit would be impatience.

"Our fundamental problem is the national one. A good deal depends on raising able people from among the Wa themselves. This depends on our winning firm friendship among them. We have done that in a good many cases, but this is not wide or deep enough yet. Many Wa still hate or are profoundly suspicious of the Hans. Their past bad experiences take a lot of living down. Some leaders are close to us but others are not, and the Wa people as a whole follow their village and clan leaders in all matters. We have not yet created the conditions necessary for the general opening of co-operatives.

"Among the Wa people themselves, differences of interest are perceptibly coming into the open and this is causing some disquiet among the leaders and those who own a slave or two. The greatest care is necessary in dealing with these inter-Wa relations, too. Above all, the leaders must have face, place and prestige. Debts will be gradually repaid, with us helping where possible and discreetly. We shall pay attention to ensuring that not a single new enslavement shall take place but it would be most inadvisable to take any direct action to free those at present enslaved. A great deal can and is being done by indirect methods.

"We have to proceed according to our situation here, which is very different from other places, as you have seen. Our method is general enlightenment, gradually winning over the leaders to our way of thinking, developing production, arranging suitable status for those who own slaves and solving such problems by aid and subsidies.

"Some leading people are already finding that there is a change in their economic situation because less casual labour-power is available as a result of people being able to spend more time in mutual-aid and co-operative working of their own land. Subsidies and other suitable arrangements must be used to ensure that the leaders suffer no hardship."

Ping Fu-chang said that during their work among the Wa some mistakes had occurred because of a one-sided subjective attitude to their backwardness. "We sometimes saw only the backwardness and misled ourselves into ignoring the progressive ingredients of the situation, and we sometimes made the mistake of thoughtlessly transplanting ideas here which were based on experiences in other places where conditions are different."

The Working Committee secretary emphasised the importance of creating a Wa administration. "We have to have a correct estimation of the Wa people, not to give ourselves airs, to overcome feelings of superiority and patronage, and avoid issuing orders. Our existing Wa working personnel must be given a free hand and our work-teams must breathe the same air and share the same fate as the Wa members.

"We have to win the confidence of the Wa people, help them to develop their own abilities, their own capable administrators and to walk alone."

During the supper party that followed this meeting, a messenger came from the market place to say that Gotgor village had accepted Little Masang's offer of restitution for the head of Aidong and peace had been made between the two villages. Already I had heard that Widow Nahung had been admitted to the Urnu Co-operative from which she hoped to get the means to free her daughter from Aiga, the slave-owner. They were little things, but concrete signs of the new "doctrines" at work. I could not think of any ways whereby events could be made to go faster in those isolated, ghost-ridden jungle villages. So much seemed to depend on the success of a few frail co-operatives, paddy farming, modern medicine, the first glimmerings of literacy among a tiny proportion of the Wa people. But these things are what the people are talking about—new, vivid and offering hope. As I left on my long trek north to visit the primitive Jingpaw people, I felt that whatever mistakes Ping Fu-chang and his colleagues might commit they would not be due to lack of thought or flexibility.

Part III

THE JINGPAW

CHAPTER EIGHTEEN

VOICES IN THE FOREST

Into the jungles again—Sex freedom a relic of group-marriage—No lovemaking within the clan—Relics of matriarchy—Kidnapped brides—M'Gaw's treacherous girl-friend—Pregnancies outside marriage—Jingpaw customs hard on women—Men must pay for divorce—Little time for work

HAPPY-GO-LUCKY and improvident, the Jingpaw[1] people feast recklessly when the food is there, drink, sing, play and sometimes fight, letting tomorrow look after itself. Young Jingpaw people like to spend their whole nights singing love songs and making love in their "communal houses", and if a girl gets pregnant, this can be settled by the sacrifice of a cow. There is no fondness for work and when people do go to the fields, it is in large groups, like sparrows; as much for the company as with any real interest in getting anything done. The mountain-top villages of the Jingpaw are not fortified. They do not cut off heads or enslave each other like the equally primitive Wa, who live only 150 miles away across the jungle as the crow flies.

There is no need to describe the journey along the Burma Road—almost to the end of the Chinese section of it—which is necessary in order to visit the Jingpaw. I would add to earlier and graphic descriptions of this famous road that it is now evidently wider, harder and better cambered than in those early days when a journey up the Burma Road was itself an adventure. It is still a magnificent experience, but no hardship or danger is involved. Cheap hostels provide excellent accommodation all the way; still cheaper ordinary Chinese restaurants can put on local specialities that should not be left out of the gastronome's experiences. In Hsiakuan, near the hot springs, is a restaurant that specialises in a local dish called Sha Guo Yu (Casseroled Fish)—the fish itself being a local one from the vast Erh Hai (Ear Lake), where every year a legendary assignation takes place between a princess and her hunter lover who both drowned there rather than give up their

---

[1] I have adopted this spelling of Jingpaw because it is closest to the sound in English. There is a Jingpaw written language, devised by an American, I believe, in which it is written Jinghpo. Evidently the designer of that language was affected by the Wade system of transliterating Han-Chinese, in which it is spelled Chingp'o. Since no widely accepted spelling exists, Jingpaw will probably do as well as anything else.

love. A big, succulent fish is surrounded in the casserole with bean-curd, pigs-tripes, sliced chicken, liver, mushrooms, truffles and other odds and ends, spiced, and the whole is simmered in strong chicken broth. For those who like to try it with any suitable fish, the seasoning used is soya sauce, dry wine, white pepper and juniper.

The road drops from grassland to bamboo, bananas and tree melons where it crosses the Salween (Lu) River, and dizzily rises again to grass-land before it falls like a snaked rope deep into Mangshih town, where pineapples are a penny each and a bunch of bananas even less. Here live the slender Tai people, and here I had the curious experience —for China—of attending an evening performance of the most famous local entertainers who put on twenty variety items, only one of which was not a love song, love dance or love scene, and that item was a traditional sword dance.

Most members of the troupe were Tai boys and girls, with a few Jingpaw. Among these was a brilliant young Jingpaw girl singer who brought the house down with a love song. I learned that she had been abducted in marriage according to Jingpaw custom, but ran away and left her unwanted husband, which is rather unusual.

Mangshih is now the capital of the Tehung Tai-Jingpaw Autonom-ous Chou,[1] inhabited by 400,000 Tai people who live on the fertile steamy plains and 80,000 Jingpaw who live entirely on the hilltops. From this they derived the name *Shantou*, contemptuously given them by the Hans—a name meaning "hilltop people". They spread over the Burma border where the Burmese know them as Kachins, though there they also call themselves Jingpaw.

To meet these swarthy and jovial people, I motored further down the Burma Road, almost to the border. At Chefang—famous for produc-ing China's best rice—I struck into the jungle accompanied by Yang Su, chief of the Propaganda Department of the Communist Party Working Committee, interpreters and a couple of pack-animals. For half a day we marched, continually uphill through narrow paths in virgin jungle.

Occasionally we met Jingpaw men and women: the men always armed with two-foot-long swords, wide and heavy at the end for slashing bamboo, and sometimes with ancient cap-firing muskets or bows with a little cup on the string for firing clay pellets; the women

---

[1] An autonomous chou is a self-governing administrative unit which may be under an autonomous region or a province and may contain counties, autonomous counties or municipalities.

usually carrying bamboo baskets on their backs. Sometimes they waved in greeting; sometimes they disappeared into the jungle to let us pass.

Pride of a Jingpaw woman's wardrobe is her skirt, a handwoven sarong skirt of wool reaching just below the knee. Its general colour is russet, with intricate zigzag patterns of black and emerald green. Above her bare feet, and leaving no leg visible between them and the skirt, are leggings of the same material. A long-sleeved jacket is usually of dark cotton cloth, but the girls who can afford it prefer black velvet above all other materials for this. A square pouch shoulder-bag of handwoven wool carries inevitably a bamboo wine bottle and a box— usually of rawhide—for betel, tobacco and lime. Jingpaw women have a great fondness for silver ornaments—great flat bangles four inches wide on the wrists, ear-rings, necklaces of many chains hung with silver trinkets and rupees. Most of those I saw were from the reigns of Edward VII and George V, when the money still contained some silver, and a few were from the reign of Victoria. Round the hips and just not falling down, are many circular hoops of thin black-lacquered rattan. Jingpaw girls cut their hair in an exact pudding-basin style. It is combed radially in all directions from the crown and cut so that the fringe just hides the eyebrows, ear-lobes and touches the nape of the neck. Married women dress no differently, but usually do their hair up and wear a turban.

Jingpaw men dress in anything that happens to be available. Their national dress is a black cotton jacket, buttoned with a rupee, and extremely wide black short trousers hanging in deep folds to knee length like a short skirt. Turbans are usually black. Men carry the same square bag and, as well as wine-bottle and betel, have a powder horn for their home-made black powder, home-made bullets and a stock of sun-baked clay pellets.

Dusk was closing in quickly when we arrived at Nungbing village, working centre for an area covering 116 similar hilltop villages, and we took our supper of rice and onions pickled with red pepper sitting round a great log fire. Overhead the high fronds of bamboo gradually became invisible. Laughing voices came out of the forest as young men and women set out for their "communal houses"—generally spaces in the forest where a fire is lit and girls and boys of differing clans meet to make love. From far away came a man's voice singing a high, lilting song and then the answer of a girl taking up the refrain.

The concept of virginity does not exist among the Jingpaw and

M

before marriage there is sexual freedom, limited only by clan taboo. On marriage, which is mainly monogamous, this sex freedom ends.

Marriage is by abduction, real or staged, but often enough real. Unless deeper study leads to a reassessment, Jingpaw customs seem to reflect the transition from group marriage and matriarchy to monogamy and patriarchy, which are now firmly established. Marriage by abduction appears to be a remnant of a late stage of matriarchy, with the abduction of the women into the household of the males. These anachronistic remnants of group marriage and abduction are hard on the women and considerably influence economic life.

With us at the fireside this evening was M'Gaw,[1] the girl singer I have mentioned as singing in Mangshih, who formerly lived in this village of Nungbing and was abducted from it one morning at a spot not 200 yards from where we were sitting. She was an expert on Jingpaw marriage rules and a great opponent of them.

Girls, she told me, are likely to be abducted at any time. A young man sees a young girl of his fancy and, regardless of whether she has a lover or not, arranges for some possession of hers to be stolen—a lock of hair, a bit of clothing, an ornament. This is tested by the sorcerer to find out whether the marriage would be propitious—which it nearly always is so long as they have not the same clan name and the sorcerer is paid well. Then the boy makes arrangements with his friends for the abduction. In many cases the whole thing is arranged in advance by a middleman and the abduction is merely ceremonial. In other cases the girl's parents may know, but the girl, having a lover with whom she might elope, is kept in ignorance. Frequently, both parents and girl are kept in ignorance of the impending abduction.

M'Gaw's abduction was of the genuine sort. "It happened over there," she pointed. "Just beyond the ghost temple." She thought she was about fifteen at the time, which was in 1954. Few Jingpaw have any idea of their ages. Her abductor, according to her, was "a horrible dissolute old man" of about thirty years.

One morning a girl friend called her out to go gathering firewood. Just outside Nungbing village a group of young men burst out of the jungle and grabbed her. "I shouted and wept," said M'Gaw, "but my girl friend only laughed. She was in the plan. My father couldn't hear and other villagers would not help because this is the custom of marrying girls.

"There were six or seven men and some women of my village.

[1] The names of ordinary Jingpaw women all begin with M' and those of men with Le.

I struggled but was dragged a long way through the jungle to a house where I had a meal and was kept most of the day. Then I was taken to the house of the man who wanted to marry me. Six holes were dug in front of the house in a line. Sheaves of tall grass were standing in them and a long bamboo through the middle of the sheaves.

"They made me walk along this bamboo into the house. I had to hand betel nut all round, carry water and cook glutinous rice. This is always done. The old folk were singing and drinking. My intended husband and I had to sit together and exchange rice and wine. The party went on singing till dawn. Then I had to get breakfast and the girls from my village took me back home. They sent the wedding gifts back with me: four cattle, a leg of beef, a big gown, silk and cotton cloth and a long silk robe like officials wear."

Her father accepted the gifts and therefore accepted the wedding, but M'Gaw loved someone else. Her husband's family kept sending for her, but each time she ran into the jungle and stayed there for several days until they went away. This went on for two years. Then a cousin brought a message that if she was really unwilling, the gifts should be returned and the whole matter called off. But two of the cattle had already been sacrificed and her father could not repay them. He pressed her to go through with the marriage. Her lover turned out to be weak and fearful of eloping.

One night, M'Gaw said the equivalent to "a plague o' both your houses" and fled through the ghost-infested paths to the hut of the Communist Party work-team. She was locally famed as a singer of love songs and was soon singing them to the public in Mangshih as a member of the multi-national song and dance group there.

M'Gaw spent a long time with me round that log fire explaining Jingpaw marriage customs and singing samples of Jingpaw love songs.

People of the same surname do not go to the same communal houses. It would be very shameful for two people, and especially close relatives of the same name, to sing love songs to each other, since this is the prelude to love-making. Most songs begin by asking the name and village of the other party, to avoid this social crime.

Unmarried girls who become pregnant suffer no social criticism and children conceived out of marriage suffer no discrimination. But the girl's price on the marriage market and her chance of a good match are sharply reduced once she has had a child. The fathers of such children seldom marry the girls, preferring to get out of their obligation by the traditional sacrifice of a buffalo. This is an unusual custom. I have generally found that in societies where remnants of group marriage exist, the birth of a child is regarded as a sign that marriage would be propitious. But among the Jingpaw, even if the girl marries the father, the wedding gifts are less than they would have been. Otherwise she remains single, continues to go to the communal house or is married to a middle-aged widower.

Despite these risks, the girls go to the communal houses because it is customary. Also, as one *ganbu* remarked: "They have no other recreations and their youth is spent in this manner."

Few girls would be so bold as to reject a marriage by abduction as M'Gaw did. I asked her why she was so opposed to marrying this man and she said: "He was old, more than thirty, smoked opium and was a lazybones who only had the price of a wife because his younger brothers had to work." She had very decided views about marriage for love, and freedom in choosing one's own partner, doubtless gathered from her associations with the work-team. She said: "I am very grateful to the work-team. Without them I would now be leading a life of misery."

M'Gaw felt sorry for her father, too. He would have to repay the wedding gifts. "But I send him 7 yuan a month from my wages and he can save it if he wants to clear off that debt." She gets 34 yuan a month as a student subsidy.

"Our Jingpaw people never had anything like finding a partner in marriage. It was always arranged by the parents and the villagers. Now it's changing slowly and some girls can find their own husbands. The villagers are influenced by the *ganbu* and more parents are agreeing to let their children marry as they please.

"I have read the Chinese marriage law, but it is not yet known among the Jingpaw," she said. "I am free and independent, myself. One day I will marry a man I like. Anyway, I'm not going back to that man."

The system of consanguinity reflects matriarchal and group marriage. All persons from the fourth generation back are called *ager*, a feminine term. The sons of brothers and the sons of sisters are called by the same term, *adzor*, meaning "sons". A dead father's concubine is taken over by his son in addition to his own wife. Uncles and nephews take over widows. These "take-overs" have priority before marrying a wife of one's own choice.

Brothers and sisters and all people of the same surname do not use the same communal houses, nor do sisters or first cousins in the mother's line go to the same house. Owing to these complicated restrictions, a girl who becomes pregnant can usually point to a certain man as the father of her child.

Breaches of the rules of sex relationships are visited by capital punishment. Incest between brother and sister is punished by death to both. If relations occur between the children of two brothers the man only is executed.

No action is taken against wives for adultery, but the husband seeks revenge or redress from the man. Both sides must be in agreement if a divorce is wanted and divorce is more difficult for the husband since he abducted the woman. For a woman to have a divorce requires only that the marriage gifts be returned. If the man wants it, he must give more presents.

One effect of the all-night singing and love-making in the communal houses is that young people have little value as labour-power until they are married. They also need considerable funds for gifts and other expenses in their affairs. At the start of a new affair, songs are exchanged throughout several nights, the boy singing of the girl's beauty and desirability and the girl expressing doubts: her family would not like it or his love would not last. The boy sings back reassuring her. Then there is an exchange of presents, usually silver coins and flowers in a betel husk, which the boy secretly puts on the girl's bed at night. If she does not want anything to do with him, she will return it unopened. If she consents, she gives him tobacco or weaves him a sword belt. All these activities leave little time for work or education and make big inroads into the family finances.

On my first night in Nungbing, I lay awake a long time on my plank bed in the new clinic. I could hear above the sighing bamboo and the chirruping and squeaking of the jungle, the faint sounds of singing far away in the forest communal houses and sometimes the squeals and laughter of the young people.

CHAPTER NINETEEN

SINISTER DEVELOPMENTS ON THE HILLTOPS

Killing to cure—The only safe piece of meat—Jingpaw's view of the Jingpaw—Primitive communism—Equal shares regardless of work done— Leaders become rulers—Recent growth of usury—Development of landed property and "money"—Foe becomes friend—Direct transition—Collective work no aid to co-operation

AS soon as I arrived at Nungbing village I had asked to see the next cattle sacrifice, and before I went to bed a message had come that a water-buffalo was to be sacrificed at dawn the next day in Bangda village, seven miles away across the ridgepaths. Tall bamboo rustled in the darkness overhead as we set off in the dew; past the village headman's long house; through the bamboo grove and its ghost temple where M'Gaw had been abducted; on to the ridges, where slash-burn cultivation had destroyed the jungle; and as we walked the mountain tops lightened and glowed pink.

All these jungle paths look alike but M'Ubi led the way—a local Jingpaw girl who had become a medical worker; a mobile jungle nurse with a big square leather shoulder case bearing a red cross. She was explaining that today's sacrifice was for a burial but most sacrifices were to cure sickness. "It takes longer than I thought it would to get my people to have any faith in modern pills and drugs. In Bangda village, where we are going now, I cured a man of malaria but his family sacrificed a buffalo just the same." I had been told on the previous evening that in Nungbing, which has sixty-five families, they had sacrificed twenty-eight cattle, seventy-three pigs and 235 chickens in 1956—more than one pig weekly and one beast every fortnight.

We overtook people on the way who were going to the sacrifice. All the villagers of Bangda and plenty of others from nearby places would turn up.

Suddenly there were shots in the distance and we started to run towards them. For all our haste, the buffalo was dead and already lying on its own skin, headless, when we arrived in Bangda. Half a dozen experts were carving it up to make sure that everyone got the right bit: slices for children, ribs for the widow and the communal pot, hind legs for the sorcerer and the local leader.

Three male dancers were very seriously prancing round the house, led by a man with a spear. They were driving out evil spirits but everyone else was busy cutting up meat, ladling blood into bamboo tubs, making skewers, preparing a tree-leaf which is used as an accompanying vegetable or firing off blank charges of black-powder in ancient muzzle-loaders. When cauldrons were steaming all over the village, out came the rice beer and spirits and I soon realised that a sacrifice is chiefly a glorious frolic, taken seriously only by the sorcerer and his helpers—for whom it is business.

Most of the buffalo was soon being digested, together with plenty of rice liquor and a bitter sauce made from the half-digested grass in a certain part of the animal's gut. Then a piece of meat was hung on a high bamboo and people started blazing away at it with muzzle-loaders crammed with home-made black powder and loose fitting lead bullets. This meat should have gone to the person shooting it down, but there was no steady eye in the village. The meat stayed up and the only knocking down was of well-loaded people carelessly firing muskets loaded with equal liberality.

There was dancing, in which wags burlesqued the still-serious witch dancers; then more drinking and eating. A fine day for one and all!

But the family of the dead man must provide for three such days by custom—buffalo, liquor and rice. The widow gets into debt, dead buffaloes cannot be used for farmwork, weeds grow while hundreds of man-days are wasted. And this is typical of the way of life of these hospitable and prodigal people.

One of the bigger Jingpaw leaders said to me: "Our people are backward and superstitious. The men are lazy and the women do most of the work. After the harvest we eat and drink without a thought for tomorrow. Every buffalo we kill is one less for working." This was Tzaudung, now a member of China's parliament and vice-Chairman of the Tehung Chou; a young man, plump and clean, wearing a wristwatch and surrounded by photographs of himself taken with Liu Shao-chi and other Chinese leaders. He served scented tea in fine porcelain, sitting on real chairs.

Taking his long silver-mounted sword from the wall he said: "If any Jingpaw goes into any house and hangs up his sword and bag, that is a sign that he wants to be fed. When he has eaten, the family where he called will also give him food to carry on his way. We eat in each other's houses till nothing is left. This communal feeling has its good side but it makes saving and progress impossible. So in the end, nobody has enough to eat.

"Our people are very hostile to other peoples. This is understandable. People used to oppress us and call us 'monkeys'. They looked down on the Jingpaw. We officials were above the other Jingpaw, but above us were the Tai officials and above them the Kuomintang Han officials."

Historically, the Jingpaw are just passing out of primitive society into feudal society. Irrigated and garden land are privately owned but cannot be sold. Other land is owned in common and can be used by whomever has permission of the leaders to clear it. There is insufficient paddy, and farming methods are of the most backward kind.

Oppressed most of the year by the need to make a daily living, the Jingpaw spend a great deal of time collecting wild berries, fruits and firewood to sell to the well-to-do Tai people on the plains below; and so neglect weeding or protecting their own poorly sown crops from animals.

Little exchange takes place among the Jingpaw themselves; every family has the same things and there are many primitive-communist features about Jingpaw life. Tillage is frequently done in common. A family makes some rice beer and other families come to help on their land. There is no payment for this labour and nobody is regarded as under the least obligation to make any return in labour or kind. Houses are built in the same way. To the Jingpaw it seems one of the obvious facts of life that if five people can do a piece of work in one day, then ten can do it more happily and more quickly, leaving more time for pleasure.

Nobody goes hungry while anyone has food. When a family which runs out of food goes to eat with another family until that one runs out, there is no thought of debt or payment involved. The Chinese People's Liberation Army has a stringent rule—which played no little part in securing mass support and enabling it to defeat the corrupt, looting Kuomintang army—that not one thread of cotton may be taken from the public without payment. This rule was not a political asset among the Jingpaw. They regarded insistence on paying for things as a sign of "bad heart". Jingpaw custom is to eat, brew and entertain for a brief period after harvest and this is followed by a longer period of picking a bare living from the jungle.

However, into these naïve and human relations came the *tzau*[1] or hill officials. Formerly these were the Jingpaw public leaders like the headmen and elders of the Wa, not in any way set apart from the people; but gradually, under the influence of the Tai system of manorial feudalism on the plains below, which itself was overlaid with the Chinese imperial feudal system, these positions became hereditary and the hill officials became a caste of rulers of areas instead of clans. Now there are some 500 families of these officials, a separate caste which does not intermarry with the other Jingpaw.

Five of the biggest hill officials each rules more than 10,000 people; small officials may rule a single village. These officials' families are equal in status—theoretically at any rate—and marry only with other officials, outside their own clans. The position of official is hereditary, passing to the youngest son of the ruler. They rule by customary law, without troops or police and with the help of smaller officials. These smaller officials, or *suwun*, carry still more evident traces of the primitive democracy which was swiftly disappearing when the work-teams went in. Some are chosen from the family which was earliest in the village, but all are now appointed. Old people can still remember when some of them were elected. These petty officials are not members of the ruling caste. Intermarriage between officials and commoners is not subject to actual penalisation—as among the Norsu, where it is punished by death—but an official person marrying beneath him loses caste, and a common Jingpaw could not afford to marry his son into an official family. There is a saying: "A melon cannot become meat, and a common person cannot become an official. There has to be a seed." Most officials belong to the Langsu and Chasu tribes, the smallest of the four Jingpaw tribes. From this derives another saying that "there are nine officials in ten Langsu families".

Hill officials have acquired wide-ranging economic privileges over other Jingpaw. Every ordinary family must provide three to five days corvée labour yearly and several *lor* or backloads of rice, which I valued at 7 yuan (about £1) yearly. In addition they get a hind leg from every beast sacrificed and every hunting quarry. There are "gifts" to be rendered on occasions of birth, marriage and death in the official's family and fees for settling disputes. A hill official must lead the ceremony of sacrifice to Mudai, the biggest Jingpaw ghost, when the villagers make "gifts" of cattle, liquor and other things to him. He

---

[1] The names of all male members of the official caste begin with Tzau and those of the women with Nang.

"helps them in farming" by conducting the sacrifice at the official temple—a thatched hut in the jungle—before the spring sowing. His land is then dug a little and before this nobody may begin farming.

Hill officials control the common land in their area. When a new family moves into the district, the official allocates their land and resumes control when they leave.

Non-Jingpaw people (Hans, Tai, Lisu, etc.), living in an area under the rule of a Jingpaw official, pay a poll-tax in money or kind. The few slaves[1] owned by the biggest officials were generally not Jingpaw people but captives from raiding and fighting other nationalities.

It may be assumed that the official caste became wealthy by the dual process of using to their own advantage the headmen's privilege of allocating the land and receiving gifts; while at the same time that position gradually became fixed by heredity rather than election. An official today, even with only one village of say sixty families, working the best land with ample corvée labour and receiving gifts and fees, is wealthy enough to be differentiated from the ordinary common family.

A hangover of the primitive communal way of living which preceded this state of affairs is the continuing legend that the hill official has the duty of feeding the poor and helping the needy. To what extent this was ever true cannot be now known. It must have had some foundation and this now provides the theoretical basis for the greater exactions gradually imposed as the caste became more and more separated from the rest of the people.

It was put to me this way by Tzaujong, ruler of twelve small villages—360 households—in the Nungbing area. We sat after breakfast, he quaffing large slugs of powerful rice spirit while I pretended to do the same out of courtesy, and talked about his position as an official. He was hunched up in a black velveteen jacket over which he wore an old Japanese army officer's great-coat.

"I never got anything for being an official," Tzaujong said. "But we officials get some reward for helping the people in farming, telling them when to begin the sowing and so on. I got more land and better land because the newly opened land goes first to the official. And some

---

[1] Presumably the reason that Jingpaw society failed to develop in the classic manner—primitive, slave, feudal—should be sought in the peculiarities of the terrain. Whereas the Norsu and Wa remained isolated from the influence of the lowlands because they lived in highland areas peopled only by themselves, the Jingpaw live interspersed on hilltops among the Tai who occupy the plains. Being usually only a few hours march from a Tai district, it was relatively easy for the Tai manorial-feudal influence to penetrate.

grain and opium, the legs of cattle and other gifts. Because I have more income I am able to help the common people when they are in need. No, there are no rules about this help. An official is also poor and so he cannot help very much. He decides how much. People may bring a little liquor and parsley and I might give a *lor* of grain [worth about 1.50 yuan or 6 shillings]. Later they may kill a beast and give me the leg.

"Among the Jingpaw, helping others was never regarded as creating debts or obligations in the past. We learned these things from the Hans about twenty years ago. They taught us that if a person borrows it is reasonable for him to return something extra to the lender. Our elders tried to stop this, but the damage had been done."

However, when I came to probe into the actual income of this old official, who is now one of the strongest advocates of the new "doctrine", it was by no means to be sneered at. His 360 families were obliged to give him three work days each—equal to 1,080 work-days or three people's work for a year; grain rents of three *lor* average (4.50 yuan), totalling 1,620 yuan (about £240) and three ounces of opium each which must represent at least half of that sum. Even assuming that a fair proportion of the households did not pay, this was still a large sum for such a place and would provide a liberal margin for his helping those who "rewarded" him for "helping with the farming".

A survey of the area around Nungbing showed that the average hill official family owned about five acres of land, mainly good fixed paddy land, while other Jingpaw owned one and a half acres of dry slash-burn land. They also owned twice as many buffaloes and ten times as many oxen as an ordinary family.

Stable property and "money" property—paddy, cattle, and opium—were being rapidly concentrated in the hands of the officials. The other point of wealth concentration—the sorcerers—get the perquisites usual in such societies: one leg of each sacrificed animal and varying fees for intervening with the ghosts. They do not belong to the official caste as a rule but benefit from their close association and so have with it common interests.

This accumulation of wealth formed the basis for the development of usury out of the primitive communal "borrowing", mostly between relatives and within a village.

When the work-team made a debt survey in Nungbing village in 1952, there were a few cases of loans made by the local official and sorcerers to people in other villages, but none to people in Nungbing itself. A few Nungbing people had borrowed from other officials and villages at interest. Most "debts" were owed to relatives and carried no interest, though there were a few cases of "buying opium shoots"— paying half a silver dollar an ounce for opium fields which would be worth 75 cents an ounce when harvested and gaining an interest of 50 per cent. in a few weeks.

Four years later, in 1956, debts within Nungbing village to local people were no less than 5,340 lb. of grain, at an annual interest of 5,610 lb.; and debts owed to other villages amounted to 7,080 lb. at 6,150 lb. interest. Interest on debts had become 4·35 per cent. of the total grain output of the village. This was still small but showed a rapid rate of increase.

The borrowers were generally people who had to cope with special events such as a marriage or a sacrifice, people who had no food and could not for some reason go to the jungle for a living and, inevitably, opium smokers whose labour power is reduced at the same time as their expenses rise.

In one family of debtors, the income for the year had been 484 yuan, which would be a very comfortable living indeed for a peasant elsewhere in China. But this family had to marry off a son and provide for this: two oxen, 200 bowls of liquor, rice, seventy eggs, dress materials, ceremonial gowns, five ounces of opium and sorcerer's fees coming to 282 yuan. Even the 200 or so remaining would be enough to live on, given the same providence as an ordinary Chinese peasant. But owing to the normal improvidence of the Jingpaw, nothing was left at the time of the wedding and the family had to borrow at interest.

This area as a whole—the Tehung Tai-Jingpaw Autonomous Chou —is a hothouse where almost anything will grow well. But where the squalid poverty of the Jingpaw was mainly due in the past to wild squandering and waste at harvest times—"eating new grains and talk- ing old quarrels"—now a few factor had arisen: the impoverishment of the ordinary Jingpaw family by usury, made possible by the increasing concentration of property in the hands of the hill officials.

While the political workers were going through the usual prelimin- ary process of "doing good and making friends", they studied these processes of change and concluded that the Jingpaw were already moving at a fairly rapid pace into a form of society that boded little good for the common people.

The problem that confronted them was essentially similar to that among the Wa and the Norsu—how to bridge the gap between this primitive way of life and what was going on in the rest of China. Previous Chinese régimes, far from trying to do anything about it, had actually engendered the caste aspects of the problem by planting Han officials over the Tai and the Tai over the Jingpaw, and drawing what tribute they could.

Among the feudal Tai people on the rich but limited farmland on the plains, the news of the land reform in the rest of China led to a general demand by the land-hungry Tai peasants for a similar redivision of the land. Tai landlords, subjected to heavy mass pressure for land reform, had to acquiesce and the land redistribution went through peacefully by agreement of landlord and peasant.

There was no such demand among the Jingpaw who suffered no shortage of land. Rent and corvée per family were negligible and certainly not a major cause of poverty, and the Jingpaw regarded their hill officials as natural rulers to whom they rendered certain services in return for which the officials performed public services and helped them in time of distress. It was essential to work with the officials. Hostility towards the Hans, who had always oppressed the Jingpaw, provided another complication.

Tzaudung, who is now an ardent supporter of the Chinese revolution and a member of the National People's Congress, was formerly by no means friendly to the Communists. In 1950 this young ruler of some 3,000 people fought the People's Liberation Army in a two-hour pitched battle, which he lost. The jungles were then swarming with runaway Kuomintang troops, bandit gangs living off the country and robbing the Jingpaw of their tiny possessions. Tzaudung, feeling that he was unable to cope with the fires burning all round him, took all his valuables and fled, making for the Burma border. On the way he was ambushed by Kuomintang remnants, his brother killed and all his possessions stolen. PLA soldiers heard of the ambush and went in pursuit of the robbers, captured them and returned all of Tzaudung's property. This made a deep impression on the young man. But Jingpaw leaders on the whole were hostile and suspicious, fearful of losing their privileges and status.

In principle the political workers decided to adopt a similar policy and method of work to that among the Wa, with variations to suit the local differences.

"From the start we worked with the officials, to win them to help us in overcoming primitive backwardness and leading the whole Jingpaw people to a better life," said Yang Su, the propaganda department chief. "The main thing was to introduce better farming methods, produce more and find ways to encourage the people to consume less erratically.

"We considered that the direct, gradual transition to socialism was possible here, without going through other social forms. This was possible because the revolution in the rest of China enabled the state to provide massive help and because of the existence of the Communist Party, which would be able to influence the situation scientifically."

Relief distributed among the Jingpaw was colossal. Up to the end of 1957, state-provided relief of 1,000,000 yuan had been given out in goods and a further sum of 810,000 yuan in "loans" (interest free and capital not returnable). Subsidies to officials to compensate for losses in privilege and corvée came to about 250,000 yuan. The total came to well over £300,000.

Farm tools were brought in to demonstrate modern farming methods and sample plots were cultivated to show the advantages of such cash crops as the valuable wax-insect, tea and coffee, and early crops such as potatoes, peas and beans. Relief enabled people to spend more time in productive farming instead of perpetuating their poverty by squandering most of their working time picking a living from the jungle.

A good deal of the relief and aid goods were wasted. Draught animals given for farming were futilely sacrificed to cure people dying from malaria, who could have been kept alive for nothing with atabrine. Much of the relief grain went into the brewing-bamboos. But relief did something to bridge the annual hunger spots and set free more man-days for regular farming. More important, perhaps, was that it broke down the hostility to the Hans.

Relief by itself could settle nothing and it was felt that the situation could only be changed radically by moving in the direction of producer co-operatives. "And rather naïvely," said Yang Su, "we had at first imagined that the primitive communal way of life—with collective working and division of the crop among those who work the land—would be helpful in setting up producer co-operatives. Actually we found that exactly the opposite was true."

The gap between equalitarian ideas and the socialist "to each according to his work" proved in practice to be very great indeed.

CHAPTER TWENTY

SHORT-CIRCUITING HISTORY

Key to many doors—Experiences from the Esquimaux—Jungle "depart-ment store"—Objections to payment for work done—Counting work days shows "bad heart"—People are all the same—The unimportance of work—Reluctance to take more than another—Co-operative members don't sacrifice—Cash crops

IF the Jingpaw had gone on developing along the lines they had taken since the latter part of the last century, the result must have been a manorial feudal system, with a class of land-rich overlords at one end of the scale and an impoverished peasantry at the other. What was sought by the political workers was a means of by-passing this process—of moving them through several historical stages in a single leap—while maintaining an alliance with the official class which would prevent destructive clashes between Jingpaw and Han or between Jingpaw and Jingpaw.

Producer co-operatives appeared to be the golden key to unlock many riddles. More paddy land would fix the arable and immediately raise the average level of productivity; common ownership of cattle would prevent sacrifices; periodic payments of income would end the phenomenon of a few months hectic eating and drinking followed by more months of time-consuming efforts to squeeze a bare living from the jungle; the labour power thus set free could raise the entire level of farming; and the common Jingpaw could develop their own leaders as an alternative political force to the exploiting official class. Other arguments existed for co-operatives as centres for educational, medical, cultural and social work.

A new form of organisation for what is called "transformation work" is being used throughout the Jingpaw areas—the Production and Cultural Stations. These are said to owe their origin to reading about work among the Esquimaux in the U.S.S.R. These stations send out work teams, set up trading systems (markets, stores, mobile buyers), develop medical services, schools, technical classes and gener-ally direct the day-to-day work among the scattered Jingpaw.

Nungbing village, typically Jingpaw, was an obvious choice for a Production and Cultural Station. Only half a day's march from

Chefang town, it is also a recognised Jingpaw centre, and, as Jingpaw villages go, a rather large one.

It is perched exactly on the highest point of a long mountain ridge, among bamboo and banana trees. A few paces across the ridge brings a total change of landscape: on one side, wild hill country spotted with irregular patches of slash-burn farmland; on the other, a view right across the flourishing alluvial plain of Chefang, major town on the Burma Road, where every available inch of ground is under China's most famous rice and every little stream turns water-wheels operating automatic pestles and mortars for husking it. Even the birds down there are fat, for they have learned to time their flight by a fraction of a second to get under the rising pestle and out with a grain of rice before it falls.

Nungbing has seen great changes. Its thatched huts, dotted about and hidden from each other by thick forest, are now overshadowed by the square, tile-roofed adobe buildings of the Production and Cultural Station. Facing the clinic where I lived, which was also the medical department of the Station, was the new "department" store— a single large shop jammed with everything dear to the hearts of the Jingpaw and covered outside with illustrations of the jungle produce which the trading team was willing to buy. A grey monkey skin, stuffed with straw, was hanging outside to dry like a grisly pub sign. The shop's long counter gave straight on to the jungle, and usually had three or four Jingpaw, mostly young, leaning on it—their sling bows across their backs, pondering no doubt what to buy for their current lady-love or how much fresh bamboo shoots would be needed to get the now indispensable electric torch. Old Jingpaw ladies, mouths as black as night with betel nut, would stand for hours fingering a length of cloth before deciding to trade their baskets of some herb, unknown to me, for enough to make the old man a new pair of trousers. Behind the clinic is the grain shop and next to it the building which houses a team of agricultural experts. On top of the ridge, with a view over both valleys, is the primary school, with a school bell consisting of an old lorry wheel, and a spare-time training class called a "half-farm, half-school". A piece of levelled ground in the middle of everything is now a new regular market every sixth day. This has reversed the previous situation. Mostly Jingpaw went to Chefang to sell; now Tai people from Chefang come to the Nungbing market to buy.

An advantage claimed for these Production and Cultural Stations

—there are seventeen of them—is that they are administrative organs equivalent to a local government. Nungbing Station is responsible for five rural districts with 116 Jingpaw villages. Being jointly operated by the Communist Party and the local governments which are in the process of formation, they are said to form a means of unifying the officials, sorcerers, ordinary people and the Communist Party political workers. As far as I know, these stations do not exist anywhere else in China. Nobody argued that they were superior to other methods of organisation. They were found useful in Tehung because of the scattered nature of Jingpaw society and have been responsible since their establishment in 1956 for getting the co-operatives set up and guiding their development by means of the village work-teams.

From the first moment the new co-operatives looked like foundering on the rock of primitive-communist equalitarianism. That the Jingpaw cannot write or count, object to planning anything and are by custom quite amazingly indolent and thriftless, were negative but easily foreseeable liabilities. But the positive objections to payment in accordance with work done were both varied and unexpected.

One of the first co-operatives established in the Nungbing area is at Lungjun. I strolled the six or seven miles there over the ridges with Liang Yung-li, the Station chief, whose name somewhat aptly means "always at zenith", for he is certainly always on hilltops and ridges. In a little village on the way a woman was weaving one of the geometrically patterned woollen sarong skirts worn by all Jingpaw women. The warp of hand-spun yarn was stretched between a stick some yards away to a frame held on her lap by a belt. She laboriously passed the weft, wound on a piece of flat wood, from side to side, producing a few inches of foot-wide cloth a day. From start to finish, such a skirt takes up to two months work, sells for anything between 21 and 100 yuan. In the same little village I saw a Jingpaw oil-press—two bits of timber in a morticed log which are driven together by wedges, squeezing out a small fraction of the oil from the seed; doing wastefully in a day what a simple screw press could do in minutes.

Lela, leader of the Lungjun Co-operative, is young and handsome, with a quiet manner and, for all that he cannot read, write or count, very intelligent. He has wide, candid eyes, does not often laugh, and seems to be in relations of unusual equality with his beautiful young wife. She was breast feeding their second child when I called, so Lela took the three-year-old and carried him round with us all the afternoon as we toured the co-operative. It was an impressive sign of character

N

that he had no fear at being laughed at for doing this "women's work". At his house were farm tools issued to the co-operative by the government: about a dozen of the broad iron shares used for ploughing paddy and a variety of "modern" iron tools, hoes, mattocks and spades. Overlooking a smooth basketball pitch, which does alternate duty as the threshing floor, is the big hut of the work-team, which also serves as the co-operative meeting place.

Lela described the knots that the co-operative was still trying to unravel. As he talked, villagers wandered in to listen and argue, squatting on their heels by the open wood fire, chewing betel and passing a pipe round.

"Our custom," Lela said, "is to look down on people who haggle over what one person does for another. We think it shows a bad heart. I may help you to build a house or open a field. But afterwards I forget it. You are not obliged to do the same for me. You don't owe me something. What grows on my land is mine but you are welcome to come and eat it as my guest.

"If several families work on a piece of land, we do not add up what each does, or calculate that this person is strong while this one is only a child and that one an old man, or whether this person worked ten days and that one fifteen. We never heard of dividing the crop un-equally and giving people who worked harder more grain, and we never had regular working hours. Our way is that more people shorten the work and the time goes better with the talk. It's not so tiring. Counting work done seemed nonsense to us and rather unfriendly."

One very old Jingpaw, an obvious opponent of co-operatives, broke in at this point. He had been fretting and fuming while Lela was talking and now he reproduced almost the identical argument I had heard among the Wa. "It's all new-fangled nonsense," he said. "Life isn't like that. I was a child, then a man and now I am old and weak. That's life and we are all the same. I don't agree with these work-points. One day I feel like working, another day I want to have a drink or sleep. In a lifetime everyone does about the same. So I say share alike and never mind what a man does on this or that day." Having got that off his chest he went back to his bubbling bamboo water-pipe.

Lela had been a leading figure in trying to get the co-operative going from the moment the idea was put out in 1955. Other people had said this was just a cunning Han trick to get the Jingpaw to grow things for them. Lela had not believed that. "They seemed to be sincere people, giving us things. They knew more than we knew and I believed them when they said co-operatives would help us." He in turn helped the work-team to persuade eleven out of Lungjun's twenty-five families to form the first co-operative there in 1956.

One of the many vexed questions which the co-operative was to meet came up immediately over planning their crops. As Lela explained: "What we Jingpaw have are all the same things. We grow the same things—what we need—and don't buy or sell among each other. If we have nothing we eat with others and if everyone has nothing we sell things from the jungle to people below on the plains.

"We think it madness to plant things we don't want, just to sell them. We prefer to plant what we want ourselves.

"But that is very inefficient," the young co-operative leader went on. "It's hard to get people to do differently. Our members got very nervous about the idea of planned planting. They thought: 'Suppose I have only one thing on my land and something goes wrong with the co-operative?' How could people have faith in the co-operative till they had tried it? We could not reckon out how much we would need of this or that, and had to get the work-team to help us to plan. This nervousness about not growing the same things on their own land as they had always done caused the members to keep land back from the co-operative at first and plant a little privately in case something went wrong."

Lela described how they first kept records by memory. One member would be responsible for remembering the number of work-points on the rice, another on the beans. When this failed, they made the records with notches on strips of bamboo and knots in string. This came to grief when the children joined the game, adding notches and knots. The work-team came to the rescue and prepared printed work tickets. Unhappily these contained the Han word *fen*, which also appears on some of the paper currency, and became confused with money. An astute well-to-do villager bought quite a lot of them hoping to make a profit at harvest time. But on the whole this method was effective.

Rate of attendance at work was low. What appeared to me to be a most heart-breaking and intractable problem for the work-team was the number, variety and lack of coincidence of days on which a Jingpaw traditionally does not work. No work is done on birthdays, but these do not occur annually. If a person is born on the third day after market day—which is usually every sixth day—then every third day after market day is a non-working day. A day is similarly marked for the death of the most recently deceased relative. Unless these chance to coincide, three days out of six are ruled out for working, for market day is also a holiday. Then there are days for the traditional sacrifices and extra ones for marriages and deaths, days for visiting relatives and, in the case of unmarried people, the time-consuming requirements of love-making. All this leaves little enough time for work and that time very hard to plan.

I examined the case of the widow M'Nang, who has three dependent children and is a strong supporter of co-operation, being one of the three Communist Party members in Lungjun. She had the usual government relief, which was consumed in the usual irrational manner, and faced the necessity of providing for her children every day. During the 183 days between April and October 1957, she spent seventy-nine days gathering firewood and wild vegetables and going to market to sell them; nine days on ghost affairs: only eight days on traditional collective work with other families not in the co-operative (it would create a bad impression for a Communist to evade these customary duties); two days on wage labour; ten days sickness and fourteen days on various other matters. This left only sixty-one days for birth- and death-days and working for the co-operative.

It was quite impossible for the work-teams to find their way through this maze of taboos and personal difficulties. They finally devised a "small contract system" by which a given task was set for a group of members who were made jointly responsible for completing it within a certain period of time—say, between two market days.

Ways had to be found to distribute income periodically rather than all at once, otherwise the members made wine, sacrificed and bought finery, found themselves with nothing to live on and had to get a living from the jungle instead of doing productive work.

In all these matters the harried work-teams had to provide the most detailed help, even to assisting people to measure how much they should consume daily in rice and oil and how much time to devote to co-operative and private affairs to get the maximum income.

In addition to all these complications, there was some quiet sabotage by the officials, who fed the new co-operators with rumours that they were only working for the Hans; that payment according to work would cause disputes between families after harvest. "Co-operatives are just a way to control the people and force them to work," the old officials said. They claimed to have seen people in the co-operatives on the plains "driven to work like cattle by men armed with rifles". Co-operative fences got "accidentally" broken, or pulled down by the irate ghosts so that cattle ate the crops.

New snags developed when the time came to distribute the first harvest. Tradition dies hard and the members who had said: "More work, more from the common crop is right," had second thoughts when this concept came into direct practical conflict with the primitive idea of "work together, consume equally". Those with more work-points felt selfish and isolated; those with few complained that they were being robbed of the produce of "their" land which they had joined to the co-operative.

"This land is still mine and what grows on it should be mine. Those who worked on it were only helping me in the traditional manner," was the commonest reaction. They said: "I put my land into the co-operative but I did not specially need the help of others." One member wept openly when he found that the rice on "his" land was to be distributed to others, disregarding the fact that pepper from "others'" land was being given to him. He threatened to burn the rice.

Poor families with little land, who had worked more, felt that they had no right to more grain than those who had more land but had worked less. And those with more land also felt that they were entitled to more of the crop by virtue of that fact. Some of the bigger land holders actually smuggled half a ton of rice out of the store and hid it.

It seemed impossible to me that a co-operative could unravel this string of Gordian knots and survive. But when the testing time came, at the beginning of 1957, not one family left the co-operative, though several had previously stated their intention of doing so. (Two families had left it almost as soon as it was formed—one being that of a sorcerer. This had left nine families to cultivate the first co-operative harvest in 1956, all of whom continued as members.)

I spent a long time with one of those who had said they would quit and afterwards remained members. This was Lemang, a young man with a wife and three children. Naturally Lemang had only the haziest idea of what he had earned before he joined the co-operative. But we sat in the work-team's house with members of the team and neighbours, including non-co-operators, discussing how much land he had worked and what other things he had done, and gradually worked out what I believed to be an approximate comparison of his income and expenditure for 1955, before he had joined the co-operative, and 1956 which included the first co-operative harvest.

Lemang's income in both years consisted of two parts: farming and jungle side-occupations. In 1955 we estimated that he got the equivalent of 61.50 yuan from rice, soya and corn; he got 54.75 yuan from cutting firewood, selling bamboo shoots and a bit of exchange I failed to understand, which involved red pepper, cucumbers and a chicken.

His income was 116.25 yuan but he spent 146.40 yuan—30.15 yuan more than he earned.

In 1956 his income had risen to 146.80 yuan from the co-operative, plus 22.50 yuan from the jungle—a total of 169.30 yuan. But his outgoings also rose, to 192.75 yuan for the year. He spent eight times as much on liquor and twice as much on tobacco as in the previous year, had a smaller deficit and more fun.

Without keeping a diary, Lemang knew that his income was more and that he went less to the jungle. His income, being from farming instead of hit-and-miss jungle roving, was more reliable. Even Lemang's 1955 income would have been enough to live on—being slightly higher than the average for the whole of China's peasantry at that time, but what is a livelihood among the Hans was penury among the Jingpaw because of their different customs.

That 1956 harvest and share-out had been a practical lesson in the advantages of organised co-operation as contrasted with what they colourfully described as "going to the fields like flocks of birds". Lela said that it gave everyone a clear idea of what was meant by "more work, more from the common pool". Co-operative property had increased.

A work-team member gave the following figures for the co-operative's land and animals:

				January 1957	January 1958
Wet paddy	.	.	.	9·2 acres	12·2 acres
Dry Rice	.	.	.	41·0 acres	49·0 acres
Oxen	.	.	.	7	12
Buffaloes	.	.	.	3	5
Horses	.	.	.	1	2

Members of the co-operative still do not regard land opened in common as being co-operative property. One member said: "If I ever leave the co-operative, I shall take out my share of the wet paddy land." Since nobody seemed inclined to leave, the question had no practical significance, though it pointed to a continuing tentative attitude.

All of the co-operative's animals listed above have been bought by government loan and are in addition to animals privately owned, which are rented to the co-operative by its members for cash or grain. Collective ownership of the cattle and the income derived from privately owned cattle form a powerful brake on any tendency to sacrifice animals. This is borne out by the facts.

Cattle sacrificed in 1956 by Lungjun village's twenty-five families numbered twenty-six, mostly to cure sickness. Of these, co-operative members killed three. In 1957 there was an all round fall. Three cattle were killed because girls had got pregnant and five were killed for funerals. Not one was killed for sickness and, as he told me this, Lela waved his hand at the medicine cabinet on the wall. One of the work-team members in Lungjun has had medical training. Of the eight cattle sacrificed, not one was owned by a co-operative member.

Refusal to sacrifice in one place has its effects elsewhere, because the customary sacrifices go more or less in rotation and people feel less inclined to carry out a commitment which others are evading.

Lungjun co-operative has agreed to accept the applications of three other families for admission. Membership conditions, which seem to constitute the rules of the co-operative, are:

New members must not be "lazybones" nor well-to-do people;

New members must invest land;

The rate for hiring a privately owned draught animal is 15 yuan annually;

Land dividends are paid, 20 per cent. of the estimated crop for paddy land, 15 per cent. of the actual yield for dry land;

No dividend is paid on farm tools (most of these had been given by the government).

In several nearby villages, the poor people had already approached the Production and Cultural Station to ask for help in setting up co-operatives. In spite of the difficulties created by primitive equalitarianism, there has been a much more rapid development of co-operation among the Jingpaw than the Wa. I could only assume that the advantages of the deeper communal traditions of Jingpaw life outweighed the practical disadvantages. The figures for the growth of co-operation speak for themselves:

			Number of co-operatives	Families	Percentage of population
1954	.	.	4 (experimental)	49	—
1956	.	.	82	1,575	6·3
1957	.	.	216	2,988	12·2
1958 (planned)	.		400	—	25·0

In Lungjun Co-operative they have evidently overcome the incomprehension of cash crops. Lela took me round their land, most of which —other than the wet fields—is at 30 to 45 degrees from the horizontal. There is a brand new coffee plantation, a tea hill and the valuable wax insect is being cultivated on a great many trees. Beans, potatoes, peas and other new crops grow well in this hothouse climate and do much to fill the gap between the grain crops. Lela went for a course of study in tea processing—up the Burma Road in a lorry to the ancient walled city of Baoshan, which much impressed him by its size and bustle. He said: "We are only growing enough tea for ourselves now but as soon as possible we shall sell the surplus." He said he applied for membership of the Chinese Communist Party after the co-operative was formed and two other members of the co-operative had joined, both women, M'Nang, the widow, and M'Puvang. His own wife wants to join, but he said this was not easy because of the children. His Communist Party branch meets twice a month and discusses "work, the co-operative, reform of the local government and political lectures on China and foreign affairs". This is one of twelve rural district branches of the Communist Party among the Jingpaw.

There will be a great demand for administrative workers in these new co-operatives, and the faster the movement spreads the less able will the work teams be to cope with every problem in detail as at Lungjun. It seemed to me that the rate of development of co-operatives was in danger of outstripping the rate of production of Jingpaw people able to write and do simple arithmetic—at any rate for a time. There is one primary school in each of the ninety rural districts and all the Production and Cultural Stations have a "half-school, half-farm" attended by villagers who are willing to learn the three R's and study modern farming methods.

Nungbing's "half-school, half-farm" has twenty-seven students, including fifteen unmarried girls. Students get a subsidy of 10 yuan monthly for a two-year course. This is more than Lemang had earned in 1955 and is therefore a very generous allowance. Attendance is erratic, as may be imagined, for the students spend a great deal of their time in love affairs. When they attend, mornings are spent in study and the afternoons working on the school farm under the teachers' guidance.

At the primary school, which was on holiday during my stay, there are 145 pupils, almost all Jingpaw. It was very hard to get pupils when the school opened in 1952, owing to suspicions over the motives of the Hans. No officials' children went so all the others stayed away. After much persuasion, a hill official agreed to send his only child, a five-year-old boy, too young to study. But he was welcomed, given sweets, petted, bathed and fed by the teachers and made so much fuss of that he kept demanding to go back to school. With the son of a hill official there, the way was opened for other children. At first the children taught the teachers the Jingpaw language and the teachers taught the children how to write it alphabetically. Now there is a full five-year course, entirely free including board, books and clothing.

There are 400 full-time Jingpaw working personnel, mostly helping the work-teams and mostly illiterate. Unless Jingpaw customs change and the youth spend more of their time in learning and less in play and love affairs, raising an educated new generation of Jingpaw still seems an uphill task.

CHAPTER TWENTY-ONE

THE CARROT AND THE GOAD

*How to get a buffalo unbogged—Penicillin and corn liquor—Jungle nurse—
Winning over the sorcerers—Officials' lapsing privileges—Differing
opinions of the tzau—Pull from the front and push from behind*

ONE wise old Jingpaw said to me: "When a buffalo gets stuck in
the mud, you hold out some food in front of its nose and push
from behind. Then the buffalo helps himself and, with some pushing
at the same time, the difficulty is overcome. That is how it is with our
leaders."

Sorcerers, who form part of the Jingpaw upper crust, are usually
clever people. From their youth they have to train their memories to
learn all the rigmarole of ghost worship, sacrifices, legend and taboo.
Having a strong vested interest in ghost worship, they are naturally
hostile to modern medicine, which is the main sphere in which the
new things affect them at the beginning. Hind legs from slaughtered
cattle comprise a large part of their perquisites.

For all that so many cattle died to make people well, health was in
a dismal condition. Malaria, dysentry, gastric ailments, influenza and
venereal diseases took toll of the living and those about to be born. A
long list of minor ailments, especially skin diseases and trachoma,
ensured that the sorcerers never lacked a small fee to eke out the bigger
ones. Sleeping as they do in damp forests without bedding, older
Jingpaw are almost universally afflicted with rheumatism. They eat
vast amounts of the hottest red pepper to make a diet of grain and wild
vegetables more palatable, and so ruin their digestion.

To prevent sick people from visiting the medical centres or sending
for medical workers, the sorcerers used all the obvious methods—
rumours that the Hans were trying to kill off the Jingpaw and that the
ghosts would exact revenge. It was a favourite device to let a serious
case go for treatment and then, when it seemed that a cure was immi-
nent, to order that treatment must now be stopped and the ghost be
placated with cattle. Fatal cases resulting from this were then blamed
on the Han doctors. One sorcerer, when a pneumonia patient was on
the mend after a course of injections, gave him large quantities of

alcohol to drink, causing his death, which was then blamed on the injections.

But persistence—especially with atabrine, sulpha drugs and aspirin—brought results because they had obvious and undeniable effects. Gradually the mobile medical teams were welcomed as they went on their circuits. Later came clinics and now all Jingpaw areas are covered medically from the seventeen Production and Cultural Stations. Medical work—as is usual among the backward communities—became the most important means of opening up all other work.

A start was made on training Jingpaw medical workers. M'Ubi, the girl who escorted me through the jungle to see the Bangda sacrifice, was one of these. In the teeth of parental opposition, she enrolled in a mobile women's and children's health team in 1953 at the age of seventeen. She was sent to Mangshih for medical study, then up the Burma Road to Baoshan for general education, and after a spell in the jungles for practical training she went to Kunming for further study. Now, as one of three full-time medical people who comprise the staff of the Nungbing Station's medical centre, she acts as nurse, mobile medical worker, midwife and propagandist. She told me innocently: "The more cattle people have, the less they believe in our medicine and the more they rely on the ghosts."

M'Ubi said: "Medical work stops people killing cattle. Where the medical work is good and continuous, as at Lungjun, the cattle live. Where it is poor, they go to the sorcerers and the cattle die. Our trouble is that we haven't enough Jingpaw medical workers and the others don't know our language and customs." In fact there were still only fifty-four medical people, including thirty-one Jingpaw trainees, in 1957, which was to be increased to eighty-five in 1958.

All this tended to leave the sorcerers out in the cold. They got subsidies and position but lost an important sphere of influence—that of intervening with the ghosts who were responsible for sickness. Because sorcerers have more ability than most Jingpaw, classes were started to train them in simple medical work with the aim of changing them from ghost-doctors into medical workers. Fortunately the main diseases affecting the Jingpaw, malaria, dysentery and influenza, responded to fairly harmless drugs, and after training to diagnose these and other common ailments, the sorcerers are given a small medical kit and go on their own rounds, their prestige enhanced and happy to pursue this new calling since the older one becomes daily less reliable. These sorcerer-doctors get a monthly stipend and loans to help them start productive farm work in the intervals of their medical rounds. This certainty seems a case of the bogged-down buffalo being attracted from the front and pushed from the rear. Some people in Tehung say that "the training of sorcerers is the surest way of ending cattle sacrifices". This may or not be true. It seemed wise of the *ganbu* to put more reliance on the co-operatives. In Lungjun, where there is a permanent medical worker, it was still only the co-operative members who entirely refrained from sacrificing cattle in 1957.

In the case of the upper-caste officials, the customary method has been followed of leaving a reasonably wide road open for them to travel along. Subsidies to them have averaged 50,000 yuan a year.

One by one their privileges are lapsing or being given up as they become salaried members of local government bodies, and take up farming on their own behalf.

Tzaudung, whose property was rescued and returned by the PLA, went to Peking, marvelled at the size of China and the hero's welcome he got, and returned to help in propaganda work among the official class. He was the first official to relinquish the poll tax. "I am better off than I was formerly," he told me. "There are *tzau* who are dissatisfied but most of us support the new things and the changes because they are better for everyone. Now we have political equality and the Jingpaw are represented in the government at every level. Now we have schools, many schools, where there were none before, and our own people are being trained in culture and self-government."

I had a different impression of another official, Tzaumo, who was absolute ruler of about 10,000 Jingpaw. He fought against the PLA and, for some time after he gave up doing that, refused to allow any *ganbu* to enter his district. Later he had to give way to the pressure from his own people who saw others getting relief, loans, medicine and schools. This stocky young man (they are often young because inheritance is to the youngest son) is now vice-Chairman of the Autonomous Chou and in charge of its civil administration. He exuded none of the warmth of Tzaudung, but in answer to questions agreed that living conditions were improving for the people. About his own situation he said: "I have given up some things. Formerly the *tzau* ruled his area and had economic advantages from that. Now my area is under unified state rule. I get subsidies and I am not any worse off. Politically my position is higher.

"But our people are not accustomed to organisation. They had the tradition of tribal life and take slowly to change. It is a matter of habit."

Tzaumo is a strong nationalist, believing that the Jingpaw ought to be called the Zaiwa people after their biggest tribe, of which he is a member.

On the other hand, Tzaudung was also a Zaiwa and had no feelings about this at all. "Even in Burma our people are called Jingpaw," he commented.

This old official said: "Three years ago, in 1954, I gave up all my privileges voluntarily. At first I was elected a rural district head and then I gave up taking the hind legs of animals and accepted only front legs. I went to Mangshih and heard lectures about living on the labour of other people. When I came back I gave up all my privileges. Later I was elected to a county position. There are nine *tzau* in my area and some still take their privileges. It is a voluntary matter."

He used to have ten cattle and now has twenty-four, he said. His five acres of paddy land have been extended to fifteen acres with government help and he gets 6 tons of grain annually out of that. "Now I have three suits, several quilts, better food and more wine," he summed up.

Enquiries at Lungjun confirmed that the giving up of privilege is patchy. Members of the co-operative and other villagers have all ceased to pay land rent in grain. Corvée labour of three or four days annually is still rendered, and also the hind legs of the dwindling number of sacrificed cattle. Land rent was voluntarily surrendered by the official, who is a member of the county Political Consultative Conference.

It seemed that the pull from the front—subsidy and political position—has to be supplemented by the push from behind by the people and the pressure of the new social forms, before some of the *tzau*, perhaps most, are willing to let go all their economic privileges. It is the combination of these two forces which provides the possibility of direct, gradual transition by peaceful means.

CHAPTER TWENTY-TWO

CONCLUSION

SUCH changes from primitive, slave and semi-feudal social forms as I have tried to describe are going on all over Yunnan Province and in many other places in China—all with their differences and similarities and at varying speeds. In all cases the changes are so rapid that no opportunity may recur to visit these places while the old and the new co-exist and thus may be studied in actual transition. As I write, a few months after leaving the Cool Mountains, slavery has already passed into Norsu history. Wa hillmen, who had never learned even to make pottery, have now set up various kinds of small factories in their remote mountains.

Whatever differences existed among these minority peoples, they had the common feature of intense nationalism. They fought against foreign penetration by the British and French and they fought against Great-Han oppression by the Chinese imperial régime and the Kuomintang. They hated the people who contemptuously labelled them "barbarians", "Lolos", "hilltop people" and the rest. Whatever divisions existed between slave and master, serf and overlord, clan members and usurping clan leaders, all were transcended by the single-minded detestation of the Han. However hated and feared a local leader might be, he could rely on his people to rally in support against the Han.

Into this complex situation, when the Chinese People's Liberation Army marched south-west in 1950, was injected the added irritant of large bands of Kuomintang remnant troops of the most diehard kind, reinforced from Taiwan (Formosa) with American aid. In such wild country, they were able to cross and recross the never completely demarcated borders, complicating China's international relations and by their ruthless banditry feeding the existing anti-Han feeling. At the same time as mopping up these Kuomintang remnants—wherever possible with the aid of the minority peoples—historic hates had to be dispelled.

But the first requirement was to clean up the Kuomintang troops. Without this, no settled situation could be created in which to solve other problems, and the borders of the new republic would be constant trouble spots. Agreement or at least acquiescence of the minority leaders in the entry of the army was necessary, otherwise there would be a chaotic situation in which the minority-Han relations would be worsened. It was not easy. Much as the minorities hated the Kuomintang, they were suspicious of all things Han, and fearful that the Communists would liquidate the "rich", "appoint the slaves as masters" and otherwise behave according to the rumours energetically spread by the Kuomintang. On the other hand, the Kuomintang were physically in their territories, ravaging and looting. A basis existed for agreement between the Communists and the minorities.

Leaders of the minority peoples were told that no changes in their social systems would be imposed on them; the minority peoples themselves would decide what would take place and at what time. Whatever changes might occur, the leaders would be adequately compensated and subsidised so that they might maintain their living standards and they would have assured political positions corresponding to their status among their own people. And this was the reasonable way out that was taken—at once by the Norsu, but only after two years by the Wa.

Two fundamental aspects of the situation were these: it was impossible to win the friendship of the isolated minorities without winning the stable confidence of their leaders; no social reforms could be smoothly carried out without denying to the leaders the possibility of using traditional anti-Han sentiments as a means to preserve their privileges.

Here was the starting point of the policy of buying out the leaders, pouring in relief, encouraging better farming methods, providing medical services, in a many-sided process which set new ferments at work. By the accumulation of many small and virtually unnoticeable changes, a new situation could gradually be brought about in which radical reforms would become unavoidable.

What changes were envisaged was set down in the 1954 Chinese Constitution:

In the course of economic and cultural development, the state will concern itself with the needs of the different nationalities, and, in the matter of socialist transformation, pay full attention to the special characteristics of each.

What this meant was indicated in Article 4 of the Constitution as follows:

The People's Republic of China by relying on the organs of state and the social forces, and by means of socialist industrialisation and socialist transformation, ensures the gradual abolition of systems of exploitation and the building of a socialist society.

As the policy of "doing good and making friends" went on, the people began to make a distinction between "good Hans and bad Hans"—the Communists and the Kuomintang. Relations improved and the stress was slightly changed to helping the poorest people with relatively massive relief and loans. While the "Hans" gave grain, cloth and money, the minority leaders continued to collect their privileged tribute and the contrast sharpened.

Now the question arose: why did the central authorities give things away while the leaders continued to collect tribute; an invidious comparison which led to pressure on the leaders from below to give up their privileges. Feudal and other dues began to be withheld and worry grew among the leaders about their own livelihood. If, at this point, the leaders had not been cushioned against economic loss, they must have opposed all reform. But subsidies provided the key—an easier way out than resistance to the growing social pressure for change.

There are three modes of transition to socialism in the Chinese countryside as a whole. Which form is applicable is determined by local conditions.

Reform: This is the method of open class-struggle applied to break the power of the feudal landlord class in the overwhelmingly greater part of China, where Han landlord faced Han peasant in a conflict uncomplicated by national differences. In this case the Communist Party, after achieving government power, used it to rouse the people against their age-old overlords and led the mass of peasants to abrogate the political and economic privileges of the 30-million-strong landlord class by force. The Han landlords ceased to exist as a class though they had an equal share of the land when it was divided. They received no subsidies, had to work like ordinary peasants for their living, and suffered a temporary loss of political rights.

Reform by Peaceful Negotiation: A similar process carried out among the minority peoples where the class divisions are clear and recognised (and resented in differing degrees) by the minority people themselves. This process, of which the abolition of slavery and feudal serfdom among the Norsu is an example, is also one of mobilising the people from above and leading them to satisfy their desire for freedom, political equality and land.

But there is a fundamental difference between the two methods in that no force is used to abrogate the political and economic privileges of the ruling class. Negotiations take place—with pressure from below—but political rights are not lost by the former ruling class and subsidies are paid to prevent any fall in their standards of living consequent on the reform. Punishment for past oppressive crimes against the people is ruled out, but offences committed in the course of the reform are subject to punishment in the courts.

Following both types of reform, there is an intervening stage during which the land is privately owned and tilled, later giving way to producer co-operatives (and now communes).

Direct Transition to Socialism: This third method is applicable to primitive societies where class divisions are unclear or of minor importance and generally not recognised by the people themselves. Land is plentiful; there is little private property in land and redivision of the land is not necessary.

These societies, such as the Wa and the Jingpaw, pass directly into social ownership of the main means of production—land—without going through other social economic forms. They go straight from tribal ownership of the land to co-operative ownership: from primitive communal working to co-operative collective working. This process pivots on raising the general level of production. Subsidising and "buying out" the leaders, and solving a whole series of problems takes place in the course of the transition. These problems include rudimentary relations of slavery, feudalism, usury, sometimes primitive democracy, and the irrational division and use of labour and means of production due to tradition and superstition.

Peaceful reform occurs within a definite, short period of time, while direct transition extends over a relatively long period and is gradual. Both are adapted as necessary to fit the local conditions. Both rely on maintaining unity between the Communist political workers and the local leaders as a means of reaching and influencing the people themselves and eventually stimulating them to impel the leaders to accept change.

I found that all such Communist workers constantly stressed the uselessness, indeed the positive danger, of applying experience from other places without consideration of local conditions. Each situation

o

is subjected to close study and a policy evolved which takes into account all visible local factors. This policy is then applied in small test areas and the results once again subjected to analysis. Errors are corrected and the modified policy more widely operated.

Once the ordinary people are stimulated to seek change, the leaders have only two possible roads to follow: either to place themselves in the leadership of the reform or oppose it. There is no third way. Leadership of the movement carries with it prestige, subsidies and the feeling that they are playing some part in helping their own people to advance. It is generally only a matter of time and explanation to win over most of the leaders. The road of co-operation is easy and leads to an expansive future; the way of opposition is hard and leads nowhere. Politically the status of the leaders is not reduced, but they become merged with the national and local government institutions and thus subject to democratic control from above and below.

To have achieved the almost incredible result of getting the Norsu slave-owners—about 35 per cent. of the most influential of the population of the Cool Mountains—to agree to the abolition of the main source of wealth, indolence and prestige, seemed to me a dramatic example of scientific and flexible leadership. No ready-made formula would have succeeded. It was possible only on the basis of a careful and accurate estimation of all the social forces and of the distribution of economic power and privilege.

The peaceful abolition of slavery among the Norsu was possible because privilege and usury were abolished at the same time (and not all usury); because the controlling group of slave-owning aristocrats was divided, isolated from mass support and politically paralysed; because those who owned fewer slaves lost both slaves and privileges but kept their land and interest on their loans; because the line of demarcation was scientifically calculated to unite at least 90 per cent. against the ruling 5 per cent.

And even those who lost were not required to lose "face", political rights or income. The rulers were thus offered both the incentive and the inexorable necessity to accept the reform, while they were denied the possibility of mobilising the people on nationalist grounds.

Old Buyu Heipo took the other alternative, fled to the hills leaving wife, slaves and everything, to conduct a futile struggle that could only have one end. He saw the folly of this and came back. A few hard-mouthed slave-owners who could brook no change, offered no serious problem to the ex-slave, ex-commoner Home Guard.

Some people were opposed to subsidising the slave-owners, but it was generally agreed that this could only increase the odds against solving a problem already sufficiently complex and that on purely doctrinaire grounds. Both slaves and masters were incapable of independent existence and equally needed help if they were to escape from each other and make their way to freedom.

In the Cool Mountains the change was rapid but into a lower social form—private ownership of the land. Among the Wa and Jingpaw the change was slower but into a higher co-operative form. Although squalor, cruelty, hunger and disease are inseparable from primitive communal life, so too are loyalty and generosity. Collective life, mutual responsibility, are natural to primitive people. This seemed to provide ground for a quicker growth of co-operatives than among the Norsu, where the motive of personal gain is deeply embedded.

All these changes are made possible by freedom to evolve policies on the spot in an extremely flexible way and the lavish state funds put at the disposal of the political workers. One of these said to me: "In a sense we are repaying the minority peoples for past oppression and the tributes exacted from them by former Chinese régimes." Because one day enlightened governments in the western hemisphere may be faced with the task of making similar restitution to other backward peoples, it seemed that there might be some value in recording these unique events while they were still in the process of transition.